MW00681689

HANGING ON TO MY DREAMS

Bouncing Back From All Rejections

To: Renaldo

[signature]

HANGING ON TO MY DREAMS
*Bouncing Back
From all Rejections*

by
Arnold Henry

"Hanging On To My Dreams: Bouncing Back From All Rejections," by Arnold Henry. ISBN 978-1-60264-812-8.

Published 2011 by Virtualbookworm.com Publishing Inc., P.O. Box 9949, College Station, TX 77842, US. ©2011, Arnold Henry. All rights reserved. No part of this publication may be reproduced, stored in a retrieval system, or transmitted in any form or by any means, electronic, mechanical, recording or otherwise, without the prior written permission of Arnold Henry.

Manufactured in the United States of America.

For my mother, Maria Henry,

who gives me the strength to

hang on to my dreams

My mother holding me on Baptism Day, 1985

TABLE OF CONTENTS

Warm-Up v
Introduction   *1*

First Quarter 3
Home Court Advantage
Chapter 1: *The Beginning of the End of My Dreams*   *5*
Chapter 2: *Childhood*   *10*
Chapter 3: *Primary School*   *14*
Chapter 4: *The Death Threat*   *19*
Chapter 5: *Inspired by Sports*   *23*
Chapter 6: *Lost*   *30*
Chapter 7: *Only the Beginning*   *36*
Chapter 8: *Basketball or Track and Field?*   *40*
Chapter 9: *More Than a Game*   *42*
Chapter 10: *Tough Times*   *49*
Chapter 11: *My Final Basketball Game?*   *54*
Chapter 12: *Unexpected Expectations*   *60*

Second Quarter 64
Taking the Lead
Chapter 13: *On to the Next One*   *65*
Chapter 14: *College?*   *68*
Chapter 15: *Sir Arthur Lewis Community College*   *72*
Chapter 16: *The Phone Call*   *79*
Chapter 17: *I Will Get There...Somehow!*   *85*
Chapter 18: *Farewell Saint Lucia*   *90*
Chapter 19: *A Military Life*   *93*
Chapter 20: *Bugle Call*   *101*
Chapter 21: *Much Needed Motivation*   *107*
Chapter 22: *My First Experiences*   *110*
Chapter 23: *A Cold Town*   *115*
Chapter 24: *Away*   *118*

Third Quarter 122
Double Team
Chapter 25: *Conquering the US Education System*   *123*
Chapter 26: *Recruit*   *125*
Chapter 27: *The Visit*   *128*
Chapter 28: *The Signing*   *133*
Chapter 29: *Before I Leave for Possibly Four Years*   *136*
Chapter 30: *Stay Out of Trouble*   *139*
Chapter 31: *Lonely*   *143*

Chapter 32: Freshman Year 146
Chapter 33: Pre-season 149
Chapter 34: Regrets 151
Chapter 35: Thin Ice 155
Chapter 36: The Right to Remain Silent 161

Fourth Quarter 168
Triple Threat

Chapter 37: I Need a Miracle 169
Chapter 38: Fighting For My Future 173
Chapter 39: The Final Decision 178
Chapter 40: NJCAA Division I 185
Chapter 41: Love and No Basketball 191
Chapter 42: Commitments 199
Chapter 43: One More Shot at NCAA Division I 207
Chapter 44: Dismiss 214
Chapter 45: Now What? 220
Chapter 46: Hanging In There 224
Chapter 47: The Final College Chapter 227
Chapter 48: Ending on a Good Note 234

Afterword 240
Acknowledgements 242

Warm-Up

Introduction

December 13, 2008

I am lying on my bed, half-naked, uncovered, and soaked in my own sweat. It is about 9:00 p.m. and the lights are off. I close my eyes, reliving the horrific moments that occurred four years ago—on this particular date and time. I had thought I could escape the flashbacks of that event by going to bed at an earlier, unusual time.

Obviously, my plans failed.

I crawl to the edge of the bed to sit, to stop thinking, to relax my frustrated brain—massage the throbbing veins in my temples.

Should I call it an anniversary? In my opinion, an anniversary recalls a special, happy day to be celebrated in the future. For instance, my birthday, February 11, 1985—thanks to my mother, I survived my father's suggestions of abortion. For sure, my father always wished I was dead; at least, judging from his absence in my life.

Still seated at the edge of my bed, I reflect on, not an anniversary, but a tragedy.

My options? I remain seated at the edge of my bed, or lie back down due to lack of inspiration, or get motivated, stand strong and face all my rejections. What will be the reward? How about transformation? From an angry, troubled boy, to a man unveiling and understanding life on my own terms; from failure after failure to achievement and accomplishment; from the bottom of the ladder to the peak of no return.

I realized that one day was all it took to make life altering changes; for my sperm-donor father to ejaculate, for my mother to marry another man, and for me to attempt to kill my physically and verbally abusive step-father.

Commitment was all it took to bring happiness and joy to my life; to play basketball for my school team; to graduate from high school; to be nominated for a national award; to achieve a full basketball scholarship from an American institution; to finally leave my broken Saint Lucian home forever.

Determination was all it took to accomplish a dream by becoming Saint Lucia's first basketball player to achieve a full basketball scholarship as a freshman at the highest level of the National Collegiate Athletic Association, better known as NCAA Division I.

But then, one incident was all it took for my dreams to be crushed; to bounce around five American schools in five years; to end up nowhere but here in Jacksonville, Florida, seated alone in this dark room, about to start writing to share with you how I was still able to hang on to my dreams.

My mother holding me at my birthday party, 1986

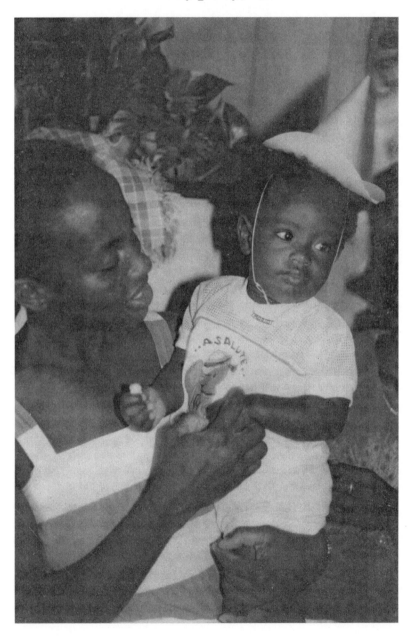

First Quarter

Home Court Advantage

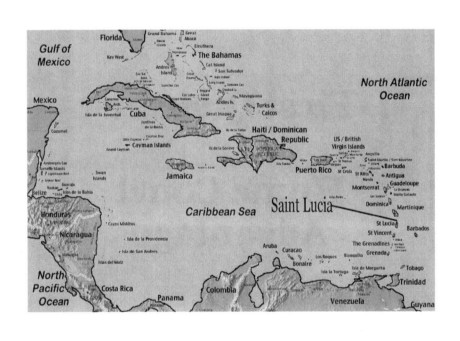

Chapter 1

The Beginning of the End of my Dreams

December 13, 2004
9:00 P.M.

I knew then that it was over—everything I had worked so hard for. It felt like my legs weren't strong enough to walk the distance, as if I was at the gym, leg squatting 1000-pounds from my shoulders. The hallways felt like they were closing in on us. With every step we made I witnessed pairs of feet hesitantly clearing our path. I found it difficult to make eye contact with my schoolmates.

My long, gray sweat pants and black hoodie helped to disguise me. But who was I fooling? I was the tallest and biggest student on the fourth floor of the Harris-Millis dormitory. It felt like the stairs would never come to an end. It was awkward walking without being able to swing my arms. My two escorts assisted me as I took longer and longer strides to get out of the building.

As one of my escorts widely opened the basement exit door, the cold breeze and snow that blew in allowed my tears to suddenly run down my face. My vision went blurry. Everything looked distorted. Upon exiting the building, fuzzy flashing lights from what appeared to be the top of a car forced me into a deep thought. *Is this it…the end? Is this all a dream? Arnold, you need to wake up.*

The noise from the door shutting behind us caused me to snap out of my hallucination. I tried wiping my eyes with my shoulders to take a better look at reality. My arms were cuffed behind me and the frozen rain melted on my hands. I shut my eyelids tightly to drain the water out and then squinted to see through the snowfall. Red, blue, and white lights flashed on top of the cop car. *This is no dream.*

"Watch your head," advised officer Sue Roberts as she opened the door to the back of the car. Sergeant Phelps held on to the top of my head and slightly pushed me into the backseat of the car.

Now seated, I tilted my head back and stared at the roof. I sniffed to prevent the snot from running down my nose any further. Tears started running down the side of my face then down my ears. As I tried to speak, a blown up saliva bubble popped. "Help me God," I whispered.

I had a strong feeling that this was the beginning of the end of my dreams—my hoop dreams—in Burlington, Vermont, USA.

5

How did I end up in this predicament? Especially after working so hard to get out of my broken home…

Home sweet home was a green, wooden house with a galvanize rooftop, located in the city of Castries, northwest of Saint Lucia. This was my Saint Lucian home since birth.

The yard in front of our house was paved unevenly. Diverging cracks made it appear as if we were hit by a low magnitude earthquake, but somehow our towering breadfruit tree stood strong (today, only the trunk remains). Our yard area was covered with rocks, weeds, and small plants that led to our three concrete steps and our home's front door. At the back of our house stood a coconut tree and next to it, a wooden shed covered with an aluminum roof. The right side of our yard was covered with dirt derived from a muddy slope that led to our neighbor's mango trees at the top of a small hill. Julie mangoes occasionally fell on our rooftop. On the other side of the house was our homemade clothes-line.

Our house was quite spacious—not too much though. And for the most part, we lived in a friendly and peaceful neighborhood. The streets were less than 100 meters away, therefore, everything we needed, such as convenience stores or bakeries, was within a 10-minute walking radius.

From the very early stages of my life, I remember flashes of my beautiful smiling mother and a monster in the form of a man, then their children. My happy world had shattered into microscopic pieces. No more sunny blue skies; no more just Mummy and me. I had to accept the fact that the storm would never cease.

Truthfully, there was no other place like home. But home was not always sweet. In fact, it was more sour than sweet; especially the late nights on my lower bunk-bed, awakened by the violent sounds that came from my mother's room.

"Bam! Bam! Boom!" Every blow would make my weary eyes open wider and wider. My heart would beat faster as if the noise was right outside my bedroom door. I would squeeze my pillow tightly, scared for my Mummy as she pleaded for a hero.

"Bang! Bang! Bram!" I imagined her head slamming onto the wooden partition that separated our bedrooms. I felt a pain on my body for every sound that I heard.

"Whack!" I felt Lucius's hand connecting with my Mummy's face.

"Aarrgh!" Her late-night-screams would wake up everyone in our house.

My youngest sibling, Marva, always started crying first followed by my younger brother, Marvin. I forced my mouth to remain motionless. I imagined all my neighbors just standing by, being spectators from their homes.

"Lucius, Lucius, aarrgh!" Mummy would cry out.

"Shut your ass up!" he would yell back, in Kwéyòl—our secondary language.

I squeezed my pillow tighter. I was too frightened to even step outside of my room knowing that I would get my share of the beating from my step-father. No one would answer my mother's cries.

I never understood the reasons for her punishments. I always felt weak whenever the thought of rescuing her crossed my mind. Lucius had a huge beard on his face and a six foot, muscular body that loomed over me.

The next day, I would creep through the house acting like I was invisible. My mother would be in the kitchen preparing breakfast. "Good morning," she would say with all white teeth when she caught me staring.

What should I say to my mother? Are you okay?

No, that would be a stupid question.

I just replied, "Good morning Mummy." She probably read the anger on my face. I just couldn't pretend we lived in a happy home.

She wore black sunglasses in the house and acted like the glare from the sun was affecting her eyes. The black marks on her skin and her swollen cheeks were another manifestation of her pain.

Seriously, how could she prepare him breakfast?

My hatred for Lucius would build. Anger and rage would sit upon my mind, ready to explode. The fingers of my hand clenched in my palm every time I noticed a bruise on Mummy's body. I wished I could punch him to death, but I never had the heart or the balls to do anything that crazy.

Making eye contact with Lucius was impossible for me. I never looked his way. I wondered if he ever looked at me.

Did he love me like he loved Marvin and Marva?

He never brought me candy when he got home from his days of fishing.

Due to my siblings' light colored skin it was obvious that Lucius wasn't my biological father. Marva had my mother's naturally straight, long black hair, and no one understood where Marvin's black curly hair came from. Lucius also had a deceased son (whom I never met), who had passed away from choking on a fruit seed. He was also the father of two other light-colored girls whom he had with two different women.

His oldest daughter, Nadia St. Brice, lived with us until she was in her early twenties. Valencia, who was the same age as me, visited us from time to time. My mother treated Nadia like her very own daughter; gave her food, shelter, and clothes for over 15 years—and got nothing in return. Valencia's periodic visits had no impact on my life.

My immediate family was my mother, Marvin, and Marva. Creating a family bond with Lucius was never on my mind. He only cared for his own children anyways. Marvin and Marva were always happy when their father was home. I tried to keep my distance from him. I excluded myself from any activity that he was involved in, like dinner at the table, gardening, or fishing. Whenever we crossed paths, I kept my eyes to the floor.

In the mornings, I greeted Lucius, "Good morning." It was not enough for him. He demanded respect from me. I thought, *a man that beats my mother will never earn my respect.* But Mummy insisted that I obey him. One day when she was fed-up with Lucius's complaints, my mother said to me, "I don't want any trouble so please call Lucius Daddy." I complied with her decision and called Lucius, "Daddy," just for her sake and happiness. Although, every time I stuttered Daddy, I felt like someone held a pistol to my head.

I grew up in Bishop's Gap, a very small, quiet community that had its tough moments. Marchand Roman Catholic Church, where I was baptized and celebrated my first communion and confirmation, was in walking distance from my home. We called our neighborhood "Da Yard." Our houses were close enough that all the neighbors knew everyone's business. Mummy was the loudest of them all. She spoke better English than me. Everyone called her "Ms. Jean," but her real name was Maria. Her loud mouth acted like some kind of advanced disciplinary device. Whenever she screamed at us it was the equivalent to a spanking—embarrassing, loud noises helped us learn from our mistakes.

Everyone in Bishop's Gap knew me as Mario. I never had to introduce myself to anyone because Mummy did that for me from miles away. "Mario! Mario! Mario! Didn't I tell you don't go playing by the road?" And of course, everyone noticed me sprinting towards the hollering voice. I would always reply, "Yes Mummy, I'm comin'!"

On the flipside, Lucius used other protocols for discipline. Whenever I disobeyed his orders, he looked at me like I just challenged him to a fight. Every vein on his body showed. If I had an option to poop in my pants I would have, but that would have caused a worse beating. "Didn' I tell you to stay your ass inside da house?" Sometimes I didn't answer his question. Why should I waste my breath? My beatings came anyways. Anything in his sight would be used as an asset for my punishment. As a child, I felt the impact of a frying pan, the branch of a tamarind tree, the side of a machete, a baton, and a belt. I didn't mind the belts though; they left cuts on my skin that healed in a few days. Getting hit with the baton was the worst pain; it caused a limp in my walk for a few weeks. The machetes made me run around the house; I feared getting slashed accidently. Running, crying, or screaming only made him angrier.

I never gained anything from his punishments, and neither did he. I never wanted to give him the pleasure of my obedience. In my mind, he was a stranger that only came around to eat, beat, sleep, and shit, but my mother kept him around for reasons I never discovered.

Did he even love my mother? Um…? If I have to think about it, then I guess not.

Did my mother love him? I intentionally distracted myself whenever I thought about it. I hoped that one day Lucius would be out of my life. But I was wrong. When I was nine years old, the unthinkable happened.

"You may now kiss the bride," instructed Father John in April 1994. This was the only time I noticed affection between Lucius and my mother. I wondered if the eyes of the Lord were open during their matrimony.

How could she be so stupid? What about the beatings? Did she even care how I felt? She blamed alcohol for his actions. I blamed "desperately in need of a husband" for her role. On their wedding day, I realized that I needed this storm to be over—I wanted to get out of the house.

My surname went from being Jean-Marie to Henry.

If my mother thought that a wedding would make a difference in an abusive relationship, she was proven wrong.

Chapter 2

Childhood

Ten-year-old youths usually view life as a way of having fun with no responsibilities. At least, that seemed to be the case among my childhood acquaintances. We all grew up running around Da Yard, playing football or cricket. However, I had visions of making it big someday. As much as I was focused and determined to accomplish success, I knew that it was not going to be easy. But the obscurity and obstacles along my way exceeded my expectations. I waited and waited for the day to come when I would be able to be on my own. Lucius and my mother's marriage crushed my hopes for any easy future break-up between them. I felt like my mother had lost sight of her own flesh and blood.

Can I really blame her though? Maybe Lucius had choked her until she agreed to marry him. Well, that's what my imagination pictured. I knew for sure I'd never seen him get down on one knee, holding a rock at the tip of my mother's finger, asking her to spend the rest of her life with him.

Expressing love was one thing that was exempt from my so-called family. I never understood my mother's reasons for keeping Lucius around except that he was the father of Marvin and Marva. Not once had I seen him caressing my mother with warm hugs or rubbing her feet after long hours of work. Neither had I noticed my mother showering affection towards him. Their relationship just seemed phony.

All I wanted was to be gone out of our household, like my cat, Puss-Puss, who once lived with us. Her disappearance was a mystery. One night, like every other night, I let Puss-Puss out the front door and the following morning she didn't come home for breakfast. I had no evidence, but I suspected Lucius was the culprit. He was the only one who I had seen kick my cat. And even though I had no pieces with which to solve the puzzle, I've lived the rest of my life holding on to Lucius as my only suspect for the loss of my cat.

When Lucius was not around, I spent as much time as possible in Da Yard with my friends—my freedom time. My first ever childhood friend was Olvin Cyril. He was the yellow, chubby kid that lived in the yellow house next to my home. But he did not last long in Da Yard. When we were seven-years old, Olvin, his mother, and older sister vacated their home and flew to New York City.

Da Yard felt empty when Olvin left. I felt like I lost my only true friend forever. It would have been great if I was able to venture along with him to the land of opportunities. Even though he was not going to be around anymore, we remained in contact as pen-pals.

After Olvin and his family's departure from Saint Lucia, his aunt, Joan, and his three cousins, Jackie, Jermal, and Jovan, moved into the yellow house.

Jovan and Jermal took Olvin's place as my companions. Jovan was two years younger than me and Jermal was three years younger than me; the same age as Marvin. Jermal was the same dark-skinned complexion as me and Jovan was the same light-skinned complexion as my brother. Their sister, Jackie, was already an adult.

Shortly after they moved in, their mother followed Olvin's family and flew to New York City. Jackie was left to take care of her two younger brothers.

After a day of school, Jermal, Jovan, Marvin, and I gathered in Da Yard to seek adventures in the Bishop's Gap area before sunset. They were my partners, my partners in crime—although we were never in trouble with the law. Sometimes people mistook us for brothers because we were always seen *liming* together. We were also involved in most of the same groups. On Saturday mornings, we were usually at choir practice rehearsing songs for Sunday's church performance. Then later that evening, we would train with our Coach for upcoming marathon competitions. And on Sunday mornings, we attended church services and sat together in the same row.

When we weren't in Da Yard breaking our neighbors' windows with our football or cricket ball, we would be trespassing into other nearby resident's yards to steal from their fruit trees: coconuts, tamarind, oranges, cherries, guava, plums, mangoes or cacao.

We sold our stolen commodities to our neighbors for cheaper prices than the Castries Market. Whenever we went out to steal fruit, we traveled together. Jovan, Jermal, Marvin, and I were all good tree climbers. We picked as many fruits as possible without getting caught; if the property-owners were to ever catch us in their trees, we would probably lose an arm or a leg after a fierce swing with a machete. Sometimes we would just relax in the trees, have long conversations, fill our bellies, and never worry about what was down under.

There was a certain Kwéyòl word that we kept our ears open for, "Yo Bouché!" In English it meant to catch someone by surprise. But to us it meant, run your butt off. And no, it was not a warning. It was said by annoying children who were intentionally trying to get us caught for their own amusement.

Whatever methods we used to climb up the trees were never used to climb down during an escape. From altitudes that might be four times our heights, a jump was the fastest way to break away. Marvin and I would sprint all the way home without looking back.

"Daddy dere?" That was the first thing I would ask Marva whenever I returned home. Luckily, I usually made it home before 5:00 p.m., enough time before Lucius arrived from whatever he did during the day. Most days I didn't know if he worked or if he just spent time in his fishing shed near the sea. He couldn't possibly have a job that involved reading because Marva or Marvin couldn't get him to read one word out of their school workbooks. It seemed like he was only good with his hands (if you know what I mean).

Unless someone needed a house built, Lucius had no work. However, let's give him praise for his extending our home with his masonry and carpentry skills. Although, after a physical fight with my mother, he yelled and threatened to remove all his nails from our home; I couldn't tell if it was the liquor talking.

At times, I wondered if he used his or my mother's hard earned money to purchase his alcohol. If Lucius knew how to keep a steady job, maybe I wouldn't have overheard my mother secretly begging our neighbors for money to send us to school. It was obvious to me that the money she earned from her housekeeping job was not sufficient to raise three children and a grown man. I never asked for anything unless it involved school. Marvin or Marva would constantly ask, "Mummy I wanna lollipop or an ice-lolly or tamarind-balls."

My mother shouted back, "I don't have money, go ask your father!"—Like that solved anything.

Who needed manufactured toys? The last time I had seen a commercial toy was at a very early age when it was only my mother and me. I had to be creative. On hot sunny days, Jermal, Jovan, Marvin, and I were in Da Yard constructing toys like Santa Claus' elves. We used resources from our environment. I used a rotten breadfruit and two broomsticks to push around a tire from a car. Some thread, a nylon grocery bag and sticks from a coconut leaf helped to build my kite. Usable parts from abandoned rusted-bicycles were mounted up to make my own bicycle. These were some of the most memorable toys that I created. But the most exciting of them all was bamboo-bursting. All I needed was a big piece of bamboo plant, some kerosene, and a homemade fire torch to allow the bamboo to explode like the cannons at Pigeon Pointe, north of the island, which were used in combat between the British and the French in the early days. The sounds of exploding bamboo sometimes indicated that Christmas was around the corner.

My Christmas day traditions were the same no matter how naughty or nice I was throughout the year. I attended church to praise the Lord, and, as a choir boy, to sing in front of the biggest crowds of the year. My mother always wrapped a tin of milk for me to bring up to the altar for the collection of items for the poor and homeless during our community's church service. And for the rest of my day, I watched and listened to the happiness of my neighbors resounding in Da Yard. Jermal and Jovan's family gave me a perfect vision of that day— through their house windows, I watched them unwrap their presents. They would receive a big barrel filled with toys and groceries from their mother, all the way from New York City. That's when I began to imagine America to be a place where all dreams were made possible.

Chapter 3

Primary School

"Mario!" shouted my mother every weekday at 7 in the morning. She yelled so loud that she probably woke up our neighbors' fowls. I covered my ears with my pillow, but it was impossible to sleep-in on schooldays. "Go buy me two-dollars bread," my mother sometimes said. I had to walk to the bakery near the church to buy fresh, hot bread for the family. On any given day, for our breakfast, my mother might prepare us bread and tuna-fish, or bread and hotdog, or bread and eggs with a cup of tea. But most of the time, we ate Cornflakes. I ate so many bowls of Cornflakes with milk that I grew up thinking that every cereal on the shelf was named Cornflakes. Same goes for Colgate; I thought every tube of toothpaste was named Colgate.

By 8:30 a.m., I was on my way to Marchand Combined School which was less than a five minute walk down the hill next to my church. It would be shameful if I was ever late for class. Jermal and Jovan both attended a different primary school than my siblings and I. We wouldn't see them until they got back home from school.

The students in my last year at primary school were all new faces. That year, the head principal introduced a new system and divided us into highest to lowest grades based on our previous report cards. I fell into the A class. All my buddies were either in the C or D class. The maturity levels of my new classmates made it seem like I was older than 10. I believed our first male teacher made the difference.

Mr. Regis was the only teacher in the entire school that could silence a room of disruptive students just by his presence. He was a dark, chubby man who never smiled, not even for the world's funniest joke. And my classmates wouldn't dare crack a joke in his classroom, we all feared getting caned. To avoid any incidents with Mr. Regis, my eyes were always glued to the blackboard and my ears were attentive to his lessons.

When I first encountered my primary school crush, Marla Foster, it was difficult to maintain focus in the classroom. To get my mind off her I tried something new: track and field. I didn't want to be known as "Tall for nothing" anymore. I wanted to be known as the fastest man on the planet. Maybe that was my route to forget about Marla and to get out of Saint Lucia—to be a track star. I wouldn't know unless I tried.

One day, I walked barefoot onto the hot, green grass at the Mindoo Phillip Park, during the early mornings of my school's Track and Field event. I was preparing to face my visions as a future runner. As I walked to the starting position, I overshadowed the seven other guys who walked in line with me. The rest of my schoolmates, who cheered from the bleachers, wore a T-shirt that represented our school's housing system (red, green, blue, and yellow). I represented the red team. The purpose of the housing system was to group and support the organization of extra-curricular activities, such as sports, in a competitive nature amongst teachers and students at a school. Every school on the island followed the same organization.

The Mindoo Phillip Park venue did not have eight lanes, or a 400 meter track, and we did not run on a synthetic surface like we had seen on the televised broadcasts of the Summer Olympics. Instead, we ran on grass in seven-300 meter lanes.

"On your marks!" shouted an official. My arms and legs trembled as I assumed my position. "Get Set!" I looked ahead at the 100 meters. "Go!" I ran like I was being chased by a man with a machete. I crossed the finish line in third place and immediately realized that running was not for me. The first and second places were probably 30 meters ahead of me.

It was my first track and field competition. The rest of the events which I participated in were: 200-meters dash, 400-meters dash, 4x1-relay, and long jump. By the end of the day I collected gold, silver, and two bronze medals. I got my first gold medal from the long jump event.

When I arrived home that evening, I surprised my mother with my awards. "Mummy, Mummy, I win four medals!"

"For true my boy. Where did you get that from, uh?"

"Today da school had Inter-house track un field ih."

"Why you didn't tell me? I would have taken the day off to come see you run."

"No, dis morning I jus' decide to run. Buh Mummy, I ran so fas' ih."

"That's good my boy. I'm so proud of you."

I had sought the same emotions from Lucius. I said to him, "I jus' wanna show you my medal."

"Okay," he replied, without even attempting to look at my hands. His face was blunt as a rotten knife.

I hammered three nails into the partition of our living room and hung up my first four medals. Just by staring at them, I visualized there were more to come. But then again, this was a one day track and field event; soon after, it was back to the books.

Marvin, Marva, and I all went to the same school. Marvin was three grade levels lower than me and it was Marva's first year. They both literally looked up to me for protection, but it wasn't necessary. We hardly got into trouble with anyone. I was known for being very quiet and even though my classmates never noticed, I was mostly quiet the mornings after Lucius and my mother's fights. These were the days I learned nothing from my teachers.

Since I had no male figure to look up to, I was my own fighter whenever it was necessary. My last fight at primary school ignited when Arthur, a student from the D class was transferred into my classroom. He was known for getting into fights and beating the living crap out of his opponents. Arthur was sent into our classroom because he needed the supervision of Mr. Regis and because of Arthur's bad reputation with the school's principal, none of my classmates would provoke a fight with him.

One quiet day at the school, everyone in the classroom was working on an assignment left by Mr. Regis before he'd stepped out; we were expected to have completed it upon his return. While I focused on the Mathematical problems, Arthur turned around and asked me, "Oye, Arnold, you have a pen mun?"

I raised up my only pen.

"Awa, dats my only pen ih gah," I said. As soon I attempted to press my pen to my notebook, Arthur snatched it out of my hand leaving a black mark across the problems I'd just solved. He then turned around and proceeded to write in his notebook. Fearful I wouldn't finish my work in time, I said, "Gason, give me back my pen please." He ignored my request and continued writing. Marla dragged her desk and chair away from me as if she foresaw the future. I touched Arthur's back and repeated, "Gason, give me back my pen please." My contact ignited his ticking bomb.

Arthur erupted from his seat, and his desk and chair went flying, breaking the silence in the classroom. My classmates jumped out of their seats. Arthur and I were surrounded by spectators. When I received a punch to the face, I answered with a punch of my own to his jawbone before he could swing again. My classmates chanted, "Yay! Hees-salòp!" (An exclamation used by Saint Lucians less than a second after something amazing, exciting, or funny has occurred. It could either be followed by laughter or amazement).

I knew that, because of my height and body size, I could overpower Arthur, so I charged and rushed him to the desks. He fell to the ground with the desks. I started landing punches to his face uncontrollably. The classroom became drop-dead-silent. My last swing was stopped by Mr. Regis. "Stop it!" he shouted with the deepness of his voice. He grabbed both of us by the shoulder. Arthur's face was red.

I dusted the dirt off of my black dress pants and buttoned up my blue uniform shirt. We were sent to the principal's office, but before I went in, I made sure to pick up my pen from the floor. That was the one fight that I needed to gain respect from my primary schoolmates; I never had to prove myself, or fight again in primary school.

It was very important for me to stay focused on my schoolwork because I was about to attempt the Common Entrance Examination, the most important academic exam of primary school. This mandatory exam was taken to determine my future secondary school—a level equivalent to the United States or Canada's high schools. But one couldn't just register for a secondary school; we had to earn it with the scores of our Common Entrance Examination. My goal was to get the best score possible that would allow me to attend Saint Mary's College—the top secondary school on the island.

From the very first day I entered primary school at the age of five, my mother always said to me, "I want you to pass for Saint Mary's College." I wanted to make her proud, although I wasn't putting in as much work as I needed to. I focused too much on having fun and disregarded my schoolwork.

Every Friday, we put down our pens for Physical Education. Mr. Regis allowed us to play basketball games after we changed from our school uniforms to our PE uniforms. I held on to my first rubber basketball during these periods. The games were played outside, next to our classroom. Our school never had a basketball court so we ran up and down on an open gravel surface area without any out-of-bounds lines, free-throw lines, or 3-pointer lines. Our pretend basketball rim was used mainly for the girls to play their netball games—it was a long metal pole that had a hoop at its peak, with no backboard. The circumference of the netball rim was much smaller than a regular hoop, but the basketball was still able to sink down.

I might as well have been playing the same position as the basketball rim because I just stood around uselessly and scratched my head whenever we played the game. Teams were divided into two groups of four. The first time teams were divided equally, I was an automatic first pick because I was the tallest boy in my class. I tried to do other stuff that could benefit my team, but there was no hope.

"Gason you real-ih lapo ih," my classmate once said to me (meaning: boy, you really suck). My interest for the game faded. Watching from our imaginary sidelines was less embarrassing.

Back then, basketball was the least of my interests. Education was my key. At home, my mother reminded me, "Mario, these boys you playing with are not going to be taking your exams for you. You should be in your books studying." I was the first of my mother's children to take the Common Entrance Examination. Whenever I opened up my notebooks and attempted to study, all the pages seemed to be blank. The fun noises from Da Yard called my name allowing me to easily get distracted. However, my mother's happiness was important to me, so I studied harder, closer to the date of the exams.

One day my mother promised that if I did well enough for a secondary school, she would get me a Super Nintendo gaming-system. That day I got all the strength in the world to study more. *Finally we could have our own gaming system.* My friends, Jermal and Jovan, had already received a Nintendo 64 from their mother in New York City. Nevertheless, I liked the sound of my mother's offer because I knew that was all she could afford.

The morning of my examination, the palms of my hands were sweating like a fat man wearing a winter-jacket on a summer's day. At the breakfast table, my nervous mother acted as if she was about to attempt the exams herself. She dropped almost every kitchen utensil she held on to. For breakfast, I ate Cornflakes, bread and salt fish, a banana, orange slices, and a cup of apple juice. Her catering efforts made me feel special, like I was at one of the restaurants in the hotel she worked at. "Good luck my boy," she said before I left the house. Her eyes were so full of tears that if she blinked they would have run down her face. Her first child was close to attending a secondary school—exactly what every mother on the island hoped for; especially for their sons.

A few weeks later, the results were in at Marchand Combined School. Every parent and examinee patiently waited as Mr. Regis publicly announced our future schools. My mother was beside me. Just before I received my results she said to me, "I am going to be very proud if you just pass for any secondary school."

"Arnold Henry, Entrepot Secondary School," Mr. Regis finally broadcasted.

"Yay, that's my boy!" my mother yelled embarrassingly. Though her loud applause and chanting encouraged me to believe that my result was perfect; my exam scores were only good enough for Entrepot Secondary School. I felt like I let her down.

Chapter 4

The Death Threat

One ordinary weekend, while Lucius and I were seated in our backyard plucking chickens' feathers, he said to me, "You mus' be waitin' for me to turn an old mun in my wheelchair eh…but I go wait for you…I go wait for da day you try puttin' your hands on me when I turn an old mun." Although the thoughts of abusing him when he became a vegetable in a wheelchair sounded like perfect payback, I'd already planned to never stoop to his level.

The situation with my biological father, or the sperm donor, was a theoretical one. Why did he never come to visit? Why did he never come to pick me up? Did I do something wrong? What about his side of the family? Did I have living grandparents, brothers, sisters, aunts, uncles, or cousins? So many unanswered questions. Maybe he was ashamed of me—that became the hypothesis of my life.

People said that I resembled my biological father. All I knew was that we had the same dark colored complexion. I wanted to know more about him than his name, Tobias. When did Tobias walk out of my life? Was he ever part of it? It was very hard to ignore his existence since he was often in the public eye because of his job as a photojournalist. However, I'd always known my mother to be both parents. I knew if Tobias was constantly in my life, or at least contributing towards child support on a monthly basis, it would have never felt like my mother was on the edge of poverty. But finance was far beyond my issue with Tobias. I needed him to be there for me emotionally—and I needed him to pick me up whenever Lucius beat my mother.

Numerous times I heard my mother in her room crying to God because she didn't have enough money to pay the light bill, phone bill, or water bill. I would have gone to my room to do the same; shedding tears until my tears-water-well ran dry. I never understood how she managed to pay the bills or provide food for us to eat, but she always found a way.

I remember one Sunday afternoon when my mother was at work for the day, Lucius was out fishing, and I was home taking care of my two younger siblings. Marvin and I had got into a disagreement which ended up in a physical fight. Lucius got home before my mother and heard about the altercation from Marva. He was fuming like a raging bull that just saw the color red.

19

"Why you raisin' your hand on my child for?" Before I could give an explanation in my defense, Lucius swung his hand across my face like a tennis player swinging a back-hand.

That was the first time he ever slapped me across my face (he'd hit everywhere else but never a slap on my face). The left side of my face felt hot and stung. My ear was ringing which made me believe that I had gone deaf. Tears came running down from my eyes. He commanded, "Make dat be da las' time you touch my children!" For some reason, at that moment, *enough was enough.* As soon as he turned around, I headed towards the kitchen counter and picked up the biggest knife we had. I rushed in his direction. But I stopped halfway, as if someone held me back. He turned, looked at me like he had just seen a ghost. The fear on his face made me wish I had done this a few years ago. I raised the knife horizontal across the room in his direction.

I shouted, "If you ever touch me again I go kill you!" I was trembling and realized that I couldn't backup my threat. Even though he stood still, Lucius's domineering nature got the best of me. I dropped the knife and ran straight out the front door.

I ran and ran on the streets, ignoring traffic and pedestrians, until I was far enough to catch my breath. Going back was out of the question. The more I walked, the shorter my strides became. My feet had acquired some tingling, sharp, and burning pains, but I kept walking like a nomad. I headed north of the island hoping a miracle would lead me to my father's residence—at these times, I wished I knew where he lived. I thought, *maybe, he would invite me in.*

Eventually, there was no more sun in the sky. It was the farthest I had walked away from home and the longest I had stayed out without anyone knowing my whereabouts.

A printed sign on the roadside said, "Welcome to the town of Gros-Islet." I had walked over twenty kilometers on tar before my path made a transition to muddy, green grass and bushes. Then I found myself in someone's tomato, yam, and dasheen garden.

"Sa ou ka fé la?" asked the deep voice that came from an open dark entrance. Seconds later, an old man charged through that front door, holding a machete, looking like he was ready to attack me.

I cried out in English. "Please…please…I'm lost. I ran away from home. Please help me." I raised my hands to block my face in case the old man started swinging.

He halted a few feet away from me. "Ki koté ou ka wèsté?" he asked.

"I live Bishop's Gap," I answered. He slowly lowered his weapon.

After handing me a cup of water and a piece of dry bread, the old man showed more generosity by giving me some money for transportation. Sitting on the doorstep of his house, I hurriedly ate and drank.

"Thank you so much," I said before departing. The old man gave me some directions to the main road. Soon after, I was aboard a public bus, headed home.

Only eight hours had gone by but the gathering of all my neighbors in our front yard made it seem like I was missing for three days. My mother was the ring leader. I approached her with my head down. "I was just about to call the police! I was worried sick about you boy!" She was furious. "Go inside! I will deal with you later!"

Lucius was not home so that kind of eased my nerves. I knew, sooner or later, I had to apologize. But apologizing to him was only to facilitate my mother's wishes. It took some time for me to meet eyes with Marvin and Marva. Instead of punishment, my mother had mercy on me since my feet were swollen from my long-distance walk.

When Lucius finally came home a few days later, I was apologetic. But from then on, the only words that were exchanged between us were good morning.

Sadly, although my threats to Lucius made him stop beating me, they did not stop him from raising his hands on others.

I was one year away from being a teenager when I finally witnessed the beating of my mother. I was fast asleep when I woke up to the sound of, "Lucius! Lucius! Lucius!" screamed, hoarsely by my mother. I jumped out of my bed and charged into the direction of her screams. I came to a halt between our living room and kitchen. Crying, Marvin and Marva joined by my side and shouted, "Daddy, no!"

I froze. Lucius was beating my mother with the wire of our house's telephone. She swung her arms around to prevent damage on her face and body. "Somebody help me!" my Mummy screamed from the floor. The bones in my body vibrated through my boiling blood. Lucius dropped the telephone and started walking away. My heart skipped a beat when his eyes connected with mine. "Police! Police! Help me!" My mother's voice regained his attention. A swift slap across her face denied her a chance to tell the police where we lived. I couldn't be a spectator anymore so I hurried to grab the biggest knife in the kitchen. I wanted him dead.

"I go fuckin' kill you," I said. "Get the fuck away from her, you pussy!" I made direct eye contact with Lucius.

"You wan a kill me, I go leave," he said. His eyes were filled with disbelief and his words were slurred.

"Mario, no!" Marvin and Marva yelled.

"Mario, what are you doing? Put the knife down!" my mother cried.

Lucius stumbled through the front door of the house. And as he exited, he slammed the door so hard that the entire house shook. A huge rock thrown by Lucius almost flew through the door. I couldn't bear to see the marks on my mother's body, so I returned to my room, uneasy, unable to sleep.

Only a few weeks went by before Lucius was back in the house. I overheard his apology to my mother. "I promise I never go drink again. I'm sorry." And just like that, my mother accepted him back.

Sometimes I wonder if my threats helped him to be a changed man. His physical abuse towards me had stopped but we were hardly seeing him at home. He spent more time at sea which was fine with me. As far as I know, the days of my mother's physical abuse had ended.

Chapter 5

Inspired by Sports

In September 1997, after a long, hot summer vacation, it was time to return to school. I started my first of five years at Entrepot Secondary School. It was like a fresh start to life: new school, new classrooms, new classmates, new teachers, new books and new uniforms.

The first bell rang at 8 in the morning. I walked through the entrance gates of the school, and was directed by a teacher to my classroom, 1R20. Upon entering, it felt like I was late by the number of students who were already seated. I kept my head straight ahead as I walked to an empty seat at the front corner of the room. From my peripheral vision, I saw my new classmates along with two familiar faces from Marchand Combined School. Everyone else was engaged in conversation.

My ears picked up laughter. I hesitated, and then looked around the classroom. I stared at a few students only to realize that all their eyes were on me. The joke flew right over my head. I investigated myself for evidence but I didn't get it. After finally scrutinizing one of the males in my classroom, I realized that I was out of fashion with my school uniform. My light-blue shirt was tucked into my tight gray pants; the bottom of my pants barely touched my black dress shoes. Basically, my image represented Steve Urkel from the sitcom, *Family Matters*.

We all wore the same school uniform, but these students broke it down into fashion. All the guys wore bellbottom-pants with a pair of black brand name sneakers (Nike, Reebok, Adidas). *This is bad news,* I thought. Wishing I could have walked back home, I rested my head on the desk. Silence was my best weapon at these not-so-humorous times. I was expecting secondary school students to have a higher maturity level, but my classmates proved me wrong. I just had to get used to it; especially since I would much rather be at school than home, even with Lucius away most of the time.

Between 8:00 a.m. and 2:30 p.m., I spent as much time as possible in the classroom. During our lunch breaks, as the moist wind blew in my face, I watched my schoolmates play soccer or basketball through my classroom's open aluminum louvers thinking, *wow, I wish I could play like them.* At lunch, most of the time, I avoided walking to the school's canteen even though my stomach growled and craved the canteen's corn pizza, peas-dal, and soft-drinks. I found it hard to

23

socialize because I felt that my attire was too embarrassing. Everywhere I walked, someone laughed at my appearance. It was impossible for my mother to afford to buy me a better pair of uniform pants or brand name sneakers. Besides, she was old-fashioned and didn't believe in brand names.

Every day I attended school, my loneliness in the classroom made it seemed like I was the only one present. I was unable to make a friend and I felt like the girls labeled me as a nerd. Since I had no other choice, I kept to myself and, for once in my life, focused on my schoolwork. I kept surprising myself by my high scores on quizzes. Spanish, music and physical education (PE) were a few of my favorite classes out of our timetable. But physical education stood out the most.

My PE sessions were taught by Mr. Lubin, a short chubby man with a black and gray beard and hair, who always wore a buttoned-up shirt tucked into his dress pants—no matter the occasion. He was also the head coach of the school's track and field team. Every class session he gave us a brief history on certain developing sports in Saint Lucia such as cricket, netball, volleyball, track and field, football, and basketball. Then we would change out of our school uniform and in to our PE gear (short-pants and T-shirt) to compete amongst each other on our school's playing field or court. Whenever he lectured, I listened to every word that came out of his mouth and applied my knowledge in competition. With Mr. Lubin's influence, my interest for sports slowly became a part of my life. But there were setbacks.

During a PE period when we were on our school's netball court playing keep-away, boys versus girls, one of my classmates passed me the ball too high. Our focus was to play defense with good communication. At first glance, I thought that it was impossible to grab on to the sky-high ball, but being so competitive I was determined. I squatted then exploded.

As I tried to catch the ball, my knee did an unusual movement while I was airborne. It felt like my kneecap popped out of place. I returned to the gravel surface with the ball in my hand but I landed on my butt. I had to drag myself to the sidelines. Mr. Lubin gave me a bag of ice which eased the pain momentarily. At the bottom of my knee a bone bulged out that would never go away—no matter how many times I iced it. I was still able to walk but my movement never looked the same—I walked like I had poop in my pants.

A few weeks later, my mother took me to see a bone doctor. The doctor said that my knee disorder was a common problem with athletes. He reckoned that the pain was going to be part of my life until my eighteenth birthday. The doctor also advised me that I should discontinue participating in sports that involved jumping.

At this point in my life, I wasn't active in any type of sports that involved jumping. I'd contemplated the doctor's recommendation and thought, *thank God I didn't choose basketball as a career.* More icing helped ease the pain as I refrained from jumping activities.

The first time I ever heard of a basketball tryout was at my secondary school. There was an open invitation for interested players to represent the school for the upcoming Inter-Secondary Schools Basketball Competition—an annual tournament held between September and December which involved all of the secondary schools around the island.

The tryout was announced during our regular morning assembly. A quick flashback of my performance in primary school allowed me to ignore the announcement. By then, I had already realized that it wasn't all about being the tallest person in the classroom; overall, I figured out that my skills didn't qualify me for a school team—I had no talent.

Out of my class, Jermeel Pierre was the only one who made the team. Judging from the basketball games played during our PE sessions, I always knew that he was good enough to play on any team. The passion in his eyes was visible. He was so good that he ended up playing on both the junior and senior teams and we were only in our first year at secondary school.

It wasn't long after the school competition began that I went to my first basketball game. I had heard so much hype about my school's team that I wanted to show my support by attending the game. They hadn't lost a basketball game since the season began. I wanted to be a witness to winners.

I took a 30-minute walk to Vigie Multi-Purpose Sports Complex where the basketball games were held. I expected that the game would at least be played in an indoor gym like I'd seen on the television. But in Saint Lucia's reality, the blue skies were the rooftop; the sun-drenched basketball court was hard as the pavement we walked on (although the surface wasn't as rough as the previous courts I had seen). The court was surrounded by a fence and behind that fence were sheltered bleachers which ran along one lengthened side of the court. And for the first time, I actually saw out-of-bounds lines, a half court line, free throw lines, and three-pointer arcs.

Before sitting in the middle of the crowd, I spotted a very noticeable face on the sidelines—my father, Tobias—who was well known on the island for his work as a videographer. He mainly took footage for HTS, one of our few local television stations. Not many people knew me as his son. When I initially saw him at the game, I approached him and stood next to him in silence until he noticed my presence with his eyes. I mean—how should I address my father? Tobias? Daddy? Our conversation lasted about a minute or less. "Here's five dollars," he said to me, slipping it in my hands like we were drug dealers.

"Thanks," I responded, then walked away pretending to myself that I was used to my father's carelessness.

I joined my school supporters in the bleachers. They stood on their feet to see every action. Through the holes of the wire-mesh fence, I watched the game already in progress. Ten minutes had gone by and my school was up by a large margin. Although we were winning, our players on the court had no mercy for their opponents. They weren't just winning the game, they were giving them an ass-whooping.

Seated on the bouncy bleachers, I daydreamed of being part of our school's basketball team. Momentarily, I found myself suited-up with our school's blue and yellow basketball uniform. At the center of the court, I joined my teammates in a huddle to discuss the next play. Jermeel said, "Arnold, we go pass you da ball so prepare to shoot it!"

"You know I got dis," I responded cockily. The referee blew the whistle. Immediately, I caught a pass from Jermeel who stood outside the lines.

"Swoosh!"

I woke up from my fantasy and realized that my school extended their lead by two more points. I was still seated on the same wooden bleachers, wishing I was a uniformed basketball player on the court.

That was the best basketball game I had seen. Who am I fooling? That was the only game I had seen. The enthusiastic chanting, screaming, and taunting students were like groupies, especially the girls who screamed for players by their first names. At one point, I even heard someone scream out, "Jermeel, you so hot!" I wondered about my ugly, pimpled face; if I was on the school's basketball team, would the girls think I was hot, too? I promised myself I would at least tryout for the team the following year.

I had only attended one game during the 1997 season. By the end of that season, my school basketball team did well, but their performance was insufficient for the Inter-Secondary School Championship title.

One morning while seated at the breakfast table before attending school, I heard the radio broadcasting that the championship game was won by the undefeated, Saint Mary's College—the only all male secondary school on the island.

By the 13th of December, right before Saint Lucia National Day, my first school term ended. As always, exams were given a week prior to the end of the term. After evaluation, all students received their report cards. I had the second best score in my classroom.

My mother proclaimed that Christmas Day would be memorable. For some reason, she was able to afford it that year. She decorated the house with Christmas lights, put up a Christmas tree, made our traditional sorrel juice and black cake, and baked the ham and turkey.

My mother wrote our names on a piece of paper, placed it in a bag, and allowed me, herself, Lucius, Marvin, and Marva to dip our hand in the bag. The name we grabbed out of the bag was the person we were obligated to purchase a Christmas present for. In order to buy our presents, my mother gave each of us forty-dollars. Since Marvin's name was on my piece of paper, I went to town and bought him a cheap, oversized G.I. Joe action figure.

Early Christmas morning we attend the 8:30 a.m. church service. After praising the Lord, we rushed home and were served a plate of finger-licking lunch cooked by my mother. Then we finally exchanged our gifts.

I handed Marvin his gift hoping he would be satisfied with it. His pleasing facial expression calmed my worries. Upon receiving my present, I unwrapped it as if I was expecting a million dollars in the box.

"To my wonderful son, Mario.
From your mother, with love."

I held on to a leather wallet. As I unzipped my brand new wallet, I noticed there were passport sized photos of Marva, Marvin, and my mother fitted inside. I was so appreciative of my leather wallet that my eyes started tearing up; the water easily dripped down onto the smooth texture of the wallet. "Thanks so much, Mummy. I love it," I said, tightly hugging her. It was definitely a Christmas to remember.

On Monday, January 5, 1998, school reopened for the second term. For some of my classmates, a new year always meant new shoes, a new school uniform, or a new bag—everything had to be brand new. I went back to school looking the same as the previous school term. And of course I had to pay for it with the usual jokes. I understood that my mother wasn't able to afford those things so I tried to not let the teasing bother me.

With the new term on the way, I decided to get more involved in sports by participating and representing within my school's sports system. Around that time of the year, track and field was in season and my school had a scheduled event. Like in the primary school level, my school divided up the student body into four team colors (yellow, blue, green, and red). This time I represented the blue team.

During our physical education class period, Mr. Lubin recommended that I participate in shot put, discus, javelin, long jump, and high jump. He said that my height and long legs would help me excel in these events with proper training. I took some of his advice and focused on shot put, discus, and javelin. My painful knee would have caused problems in the jumping events.

After a discussion with my mother, I was allowed to stay after school hours for track and field training with Mr. Lubin. I attended training every day. I treated my events like I had found a new best friend. No one had to encourage me to become better; I wanted to be the best for myself.

From my training sessions, I learned the basics. My technique was not superb but I was ready to represent my team at the Inter-House Track and Field Competition. By the end of it all, my hard work helped me win two gold medals for shot put and discus.

Whomever was awarded medals was selected to represent the school at the upcoming Inter-Secondary Schools Track and Field Meet. I was thrilled when Mr. Lubin announced my name.

The games took place at the usual, Mindoo Phillip Park, not too far from my home. About 21 secondary schools from around the island filled up the bleachers with students of different color-coordinated-uniforms. Each school had their own ways of showing support by using homemade musical instruments such as buckets, sticks, and glass bottles for drumming, while the students chanted out their own encouraging lyrics.

The event started around 9:00 a.m. and ended about eight hours later. Since I was not involved in any races, my focus was on my two events, shot put and discus. It was my first time facing other secondary schools. I received no awards. I felt discouraged, but thoughts of a brighter future played in my head. I knew that I had more work to do and giving up now would have labeled me as a quitter. I was not a quitter.

One school night, I was sitting in the living room watching basketball on HTS television station when I witnessed greatness. On that court there were five players dressed in red uniforms and the other five players were dressed in white. One person in particular stood out; his tongue too. I had never seen such amazing and breathtaking skills from anyone in a sport. The number 23 was on the back of his shirt and above it read "Jordan."

I sat on the edge of the chair. I froze to prevent the sounds of creaks coming from our wooden chairs and floors. My eyes were focused on the television screen—like a sniper aiming at his shot. It was minutes passed my bedtime. My mother tried to break my focus. "Mario, it is after 10 o'clock, go to bed."

"Mummy, please jus' now, I jus' wanna watch dat."

It was my first time witnessing the legendary Michael Jordan from the Chicago Bulls play a NBA game. I had heard friends and classmates mention his name on numerous occasions. But on that night, thanks to our local television station, HTS, I was able to watch my first NBA game.

I knew the Utah Jazz was hosting the Chicago Bulls because their logo was printed on the court. The score was close. It seemed like the Utah Jazz were leading by one point with a few seconds left. Utah Jazz had possession. The commentators on the television announced, "Stockton inside to Malone."

"They doubled him."

"Jordan knocks it away from him, Jordan got it."

The crowd looked in awe, gradually ceasing their offensive chants, and then reverberating to defensive tones.

The commentator continued, "The Bulls can win it…the Bulls can win it." By his reaction I knew that the game was intense. With less than 20 seconds left, everyone in the building was on their feet.

"Here comes Chicago, 17 seconds from game seven or from championship number six."

Number 23 dribbled the basketball down the court then hard to his right. His defender was playing him tight. To the defender's surprise, Jordan quickly maneuvered and dribbled the ball from right to left leaving his defender motionless. As Jordan jumped to shoot the basketball, the defender tried to recover but it was too late, the ball had already left Jordan's hand. The basketball flew through the hoop hitting nothing but the bottom of the net.

I whispered, "Wow."

There was a lot of disappointment in the audience as Utah took a timeout. There were still 5 seconds left and Utah Jazz had ball possession. A small white guy had all the pressure on him. He shot the ball behind the white arc. He missed. And just like that, the game was over.

The Chicago Bulls won the 1997-1998 NBA Championship. Jordan ran up to his coach, Phil Jackson, hugged him and screamed, "I had faith! I had faith!"

Chapter 6

Lost

After my third school term, I had two months of summer vacation. I spent most of my time at home playing my Super Nintendo. Surprisingly, Olvin returned to Saint Lucia for a visit. We reunited, reliving our youthful moments in Da Yard, then soon after, it was back to school for me.

Before I started the school year in September 1998, I ensured that I was up-to-date with the latest trends—no more tight pants. I felt more relaxed at school. In fact, it was easier to be sociable and I was no longer hiding in the classroom.

One Monday morning, during our weekly assembly, our school principal, Mrs. Ifill, announced, "Basketball tryouts will be held today at 2:30 p.m. for the upcoming Inter-Secondary School Basketball Tournament." Immediately my knees felt weak and my heart raced. I felt like Mrs. Ifill directed her announcement only to me.

Afterwards, I returned to my classroom, but my mind was still at the assembly. Everything around me seemed silent. I sat at my desk while my body shook constantly. My eyes stared longingly at the wall clock. During every class period, as my teachers lectured, I pretended to be taking notes. Recapturing the day when I'd attended my first school's basketball game, I thought, *you promised to try-out.* How could I make the team when the last time I held a basketball was in primary school? I still decided to give it a try.

As soon as the last school bell rang, my heart raced faster. I stopped Jermeel before he stepped outside of the classroom. He was the only one I knew on the basketball team. "Oye Jermeel, I tink I go try-out ih," I said. He chuckled slightly.

"Boi Arnold, you sure?"

"Yeah ih gah. Buh wha'? You eh tink I good enuff or wha'?" I asked.

"Awa, I eh say dat uh. You should come try-out."

I went to the boy's bathroom and quickly changed out of my school uniform and in to my shorts and white sleeveless top. Then I went and sat in a nearby classroom amongst the numerous players who showed up. We all listened to the school's new head basketball coach, Dexter Cumberbatch, who was average height, with a toned body shape and a clean haircut. Coach Cumberbatch also worked for the Royal Saint Lucia Police Force.

He provided us with a very detailed description of the history and the fundamentals of basketball. He covered topics such as dribbling, shooting, layups, and defensive techniques. Everything was new to my ears. Most of the words sounded like a foreign language: crossover, jumper, finger-roll, hook shot, and help side defense.

Coach spoke for about 45 minutes, then we walked onto our school's tar-gravel basketball court—the same surface where our teachers parked their vehicles during school hours. We were divided into two lines at the half court line in preparation for a layup drill. Coach demonstrated precisely, "I want you to dribble the ball to the basket. When you get close enough, jump off your left foot and lay the ball up with your right hand." He pointed to the left line then continued, "Whoever is in front of this line needs to rebound the ball after the layup, pass the ball to the player on the right line, then sprint behind the right line."

Since I was a visual learner, I decided to be the last player in the very long left line. I wanted to observe the experienced players. The layup drill started going at a fast pace. As I examined the players' layup styles, my head shifted back and forth like I was at a ping-pong match. Their fast movements made it look very easy.

When I was upfront, I easily ran up, rebounded the ball, and passed it to the next player in front of the right line; I thought, *easy*. Smiling, I sprinted to the back of the right line and watched some more examples of the players who demonstrated the layup drill. My position in line kept on shifting closer to the basket after every layup. I bit my nails. For every player that seemed decent, I noticed Coach wrote their name on a piece of paper.

"Let's make this," I muttered.

While I was on the run, I tried dribbling the ball with my fingers like Coach demonstrated earlier. But the palm of my hand did all the ball handling—I thought I would never get to the basket. Jumping off my left leg, I raised my right hand and proceeded to layup. My body felt weird from the awkward motions. The ball left my hand and flew over the backboard. My knees hurt when I landed.

"Whahahaha!"

"De mun air ball a layup!"

Everyone started laughing at my ugliness. And as if I wasn't embarrassed enough, one annoying voiced yelled, "Look at his shoes! You tink you going to church mun?"

"Hahaha!"

Their continuous laughter made me feel like running home. But I jogged to the back of the left line with my head down—I was on the verge of crying. Eventually, I found the courage to keep my head up, hold back the tears, and continue the drill. But I wasn't doing any better. For every layup I attempted, I felt as if I was setting myself up for more failure and laughter. The pain from my knees couldn't match the hurtful comments coming out of the experienced players' mouths. "Oye you suck...you tall for nutting." By the end of try-outs, Coach hadn't asked me for my name.

Ignoring all traffic and friends in the community, I speed-walked home. When I arrived in Da Yard, Jermal and Jovan tried talking to me. "Oye Mario, wham to you?"

"Nutting gah. I going to bed," I responded, without coming to a halt.

"Haha, oye it's just 6 o'clock."

"I doh care, I tired. We go sight later," I said, walking into my home.

I ran up to my mother in the kitchen who was preparing supper. "Good afternoon Mummy."

"Good afternoon Mario." She noticed my sweaty shirt and disappointed face. "What happen to you?"

"Nuttin' uh, I was at basketball try-out." Her face lit up.

"For true. Did you make the team?"

I stared at our kitchen carpet. "Uh, I doh tink so," I replied. The light on her face slowly faded away.

"Well, next time work harder my boy."

The following school day, as soon as I entered my classroom, a few of the guys laughed in my face. I noticed Jermeel as the ring leader and figured that they were ridiculing my awful basketball try-out performance. I put on a fake smile and laughed along. This was the only way to stop them from making fun of me.

During the season, I showed up at the Vigie Multipurpose Sports Complex once more to show my support for our school basketball team. This time, the crowd was thicker because they played a rivalry game against Leon Hess Comprehensive—a secondary school located a few minutes from mine. Half of the bleachers were filled with our school's gray and blue uniforms and the other half were filled with green and white uniforms. The school spirit was intense; everyone chanted on their feet the whole time.

Throughout the game, all my attention was focused on the opposition team because the majority of the students chanted for "White Mike," who was one of the best players I had seen locally. It was easy to spot him, due to the fact that he was the only Caucasian player on their squad; hence his nickname—White Mike. His style was unique and his basketball skills surpassed everyone's. I was impressed by his offensive techniques. There was no one on my school's team who could have defended against him one-on-one. He was the first basketball player I witnessed single-handedly demolish his opponents. White Mike carried his team to victory for that game. But personally, I was happy I got a chance to see him play.

Again, all the excitement from the game motivated me to pursue basketball. I was tired of being a spectator—my mind and body wanted to capitalize on my height and get involved on the court.

Back at school, I became close friends with Lance Vincent and Dudley Joseph. Lance lived in Dennery, a small town located on the south-east side of the island. He was the short, quiet guy in our classroom. Dudley was from Choiseul, a small town on the south-west side of the island close to the world's only drive-in volcano. He was tall, dark, slim, and put on a smiley face. Lance and Dudley both spoke Kwéyòl fluently. They were the only guys who I shared personal stories with. I had a closer friendship with Dudley after he moved from Choiseul to Marchand with his mother, Sylvia Joseph (better known as Iya). She believed in the Roman Catholic religion and had a strong faith in God. They lived in a small wooden house less than a five minute walk from my home. Since I was now a teenager, my mother had given me permission to go over to my friends' homes. Iya was very protective of Dudley so he wasn't allowed to roam the streets like I did. I also became good friends with my old primary school classmate, Kendell, and his older brother, Java.

I had no reason to hang around Da Yard anymore—it had become quiet, boring, and lonely after Jermal and Jovan migrated to New York City. Unlike Jermal and Jovan, Kendell and Java were also fans of basketball. One day after school, we all ventured to The Summit, the only public basketball court available in our area. It was located up a steep hill in the Entrepot community; very close to my secondary school.

Walking to The Summit was tiring. On arrival at the court, I discovered its condition was the poorest I had seen on the island. The court surface was made of rock fragments and pebbles. The rims of the baskets were bent and wobbly with no nets attached. And to make matters worse, there wasn't a fence surrounding the court; all loose balls had to be chased down-hill while dodging moving vehicles.

It was my first time at The Summit. I noticed the court was divided into two groups. On the better end of the court were the bigger, talented, and older players. And on the worse half were the players my age. We didn't have any other choice. Looking at the other half of the

33

court, I noticed Jermeel. "Oye, Jermeel!" I shouted. He did a double-take.

"Arnold gason, wha' you doing dere?"

"Tryin' to get to your side of da court," I replied.

Kendell and Java were more experienced basketball players than I was. We started playing, *21*, a game where every man plays for himself—no team work is necessary. Since I was new to the game, I had to quickly pick up on the rules. For every basket I scored I was awarded two points and then had an opportunity to add three single points at the free throw line. But I had to score at least 5 points before someone scored 13 or else I had to sit out for the remainder of the game. The game was over when someone reached 21 points.

Every game of 21 we played, I sat out when someone scored 13 points. After my second game, one guy said to me, "Oye, how com' you so tall and you cah even score 5 points?"

"Gason, doh mind dat. I jus' startin' to learn. Dat eh nutting," I replied.

"Da mun just big for nuttin'," someone else interrupted.

I wanted to prove everyone wrong.

When there were enough players on the court, someone shouted, "Teams!" Two pairs of four players were selected to play—a four-player team versus another four-player team. Initially, of course, I was not chosen. I had to wait until the end of a game when a team had scored 10 points. Winners stayed on to play another game while the losers were kicked off. Every game my team played, we lost.

By 6:00 p.m., the sunset and the games slowly died down. 30-minutes later, the court was blacked out.

After my first evening at The Summit, basketball was my drug. I felt like I needed to play to keep a smile on my face. Every weekday I rushed home from school, leaving Marvin and Marva at home, and walked up the hill. This was my regular routine: wake up, go to school, play basketball, then head back home to do the same thing the following day.

On weekends we played in the blazing 90 degrees Fahrenheit sun from noon until six in the evening. The more I played, the more I felt like my skills improved.

When I was tired of being called, "Big or tall for nuttin'," I slam-dunked my first basketball on that court. The only problem I had to overcome was my painful knee. I constantly iced it to ease the soreness after I played; day by day it got better and less agonizing.

I became so confident with my improvements that one day I mentioned to Java and Kendell, "Gason, I tink I go play in da NBA ih."

"Gason shate you talkin'!"

"Nah, nah!" I said. "For real-ih gah, I tink I go make it for true."

Kendell brought me back to reality. "Oye, you know how much people tryin' to play in da NBA mun?" I choked and then looked at him puzzled. He continued, "Exactly, not everyone can play dere!"

Reflecting on Kendell's statement, I thought, *why can't anyone play?* His comments motivated me to never miss a day on the court. I believed that hard work would make my dreams come true.

Back at home, Marvin, Marva, and I were watching wrestling one Sunday night when my mother bawled out, "Where is Lucius uh? Up to now his not back from fishing?" The tone in her voice made it seem like she predicted a catastrophe. It was about 9:00 p.m. and Lucius was expected to be home about two hours earlier. I looked out the window but all I saw were thick dark clouds in the skies.

"I doh see him outside uh," I replied.

The later it got, the more worried my mother was. While I went to bed in a happy mood, my mother stayed up all night calling Lucius's closest friends.

Two days went by and Lucius didn't show up. The story was shared with our local television and radio news stations—the headlines read, "Two fishermen lost at sea." There was a mass search of the Caribbean Seas. Our neighbors showed their sympathy by visiting my mother throughout the days.

After a few days of heartache and pain, our home phone rang and Lucius's voice was on the other end. My mother cried out, "Lucius, I was worried so sick about you!" Marvin and Marva ran to the living-room, while I lagged behind. They acted like a new-born was added to our family. I was hoping for Lucius's death announcement. We tried to eavesdrop on their conversation, but it was hopeless.

The phone call lasted about 30 minutes. Marva, Marvin, and I waited patiently in the living room until we were told the story. My mother summarized, "He is in Columbia. He was lost at sea for two days and got found by Columbians who worked on a ship."

"Daddy comin' back home?" Marva asked.

"The Columbians are going to return him back to St. Lucia this weekend."

Minutes later, everyone in the community heard about Lucius's phone call. Hours later, the news broadcasted the good news.

My one week of pretending to be the man of the house was over.

Chapter 7

Only the Beginning

In the summer of 1999, I found a second home—The Summit. Whenever I stepped foot on The Summit, all worries were set free. Besides basketball, the only things that came first in my life were my school, my mother, Marvin, and Marva.

At home, before I headed to The Summit, I peeped through our side window to detect any movement on top of the hill. If I saw anyone, I ran so that I could get in as many games as possible before sunset. If no one was on the court, I would go anyways—a normal day or holiday; sunshine or rain; sometimes even in the darkness.

On my way to The Summit, as I journeyed the streets of Bishop's Gap, through Bagatelle, then up the steep Entrepot Hill, I always reminded myself that I would never end up like the nappy headed boys and the men who spent most of their time sitting in a corner consuming drugs. Whenever I walked down their road I could hear my mother preaching, "Mario, please stay away from them boys by the road eh." All my life, I treated their path like a no-entry lane. When they first noticed I bounced around a basketball, maybe they knew that I was already high on life, not even alcohol was in my system, because they left me alone.

Upon arrival at The Summit, it felt like stepping onto a new planet, although from the edge I could see my home together with all the houses and trees next to the Catholic Church. My new found basketball friends, Hakeem Yorke and Kern Constantine, were on the court as much as I was. They lived so close that I could see their homes from anywhere on the court. They were the ones that made our pickup games fun, competitive, and interesting. We all had one common goal—to play for the secondary school that we attended.

September 1999, the start of my third school year at Entrepot Secondary School: same classmates, different classroom. My attitude had changed. I acted as if I was attending a school just for basketball and making the team was my final exam—only basketball crossed my mind. An entire year had gone by; the wait was over.

I hardly had any real friends on the basketball team so the day of the tryouts, I tried to encourage Dudley to tag along with me.

"Oye Dudley, I tink you should come tryout mun."

"Awa gason, cricket is my sport. Basketball eh my ting."

"Irie, I go jus' go by myself den."

Here I was, standing on the same right layup line—déjà vu. But I felt like history could only repeat itself if I allowed it to. I looked more like a basketball player with my basketball shorts, a jersey, and a pair of Nike shoes that my godmother had purchased for me in New York City.

Coach Cumberbatch held his pen and a piece of paper in his hands in search of talent. It seemed as if it was the same pen. Seeing many familiar faces in line made the butterflies in my stomach flutter. To distract my nervousness, I muttered, "Come on, stay focus. Come on, stay focus."

Suddenly, I was upfront holding the basketball with a tight grip. Staring at the rim, I dribbled the ball with my fingers while flexing my wrist towards the open lane. The rays from the sun were slightly affecting my sight. I felt like everything was silent, moving in slow motion. For every time the ball touched the gravel surface, my heart also beat at the same rhythm. When I was close enough to the rim, I vertically exploded, gripping the ball tightly with both hands, then sunk the ball through the hoop. As I hung on to the rim, I finally heard a small applause from the players. I ran to the back of the line smiling with my head up.

"Hey, what's your name?" Coach asked without any hesitation.

"Arnold," I replied.

He jotted it down on the piece of paper. From the back of the line, Benny, one of our infamous school clowns asked me, "Oh you tink you a good player now, huh?" It was always hard to tell if he was serious or not. He kept looking over my head as if something interesting was going on behind my back. It turned out that Benny was just surprised at how tall I was. At the age of fourteen, I was about six foot four and my shoe size was the same as my age.

After two hours of basketball tryouts, and making the team, I was so thrilled that I told everyone on my way home. Nothing could have wiped the smile off my face.

"Mummy, Mummy!" I yelled as I ran through the front door. She startled, held her hand across her chest then asked, "What happened boy? You made me jump."

"Sorry," I paused to catch my breath, "I'm on da school basketball team." My mother clasped her hands together and smiled with all white teeth.

"That's my boy! That's my boy!" Her reaction could have been heard by our neighbors. She continued, "But what about your knees?"

I rolled my eyes, turned around to give her my back and quickly responded as I tried to walk off to my bedroom, "Ugh, it gettin' better."

"Mario." She said to get my attention back. I was now staring at her index finger moving up and down in a warning gesture. "You remember what the doctor said eh. Just be careful. I don't have money for surgery eh."

"Mummy, doh worry. It not hurtin' dat much anymore," I said, and then proceeded to my bedroom.

Following a shower, I rested on my bed. I placed both of my hands behind my head and gazed at Marvin's top bunk-bed. Soon I envisioned myself at the Vigie Multipurpose Sports Complex surrounded by cheering female fans as I represented the Entrepot Secondary School basketball team. As I warmed up on the layup line, I looked at Marvin amongst the rowdy spectators. He shouted from the bleachers, "You made the team!" I nodded my head and pumped a fist in the air as a sign of victory. "Oye, you make de team?"

My imagination faded as I realized Marvin had actually asked me the question. Still staring at the bottom of his bed, I answered, "Yup."

Basketball was officially part of my life, though I felt like it still wasn't enough. I was ready to learn as much as I could from Coach Cumberbatch and the experienced players. Every practice session I'd arrive 30 minutes earlier than the scheduled time. My early arrival was to ensure that I was physically and mentally ready to advance my knowledge of the game.

For the period of practice, Coach Cumberbatch expressed no tolerance for negativity and lack of discipline. His attitude allowed us to develop strong team chemistry. I was part of a family that I loved.

Every weekday, between the hours of three and five in the evening, I was introduced to some new basketball drills and techniques. Since I was aware of my visual learning abilities, I always started drills from the back of the line so that I could witness ample demonstrations from my teammates. In next to no time, my offensive and defensive strategies were tossed up a notch. And my basketball I.Q. had dramatically increased.

As a team, we practiced for about two to three weeks. Then it was the commencement of the 1999 Inter-Secondary Schools Basketball Competition. Since I was under 16, I played for the junior basketball team; while the better players played for the senior team. Jermeel was still a junior who played for the seniors.

According to the schedule, my junior games always started about 2:30 p.m. while the senior games started a little later when the sun was less of an eye distraction.

The secondary schools participating in the competition were divided into different groups organized by the sponsors. I never understood the logics or the system used but in order to be in a good position for the post season playoffs, we had to win close to all our games. And then to be the champions, we had to win the rest of the games.

This was my very first experience with competitive team basketball. There were smaller audiences in the bleachers during our junior games. Tobias always took footage of my games. But it was not like he came to show his outside-child support; he was just working like any other day.

My lack of experience allowed me to start every game on the bench. Whenever I had the opportunity to play, I tried to contribute as much as possible to my team and at the same time tried to impress Tobias. But being a novice to the game, I fumbled the ball on many possessions—my bones shook, my heart beat vigorously, and my hands felt greasy. My contributions to the team were limited. At times, I felt like my team would have been better off without me. However, I knew this was only the beginning.

My junior season ended shortly after losing the quarter finals to Vide Bouteille Secondary School. I thought, *I'll be better next year.* Our senior team had also advanced. And even though White Mike was missing, they lost in the quarter-finals to our rival, Leon Hess Comprehensive Secondary School.

Both the 1999 junior and senior championship games were won by the famous Saint Mary's College.

Ten minutes per game was my average throughout the season. I took that experience and utilized it to better myself while playing games at The Summit. The older guys on the court had seen my improvements. Eventually, I made a transition to the side of the court where everything seemed better. I was appreciative to be playing amongst the older, experienced guys. Their competitiveness helped my skills considerably. Furthermore, Kendell, Java, Hakeem, Kern, and I traveled to different locations around the island for one-day tournaments, to broaden our basketball experience against other more talented players.

Chapter 8

Basketball or Track and Field?

While computer-users worried about the possibilities of Y2K and the upcoming new millennium, I was more concerned about whether or not I should focus on basketball or track and field.

Another school year had gone by; things were a bit different. Since the most important secondary school examination was going to take place during the following school year, all fourth year students were divided into different classrooms. The majority of the subjects I chose were sciences; therefore, I was placed with classmates with the same academic interests as me. Dudley had chosen business classes; as a result, we weren't classmates anymore. But Lance was still with me.

My schoolwork had taken priority; I'd become more serious about preparing for the day of the prominent Caribbean Examination Council, better known as CXC. There was a level of respect for these exams because our results determined our future on the island. They were the equivalent to an America high-school diploma. If I had no CXC papers, then it would be difficult to obtain a successful job or have sufficient prerequisites for college. These island-wide exams were taken by the end of our fifth and final school year. And as always, I was preparing myself because I wanted a positive future.

In my new classroom, a few seats ahead of my desk, sat the shy and soft spoken Levern Spencer. I felt honored to be in her presence because I respected her as a person and as an athlete. She was definitely a Saint Lucian idol for the successes she brought upon our island at her young age. Levern had some good qualities, smart, strong faith in God, and obedient, however, she was also known as the island's consecutive Sport Woman of the Year for her brilliance in the women's high jump event. No female in Saint Lucia have ever accomplished the heights that she had leaped over. Not just locally, but regionally, she was on top of the charts.

Levern was my track and field teammate, and we trained together at the Mindoo Phillip Park. The Saint Lucian Athletics Association had hired Jouge Acostarico, alias Noup, a Cuban field event coach, to assist in improving and strengthening the development of field-event athletes, mainly in the areas of shot put, discus and javelin. Mr. Lubin had told me about the exciting news and trusted that I would excel in the hands of Noup's training sessions.

HANGING ON TO MY DREAMS

My successes from the 1999 Inter-Secondary School Track and Field Competition had placed me amongst the top under-16 shot put and discus throwers on the island. I had received my first national medals from these events that year. And as a result, I was included in the select group scheduled to meet after school under Noup's coaching supervision.

When I first met Noup, he used a lot of body movements to communicate as his spoken English was very poor. He was a few inches shorter than me with a tan complexion and a round clean-shaved bald head. We tried our best to teach him English; after all, his services were greatly appreciated.

Sometimes Noup would share his communist experiences on the island of Cuba which was under Fidel Castro's leadership. Noup's homeland stories made me respect him more as my Coach. Every weekday afternoon from three to five, my new national teammates and I met with him. I was first introduced to weightlifting during his sessions. Every week my muscles felt tighter when I flexed. My knees felt stronger from all the drills my body was getting used to and I was slowly perfecting my shot put and discus techniques.

Ultimately, I started focusing on only shot put after Noup decided that discus wasn't the best fit for me; although if I had a choice, I wouldn't have chosen any field events. Playing basketball brought more excitement to my life. But shot put was another way to escape my family's hardship.

In the new millennium I demonstrated my progression and faith in Noup's training sessions. On the island, I was making a name for myself in the junior male shot put event. The previous year, I had only thrown the eight pound shot put a distance of 10 meters. Ever since I'd been under Noup's program, my personal best went up to over 12 meters. And in the discus event, which I barely practiced for, I always finished in the top three. My medal collection at home was gradually increasing. My mother was proud.

After each training session at Mindoo Phillip Park with Noup, I jogged for 15-minutes up the Entrepot Hill to The Summit to play some basketball games before sunset.

Chapter 9

More Than a Game

"Basketball...very hard! Track and field...better opportunity," Noup said to me on the day I told him that my basketball practice for the upcoming 2000 Inter-Secondary School Basketball Competition would conflict with my track and field training sessions. In other words, he wanted me to quit basketball to focus only on shot put.

"Noup, I cah do dat," I said to him, shaking my head. "I doh wanna disappoint my teammates." As his eyebrows came together, he shook his hand and gave me his back. At that point, there was nothing Noup could have done. Whenever I had a chance, I still attended his sessions; nevertheless, it was another basketball season, and this time I wasn't allowing my team to go down in the quarterfinals like the 1999 postseason.

A week before tryouts, Jermeel and I had a conversation outside our classroom. "Boi! You eh see de mun yet?" asked Jermeel.

"Who...Ed? Awa uh. Buh I hear about him ih. I hear de mun about six foot eight ih."

"Oye, de mun is a beast," Jermeel said.

It wasn't until a week later, during basketball tryouts, that I first saw the so-called "beast." Our new teammate, Ed Desir, who was an automatic selection, was a transfer from Soufriere Secondary School—located south-west of Castries. He was a fifth year student. To me, Ed was like a big, black giant with the personality of a child. He would have blocked my sunlight if I stood next to him. With his addition, our senior team was looking like an unstoppable powerhouse.

That year, I was still under 16 so I was still allowed to play on the junior team. Coach Cumberbatch announced the 2000 basketball squads. He thought that it was in our senior team's best interests for me to be added to the senior roster as well as the junior. Dudley had finally taken my suggestion to play basketball for the school and he was now my teammate on the junior lineup. He wasn't a skillful player but he used his height to be a decent rebounder. Jermeel was one year older than I was, so he was only allowed to play for the senior team. His point guard senses and experience would have been a great assistance to our junior team. I was the only returning junior player so I felt like it was my duty to carry the team on my back.

On the senior side, Coach Cumberbatch permitted me to start the senior season as Ed's backup center. I was the only junior playing for the senior team. Coach had seen my improvements so he utilized my skills and height on both teams. I was the tallest player on the junior team but the second tallest on the senior team when standing next to Ed.

"Dat is papicho; dat eh fair."

"He cah jus' transfer and come play for Entrepot Secondary School; dat is shate!" These were the angry voices of the many players and coaches from other schools who were threatened by Ed's presence on our team. The possibilities of my school winning a senior championship were at an all-time high. The drama had created a controversy over whether or not Ed should be allowed to participate in this year's competition. For a brief moment, our fans panicked; however, no rules or regulations were broken.

The basketball gossip had only created hype and excitement for our team; the audience could not wait to watch our basketball games. We were ready to give the fans what they wanted, but we all kept in mind that there was a bigger goal—the championship trophy.

As the season got underway, both of our school's basketball teams were on winning streaks. I realized that all the time I spent at The Summit made me feel more relaxed during these games. All the wins we had accumulated made us some of the strongest junior and senior teams on the island. Not even my basketball acquaintances, Hakeem and Kern, who both played for different schools, were any competition for us.

For the junior team, I led my team in points, rebounds, steals, and block shots per game. No more bench warming; I was a starting center. But this wouldn't have been possible without the inspiring performances by Ed. On the senior team, it was his show. I was only a backup center; the one who averaged about 10 minutes a game to allow Ed to get a short breather. Ed's defensive ethics were similar to the four-time NBA Defensive Player of the Year, Dikembe Mutombo. And of course, Ed emulated Mutombo's infamous waving of the index finger after every block shot. He was also an outstanding, strong, offensive post player with great foot work.

For every game we won, more and more spectators showed up for our following games. We weren't only defeating teams; we were blowing them out by 20-point, 30-point, even 40-point leads. We were the only senior team scoring a total of 100 or more points per game.

With all the excitement in my basketball world, I wondered if Tobias was proud of my performances. It was hard to determine if he came to support my games or if he was just shooting his usual footage for the media. How could my father be so close, yet so distant? Since he never introduced me as his son to anyone, I took it upon myself to do so.

At random times, I would ask my friends, "You know Tobias is my father?" And everyone's first response was, "For true? I never knew dat, uh. Now I see da resemblance." I failed to believe I looked like him. To me, he looked like an old man who always wore video and digital camera cords around his neck. Though I never seemed wanted in his presence, I always felt the need to say hello. Standing next to him made me feel like a lost puppy begging for his attention. But all I got was his expected five dollar donation. In due time, I figured there was no hope trying to establish a real father-son relationship with Tobias. Basketball almost filled up the fatherly-love missing in my heart.

With our perfect regular season, it was time for the post season playoffs. Quarterfinals and semifinals were a breeze—we still hadn't faced any competition. We dominated in every aspect. There was only one more secondary school blocking our championship road to victory—the defending champions, Saint Mary's College. We were the only two undefeated junior and senior teams who made it all the way through to the finals.

The championship game, Entrepot Secondary School versus Saint Mary's College, was the highest anticipated game of the season.

"Boi, Entrepot go take dat championship ih!"

"Nah mun, no team cah beat Saint Mary's College."

The championship game had established a debate amongst fans. They had already determined the outcome of the game and the majority of them suspected that Saint Mary's College would be the victor. My junior team played first.

This was my first ever basketball championship game appearance. Before our 2:30 p.m. tipoff, my teammates were sure, "Dats our victory." But on the court during our warm-ups, sloppiness and butterfingers exposed our nervousness.

On the other half of the court, our opponents in the red uniforms demonstrated organization. Yet their over-the-top confidence was sickening to me; they boasted for their fans, taunted, and held their heads up high like they had already won the game. To make it worse, their supporters in the bleachers outnumbered ours which made it hard to ignore their rowdiness and disrespectfulness. The early game made our supporters late because school was still in progress. No one expected us to make it this far—our principal hadn't implemented an early school dismissal so that our schoolmates could have showed their support.

Coach Cumberbatch's game plan wasn't any different from our regular season games. The set plays we ran started from the "inside-out." Meaning, after a series of screens to get a player open, the first option was to pass the ball to the post players, who sat inside the painted area, and, if possible, took the basketball strong to the basket; otherwise dish the basketball back out to a guard who stood beyond the 3-point arc. I played on the post area, therefore, most of the time, I was the first option.

It was two-20 minute halves of intense action in the hot, blazing sun. The game started very sloppy on our end; we created plenty of unusual turnovers. It must have been the butterflies kicking in. Saint Mary's College played a tight-zone defense which made it very difficult for my teammates to get the ball inside to me. Saint Mary's took charge of the game early on, and by halftime, they were leading by double digit points.

Being down at the half for the first time that season had everyone on our bench speechless, including Coach. We sat on the bench for 10 minutes staring at the ground; we blew off steam and rehydrated as fatigue had the best of us. Even the small number of our supporters who showed up had given up cheering.

To commence the second half, Coach finally called us in a huddle and we listened attentively as he tried to revitalize our hope. "We can get back in this game! It's not over! Let's fight!" Coach's speech had my blood pumping once again.

We piled up our hands in the middle and shouted, "One, two, three! ESS accomplish!"

In the second half, we responded with a strong full court 1-3-1 defensive press. We were now the aggressor, forcing numerous turnovers and converting them into points. To hype up my team some more, I slam-dunked the basketball through the hoop which also awarded my point guard with an assist. Four back-to-back field goals made from our shooting guard and small forward put us back in the game.

It was hard to determine the scores at this point because all the scoring and statistics were calculated by hand and were only seen by the officials who sat at the sideline table, but it was evident that we were still down.

A timeout called by SMC's head coach, better known as Flyin, allowed our starting five to catch their breath. The musical noises from their supporters had also died down. The bleachers started to fill up with our late supporters. Coach yelled to the officials at the scoring table, "What's the scores?"

"Entrepot down by four points," the score keeper replied. Coach Cumberbatch quickly drew up a game plan.

"Let's go Entrepot!" echoed across the court from the stands. We fed off the crowd's energy.

With all the confidence in the world, we stepped back into the game. One out of two free-throws made by Dudley cut the SMC's lead to three points. We executed a defensive stop and our shooting guard nailed a three-point jumper from the wing to tie the game. SMC woke up their fans with a slam dunk of their own. I answered with a drop-step-layup to tie the game once more.

As the game was near to the end, our defense became sluggish. This got us into foul trouble. Exhaustion allowed us to crouch over, placing our hands on our knees. My legs felt heavy. SMC immediately reacted to our weakening point, took over the game, and never looked back.

When the referees blew the final whistle, I walked off the court with my head down blaming myself for our lack of energy. I saw the movements of my teammates and Coach's lips but their sounds weren't emitting in my universe.

After the game, we were awarded our second place medal. An announcement registered in my ear that made me feel even more like all my hard work had been for nothing. "Averaging over twenty points, ten rebounds, and seven blocks per game throughout the regular season—the overall most valuable player award goes to, Arnold Henry."

Following the award ceremony, Tobias asked Coach Cumberbatch permission for a group photo. After the shot, he faced me and said, "You look tired out there today."

I wanted to scream, "Shut the fuck up," but I listened. And before I walked away, he reached out his hand and gave me five dollars.

On arrival to my home, my mother, who spotted me through the window with my trophy in my hands, busted through the front door, shouting, "My boy, your team won the game?"

"No Mummy, we lost. Dats jus my MVP trophy."

"Aw, I'm sorry to hear that. Next time baby."

I sighed then murmured, "Yeah."

"Sorry I couldn't make it to your game. I had a lot of rooms to clean at the hotel today."

"Dats okay. I understan'. Next week is da senior finals at 4 o'clock," I said.

She slammed her hand on her forehead. "Oh yeah, for true…I just remember. I will make sure I come to that game."

One week later, I was the only suited junior player amongst game-face-ready senior players. The game was at the same venue where we battled for the junior number one spot, but this time, the court was surrounded by four times the number of students and supporters than had appeared at my junior game. The overcrowding of the bleachers meant spectators were only a few centimeters away from courtside. They were so close that their body heat invaded the Friday dull, gray late-afternoon skies. My mother and Marvin stood on their feet and cheered through the metal-mesh-fence, from behind our bench.

From the jump-ball to the end of the first half, I was seated at the edge of our team bench, watching the action, and waiting for Coach Cumberbatch to holler my name. Ed was playing one of his best games, so my contributions were barely needed. From the get go, the game seemed like a heavyweight boxing title match because of the unusual physical contact, all together with the fans' encouraging chants.

"Let's go Entrepot...Let's go," cheered our supporters.

The electronic scoreboard which was switched on for the first time that season read: 29-25 in our favor—we were up by 4 points—which was our lowest scoring and the smallest lead at halftime that season. Obviously, we had met our first real competition in Saint Mary's College, the eight time back-to-back defending Inter-Secondary School Senior Champions.

When there were only 20 minutes left in the game, the pressure was on both teams and tensions were high. Coach Cumberbatch received his first technical foul after trying to argue a call with the referees. There were near fist fights between players, and when it seemed our bodies weren't wet enough with perspiration, it started to drizzle causing a ten minute game delay.

The rain eventually eased up as the daylight slowly faded away. The court's surface was dried with sponges, mops, and brooms. Our proud fans screamed louder and louder for every descending second on the game-clock; for every made basket, ESS supporters chanted, "Another one in their face...another one...Po! Po!"

When I finally played my two minutes of action, I represented my school proudly and scored two points, at the same time. Though I got ticketed with three quick defensive fouls, I held my ground long enough for Ed to catch his breath.

"Go home college...go home...go home college...go home," more chants were fired at our opponents.

After a long, fierce battle, the crowd shouted at last, "Three, two, one!" And the majority of our supporters from courtside stampeded the court. Even other non-Entrepot students joined in the celebration. The victory was ours.

In the midst of the jumping and screaming, I spotted my mother in the darkness. I quickly ran up to her and yelled, "Mummy, Marvin, we won, we won!"

She screamed along with me, bouncing, giggling and clapping. "That's my boy, that's my boy!" Marvin smiled.

During the award ceremony, as I held on to the championship trophy, I felt like nothing else mattered. The gold medal around my neck and the sponsorship hat on my head reiterated our victory. Amongst all the activities going on in the crowd, my ears overheard the voice of a hypocrite. "That's my son!" When I turned around to face the familiar voice, I saw Tobias pointing me out to one of the male sponsors of the competition.

"That's your son," the man repeated. "Tobias is your father?" he asked me seconds later, as if my father's comment wasn't enough evidence.

I nodded slightly and stuttered, "Ye...ye...yeah." I scratched the back of my head, flashed a fake smile, and then turned to continue celebrating our victory with my teammates.

Chapter 10

Tough Times

The first year of the new millennium came to an end with devastating news.

New Year's Eve, I woke to the sound of my mother's cries. I quickly jumped out my bed, ignoring the sleep in my eyes. Lucius wasn't in sight in the kitchen so I felt she was safe from harm. She stood very close to her electronic radio as if its maximum volume wasn't loud enough. She grasped her forehead and cried out to God in Kwéyòl, "Bondous!" Bondous!"

"Mummy! Wha' happen'?" I asked. She switched back and forth between stations in search of better news coverage.

"Listen to this…so sad," she replied. I paid close attention.

"During a church ceremony at the Cathedral, in the city of Castries, a group of men burst into the church with machetes," said the radio broadcaster.

I thought, *what da…wow that's crazy.*

"The men slashed the members of the church's congregation with their machetes, doused them with kerosene and set them on fire," the broadcaster continued.

During a church service? I couldn't listen any further. *What is my island coming to?*

A 72-year-old Irish nun was murdered and at least 13 victims were injured in the incident. Two suspected men were arrested later that evening in relation to the crime. When authorities asked the suspects the reason for their demonic actions, they responded that they were prophets sent by Haile Selassie. The late Haile Selassie was an Ethiopian emperor worshipped as a god by Rastafarians. The Rastafarian leaders of Saint Lucia said that they weren't affiliated with the church invasion.

I was disheartened by the whole situation and prayed for peace on the island. My people truly needed more prayers, especially since our crime rate was slowly increasing.

To prevent myself from getting entwined in the wrong crowds or having conflicts with the law, I continued to stay active in sports. After celebrating the victory of being the 2000 Senior Inter-Secondary School Basketball Champions, all my focus went back to shot put training with Noup. With my accomplishments from participating in local track and field events throughout the year, I was hoping that I would be given an opportunity to represent my island like Levern Spencer.

During an intense workout at Mindoo Phillip Park, the president of the Saint Lucia Athletics Association, Mrs. Patsy St. Marthe, gathered us for a brief meeting. Whenever she came to visit us with her professional attire, it meant business, although her presence was charming. Being the first female president of the athletic association, she was one of the sweetest, proudest presidents. She took the job seriously. Some of her motivational speeches influenced me to work hard throughout my track and field years.

Her presence at our training session felt like my wishes were about to come true. All eyes were on Mrs. St. Marthe as she announced the participants for the 30th Carifta Games. The Carifta games were an annual junior track and field event for countries associated with the Caribbean Free Trade Association…mainly islands from the Caribbean.

"The following athletes will be ambassadors of Saint Lucia…this year, Barbados will be hosting the Carifta Games," said Mrs. St. Marthe.

Mrs. Marthe had called 10 athletes, including Levern and I, to represent the island. She said that we were the top athletes who had official qualifying times and distances.

I thought to myself, *a perfect opportunity to bring home a medal.* But worried Noup snapped me back to reality.

"Com' on Arnold! You need work…hard…very hard competition. Everyone…very… very… strong!"

That same training day, I held and stared at the 12-pound, round metal shot put as if it was a crystal ball. I needed to push the shot put to distances that I had never landed. I called on my tenacity, worked hard in the weight room, and tried my best to perfect my throwing technique.

On the island, I was one of the top under-17 shot put throwers, but I could imagine the competiveness that the other islands would bring to the table.

In April of 2001, my nine teammates and I, alongside Mr. Lubin, Noup, Mrs. St. Marthe, and a few others, left for Barbados aboard Liat Airlines. My mother was more excited than I was for it was my first time representing my country and my first time on a plane. Before I left home, she said, "Make us proud my boy. Bring back home a medal. And good luck."

"I go try my bes'," I said.

Onboard the aircraft before we even left Saint Lucia, the captain said, "We will be landing in approximately 30 minutes." I had enough time for a short nap. The smooth plane ride made me relax and, before I knew it, my mind wandered and I found myself standing on a medal podium as I glanced at thousands of Caribbean supporters.

The sounds of the captain's voice snapped me out of my dream. We had arrived at our final destination. Another twenty minutes and the plane ride would have been the same amount of time it took to drive from the north to the south of Saint Lucia.

In Barbados I realized that not all islands in the Caribbean are the same. I lived on a mountainous one, but Barbados was as flat as the airport strip the plane landed on. The majority of the island was scrubby. The Barbadian people had a slightly deeper accent which made it difficult for me to converse. But they were friendly, for the most part. Saint Lucia and Barbados had almost the same history as we were once both ruled by the British.

I discovered that my team shared the same hotel with the Bahamas, Bermuda and Jamaica teams. Our team size was noticeably smaller because Saint Lucia couldn't afford to bring more athletes. Our plan was to make Mrs. St. Marthe proud by finishing, at least, in the top three places. To me, this wasn't a free vacation; it was a business trip for athletes.

Saturday, April 14, 2001, I awaited my fate as I faced competitors from nine different islands. In all, there were about sixteen of us. Although I was the tallest amongst the under-17 shot put throwers; my opponents looked like body builders straight out of a magazine.

The stadium's seats seemed to be sold out and that made my nervousness kick in. The thunderous crowds were the perpetrator of all my fears. It felt like all eyes were on me.

Before we competed, the officials instructed, "You will be given three throws in the first round…and then, the top eight distances will be chosen to advance to the final round…in addition, these eight finalists will be given an extra three throws."

I felt too intense so I jogged on the track near the shot put area to loosen up my muscles. I repeated to myself, "You can do it….You work hard…You can do it!" In the midst of trying to pump up my energy with my motivational words, I choked as I witnessed the performance of my opponent from Martinique.

"14.19 meters!" the official shouted. I had to ask him to repeat himself. "14.19 meters!" As I stared into space, my eyebrows raised as my mouth dropped. I couldn't believe it.

"Arnold Henry…Arnold Henry."

"Huh?"

"You up." The official brought me back to my senses. I undressed out of my blue, yellow, black, and white warm-ups, picked up the shot put, and approached the throwing area which looked more professional than the amateurish circle I was used to. I walked into the circle, glanced out into the open green grass, and breathed in and out. I heard Noup's cheers from behind the fence which separated the coaches from the athletes.

I sighed then whispered, "Dis is it." With fierce concentration, I took my stance within the circle. After a slight pause, I executed my technique, pushing the shot put as hard as possible, simultaneously roaring like a lion.

"Arnold Henry, 11.81 meters!" shouted the official. I walked out of the circle, pretending there was pain in my fingers that caused me to throw the shot put at such a short distance.

I tried my best to avoid Noup but I saw him shrug his shoulders and raise his palms to the blue skies. "Bad!" I shouted. He covered his eyes with his black sunglasses as if he was embarrassed to see me.

He pointed back two fingers. "Push!" I nodded.

My other two throwing attempts didn't mark any better distances. After the first round, I placed twelfth, throwing 11.81 meters. I didn't even top my local personal best. I had an opportunity to redeem myself with the discus throwing event. But how could I when I barely practiced for it? Surprisingly, I threw 34.17 meters, a personal best that allowed me to place eighth amongst fourteen discus throwers.

By Monday, April 16, 2001, it was official: I was to leave Barbados with zero medals.

Out of the ten of us, Levern Spencer was the only gold medal recipient. She soared over a height of 1.79 meters in the under-20 girl's high jump. Her mark had tied Carifta's high jump record, and smashed her local national record. During her jumps, when she was the only jumper left, islands from all over were cheering her on as she attempted to break the record—this was a true inspiration because it felt like she unified the entire Caribbean nation.

On our way back to Saint Lucia, Mrs. St. Marthe expressed how proud she was with our overall individual performances, and with us as a team. On arrival at the Saint Lucia Airport, we were greeted by the Honorable Mario Michel, Saint Lucia's Minister of Education, Human Resource Development, Youth and Sports at the time. He expressed to us that we made our island proud. But most of the praise went out to the only returning gold medalist—Levern Spencer.

The Carifta games made me realized that I had to work harder in order to be a great athlete. I appreciated the experience because I learned that somewhere out there, others were working twice as hard as me. I was willing to push myself and go the extra distance.

"Next time you will do better," my mother advised. She always knew the right things to say when I was down.

Every night, before I slept, I thanked the Lord for blessing me with a strong mother. Her strength was my strength. Her weakness was also my weakness.

My mother suffered from ankle pains that the doctors and experts could not explain. There weren't any inexpensive medications available for purchase that eased or healed the periodic pains—only soft-candle and heat was used to lessen the swelling.

By the sounds of my mother's cries, I just knew that the ankle caused her a lot of pain. I felt helpless and weak. She would lay in her bed, screaming like a baby needing attention and all I could do was watch speechlessly, fearfully. But most of all, I felt useless. I always asked, "Mummy, you need anyting?"

Her responses would be, "No, thank you," or "Can I get a glass of water?"

I was only strong enough to show sympathy for a moment, but when I couldn't hold the tears in my eyes any longer, I allowed them to flow down my face—mainly under the covers of my bed.

Doctors suggested that her leg be amputated but my mother didn't want that. Every day it seemed to get worse. Her ankle was black as tar. Each time I found the courage to examine her, it seemed like a mole was digging through her ankle. The color slowly changed from black to pink. The bone became almost visible underneath the skin. There was nothing Marvin, Marva, or I could do except be on our best behavior and be as quiet as possible.

The majority of the time, Lucius was not around to show Mummy the support that she needed. What kind of love was that? As her eldest child, I felt the need to find a cure, but instead, I just got used to her weeping. I prayed to God (the one true father who has always been there for us from the beginning), pleading every night, hoping He would answer my prayers.

Times got harder for our family when my mother lost her job because she took too many days off. Her ankle limited her from standing for long periods of time and, as a housekeeper working in a hotel, she needed to be able to stand on her feet to clean the rooms. As a result, there was less food on the dinner table.

Soon after, one of our newly moved-in neighbors, Rosalie Duplessis, witnessed my mother's struggles and decided to give my mother a job as a nanny for her newborn and only son, Kobie Lynch. Every weekday, before Rosalie left for work, she dropped off Kobie at our home at about eight in the morning. She picked him up after six in the evening. Little Kobie was barely two-years old when my mother started babysitting him. The small amount Rosalie paid my mother barely got our family through our tough financial times. We hung on by a thread.

Chapter 11

My Final Basketball Game?

By September 2001, I had started my fifth and final year of secondary school. With the most important exam approaching, I felt the need to act like a nerd; sitting behind my books more often—being studious. The CXC was less than one year away.

What does the future hold for me after graduation? Where will I be in the next year or two? One way or another, I sought a pathway that led to better opportunities. *What exactly were my goals?* To somehow end my mother's days of struggle? To excel at sports? At basketball?

Marvin had just entered his first year at secondary school. His low score from the Common Entrance Examination resulted in a placement at one of our island's bottom schools—Bocage Secondary School. My mother's second child was about to start the journey I began four years earlier.

I had one more opportunity to play inter-secondary school basketball. At 16-years old, I was now a senior player with a championship to defend.

Entering my last secondary school basketball tournament, I was not only a two-year-experienced player, but I'd gained some regional exposure that past summer. In August 2001, one month before school reopened, Ed and I were selected from our school's basketball team to participate and represent Saint Lucia at the Windward Islands Secondary School Games. The four colonies making up the Windward Islands are: Grenada, Saint Vincent, Dominica and, of course, Saint Lucia. I was the only junior player on our squad.

That year Grenada hosted the games, which mainly consisted of five sporting disciplines: basketball, track and field, volleyball, netball, and football. Each of the participating teams was allowed a maximum of 48 athletes. Because of this, it worked to the advantage of any country that possessed versatile athletes willing to play in multiple sports. For this reason, I was chosen by the sports committee to participate in both track and field and basketball.

The games lasted for about nine days. At the end of the tournament, after the scores were tallied, we were tied for first place with the Grenada team. I had contributed points to our team by finishing in the top three in my discus and shot put events. Our basketball team, coached by Derek Browne, had finished in second place. Although I didn't play many minutes, I gained plenty of knowledge under Coach Brown's leadership. I also had the opportunity to learn from the better players. The entire trip was the most amazing journey I'd ever taken.

It was my first time facing non-local basketball opponents and I capitalized by carrying my learning experiences to the 2001 local Inter-Secondary School Basketball Tournament. Ed had graduated. By word of mouth, I heard that he had gotten a full basketball scholarship from a college in America. We had lost a few other key players as well. Out of my fourteen teammates from our championship team, there were only four returning players, including me. And even though critics claimed that we wouldn't be able to pull off back-to-back championships, I thought differently. I believed we had sufficient talent in our newly built team.

I was now the senior team's starting center, Jermeel was still our starting point guard, Dudley continued to play, and we had Denver Joseph, a returning player who was an athletic, sharp shooter. With Ed's absence on our team, I was now the go-to guy, as well as the tallest and biggest player at six foot five and 190 pounds. I also had an afro which might have given me an extra inch or two. A few of my teammates were convinced I had filled out and now had more muscular arms, shoulders and chest. For a while I was known as "Big Arnold." I figured my time spent at the gym with Noup helped build my muscles.

The previous year, as a junior, I'd led my team to the basketball championship game with unforgettable memories of defeat. As a returning senior, my goal was to overcome my failures.

Although we had a completely different team, we sent a strong message by blowing them away by a double-digit difference. All throughout the regular season, we were the only team scoring at least 100-points per game—just like the previous year. My recorded season stats per game were: scoring over 30 points while snatching over 15 rebounds, blocking over 5 shots and stealing over 5 balls. My best single game performance was when I scored 38 points, grabbed 18 rebounds, intercepted 16 passes, and rejected 5 field goal attempts.

I wasn't too surprised with my improvements because, after the Carifta games, I'd devoted all my free time to practicing for basketball; while spending less time at track and field practice. Every day I ensured that I was the first one on the court and the last one to leave. Hakeem and Kern, who spent as much time as me at The Summit, both played in the tournament, however, their teams weren't as great as mine.

With a perfect regular season, we were ranked number one. I was convinced we had enough material and desire to be repeat champions. We were unstoppable; proving ourselves to each opponent, ensuring that no manmade brakes could ever slow us down. Well, until one cloudy Wednesday when we were put to a toughness challenge. In other words, we had caught up to our community rival at the semi-finals—the relentless Leon Hess Comprehensive Secondary School (LHCSS)—our toughest game of the season thus far.

Leon Hess came out fighting from the moment the first whistle was blown. Their strong defensive pressure tactics took us by surprise; we underestimated their smaller size. We may have been bigger, but they were quicker.

With less than five minutes left in the game, we had yet to overtake their single-digit lead. Coach Cumberbatch called a timeout. I saw the fire in his eyes. He drew up a quick offensive and defensive strategy before we re-entered the game. "Arnold…you ready?"

"Yeah, Coach…I'm not losing dat one."

"Entrepot ball!" the referee hollered.

Jermeel controlled the ball to the half then swung it to the right wing for Denver who bounce passed the ball to me on the post. Without thinking, I drop-stepped in the direction of the rim, gripped the basketball tightly, and then exploded in a layup. As the ball sunk down through the net, my teammates shouted, "And one!"

"Fweeeeh!" The referee blew his whistle indicating a defensive foul. I was awarded a free-throw which I scored.

Three minutes were left in the game. As I backpedaled to my position on our 1-3-1 full court press, I pumped my palms to the blue skies, signaling our supporters to raise some hell from the bleachers. They responded with an upbeat tempo. Then in came Leon Hess on the offensive end. Our defensive pressure forced their point guard into a double-team. Denver stole the ball and converted it into two points. In resounding chants, fans from the bleachers bellowed, "Let's go Entrepot! Let's go Leon Hess!"

Once more, relentless Leon Hess tried breaking through our tight defensive press, but it only allowed them to force another turnover. This time I intercepted the pass and sprinted to the basket like I was being chased by a pit-bull. After I dodged everyone, I slam dunked.

"Let's go!" I shouted to my teammates, but it seemed as if it was quite impossible to hear me over our fans' cheers.

Leon Hess wasn't able to keep up for the final two minutes. We went on a run which allowed us to gain our first lead of the game.

"Fweeeeh!" The referee blew the final whistle. My life seemed to be in slow motion as I collapsed to the ground, holding my fist in the air, shouting, "Yes, we won…yes, we won!"

I was so beat that I couldn't stand straight while doing an interview for my father's television station. My legs felt weak and I heard my own heartbeats. Tobias held the camera inches away from my face as HTS sports anchor, Winston Springer Junior, held the microphone to his mouth and asked, "Big Arnold, what a magnificent performance during the last stretch. How does it feel advancing to the championship game for two years in a row?"

"Um, it…it…" I paused briefly to gasp some air so that I could speak proper English, "It's the best feeling. I want to…um, give credit to Leon Hess for giving us a good run. Their defensive pressure surprised us…But, um…my coaches, teammates, and I wanted it more." I inhaled then exhaled.

"Okay Arnold, good luck on Friday," the sports anchor said.

Tobias turned off his camera then faced me. "I see y'all almost lose the game," he said.

"Uh, yeah," I replied, although I really wanted to say, *just give me my five dollars already so that I can start walking home.* But this time, there was no money for me.

"I will see you Friday," he said.

After he departed, I was irritated that he didn't even have the decency to drive me home. Maybe he didn't want me to get used to riding in his car (which I never did), or maybe he didn't want me to get used to luxury.

At least Dudley waited for me so I didn't have to walk home all alone. He was not only my teammate and schoolmate, I considered him my best friend.

"Mummy…Mummy…we won da semifinals!" I shouted as I made my way through our front door. She, Marvin, and Marva were all seated in the living room, watching our local news coverage. She congratulated me.

"When is the final game?" she asked as she flipped through the channels.

"Um, dis Friday at 4 p.m."

"Okay, I will come see you play if my leg is not giving me any problems." I stared at her bad leg, inclined on top of a chair. She broke my concentration. "Who will y'all be playing?" I turned my head away from her disturbing leg and was finally able to smile again.

"Mummy guess," I hinted, "remember last year?"

"Oh, oh, oh, Saint Mary's College?"

"Yup, dats right."

"These boys are tough." She padded around her ankle then added, "I will try my best to make it to your game."

My final secondary school basketball game was on a windless, bright, blue-skies evening. As my teammates and I warmed up, I couldn't help but think that the atmosphere reminded me of last year's senior championship game. The Vigie Multi-Purpose Sports Complex was filled with students and supporters from around the island; their chants were so loud that I

57

could barely hear myself speak. My mother, Marvin, and Marva came out to show their support as they stood at the opposite end of the court from the disorderly students. Tobias stood on the sidelines to capture the game with his camcorder. Many of my basketball buddies from The Summit attended: Kendell, Java, Hakeem, and Kern. It was obvious, and understandable, that Kendell supported his school—Saint Mary's College.

During warm-ups, my thoughts repeated, *all we need is just one more win...one more win...to be crown repeat champions.* On the other half of the court was the island's most popular basketball team, suited in their usual red jerseys and shorts. They looked fearless, overconfident, and they acted like the return of the championship title we'd borrowed was months overdue. But I felt like Entrepot was the rightful holder of the senior secondary school championship title.

My heartbeats increased as I prepared for the jump-ball with Saint Mary's College star player, James Mason. His face wasn't new to me. In fact, James and his junior team were the reason we'd lost the junior championship game the year before. We had already established a friendship, but in a game like this, we were considered enemies. A quick glance at his eyes revealed the seriousness.

"Fweeeeh!"

From the moment I won the jump-ball, tipping it over to Jermeel, I went into a championship state of mind. The sounds of wood slamming onto buckets and the crowd's chants were no longer vibrating through my ears. The hundreds of students who came out weren't visible anymore. The only fans I cared about were my mother, Marvin, and Marva. Well—and the other players.

SMC started the game with high intensity. Offensively, they sprinted on most possessions, receiving plenty of effortless fast-break opportunities. Defensively, we were pressured with their full-court-press. As a team, we struggled to keep up with their more experienced and versatile players. While we forced up difficult shots, they displayed better team chemistry by passing the ball until they ascertained a higher percentage shot.

At one point in the game, as I tried to block James, he threw down a one handed tomahawk slam dunk on top of my head—a maneuver that caused me embarrassment. But I stayed composed and responded by slam dunking a two hander on one of their centers. For every basket I scored, I noticed my mother in all white teeth which boosted my will to win. But as the last seconds were winding down on the game clock, I started witnessing more and more frowns.

Saint Mary's College reclaimed the Inter-Secondary School Senior Basketball Championship.

I finished the game with 29 points and 21 rebounds. It was my lowest scoring game that season.

"You fought to the finish," said Coach Cumberbatch, trying to placate us before the award ceremony.

Our team was awarded silver medals. Then, after SMC received their gold medals, the announcer handed individual trophies for different categories.

"The most blocked shot award of the season goes out to...Arnold Henry!" I heard my mother's cheers in the background as I accepted my award. "For the first time in school history we have two winners for the season's Most Valuable Player award." The announcer stated factual stats then announced, "James Mason and Arnold Henry will be sharing this year's MVP!"

Finally, SMC received their championship trophy. I stood in the midst of the crowd and stared at it with a jealous eye. A tap on my back broke my concentration.

"Arnold," said an unknown voice. I turned around and, to my surprise, it was a young lady.

I gave her a big smile then stuttered, "Ye...ye...yes."

"Hey, my name is Makeddah John."

"Oh hi." I shook her hands. "Wassup?"

"My shy friend has a crush on you," she said.

"Who?" I asked. She pointed to a skinny, dark-skinned young lady who stood by herself in the distance.

"She's over there. Come say hi," Makeddah demanded before she walked away.

"Okay, I comin'." *A girl finds me cute?* I couldn't believe it. I was about to make my way to say hi to Makeddah's friend when the sight of the championship trophy regained my interest. I wasn't in the mood to socialize so I just ignored Makeddah's request and turned towards my mother, Marvin, and Marva who awaited my attention. Marvin snatched my two trophies out of my hands to examine them.

"It will be okay my boy...you played good...someday you will get a bigger prize," my mother said.

The days of secondary school basketball were now over. At first, I felt like I had no more reasons to pursue the game. But reflecting on the past three years, I realized that I had developed such a love for it that I just couldn't easily let it go. Feeling hopeful, I was sure something good was approaching my world.

Chapter 12

Unexpected Expectations

By the second week in December 2001, all schools on the island were closed for Christmas break. Da Yard was being overtaken by the next generation of children. When I was at home, I spent most of my time studying for the CXC. Sometimes it was hard to maintain focus on my studies when my mother had another episode of leg pains because her moans interrupted my thought process. Little Kobie was confused. "Nanny...why you crying?" he would ask my mother in the cutest kid tone.

"I'm alright Kobie...my leg just hurting me." Kobie was young but he was polite and caring, just like his mother, Rosalie.

"Nanny, you want me to rub it for you?"

She would smile and say, "Aw, it's okay my boy. Nanny will be alright."

Where was Lucius? The only time anyone saw him was at night. Usually when he keyed his way through the front door, I would be the only one up watching television in the living room. "Goodnight," he would say. Every night I had to force out the D word. "Goodnight Daddy."

My mother always saved him a plate of food from dinner. He would eat his belly full, and then sleep for the night in the living room on a piece of mattress. The next morning he would be gone before anyone was awake.

Why did Mummy and Lucius sleep in separate rooms? They were the only ones who knew their relationship status; we children never bothered to ask. I guess we were used to seeing them apart.

Christmas day, after a wonderful church service, I was studying in my bedroom when I heard my mother say, "Huh...who?"

An unclear masculine voice replied, "Mario...brother." I thought, *maybe it's just one of my friends trying to borrow my Super Mario Brothers cartridge.*

"Mario! Someone's here to see you," my mother called out.

"Yes, Mummy...I comin'!" I answered.

Ugh, why would someone come over to ask for a damn cartridge on big Christmas day?

I hurried to the front door, but when I noticed the guest's face, I stumbled. My mother stood comfortably next to this man like he was no stranger. They were both smiling as I took smaller steps in their direction. I was certain that I had never met this presentable, light-skinned, averaged height man who looked like he was in his early thirties.

"Guess who's that?" my mother asked.

"Um…" I was searching for hints.

"Your brother!" My mother blurted through her enormous smile. I stared in disbelief.

At first, I was hesitant and wasn't sure how to react. But I couldn't erase the large smile on my face. I shook his hands, wishing it was a hug, and introduced myself.

"Mario."

"Kervyn Tobias."

"Kervyn as in…Kervyn Tobias…as in da son of Tobias?" I wanted it to be clear. He chuckled.

"Yes."

That was when I realized that Tobias wasn't my father's first name, it was actually his last name. I briefly looked back at my mother's smile, and then back at him.

"Excuse me…I have some food on the fire," my mother interrupted.

I joined Kervyn on the doorstep. "How you find me? How you know I exist?"

He pointed to a nearby house. "My girlfriend, her name is Silka, she just moved into that house," he said.

I pointed to the same house. "Oh, over deh? Dats your girlfriend?"

"Yeah, she told me that Tobias's son was in the area so I wanted to link up with you."

I slammed my palm to my forehead. "Oh yeah, I remember I talk to Silka da other day."

"Irie…you know you have three other brothers, right?"

"Oh yeah, I hear sumting about dat…but to tell you da truth, I eh really know to get in touch with y'all. My mother always mention to me how I have four olda brothers and how y'all went to Saint Mary's College then studied in Cuba…but dats all I knew about y'all."

"Well it's nice to finally meet you. We will keep in touch from now on."

"Yeah, I'm so thankful for you coming to see me. You made my Christmas day."

"Oh." He handed me a wrapped box with a bow on the top. "That's for you."

"Oh really, thanks so much," I said, holding back tears. I couldn't show my big brother that I was a cry-baby.

"I will check you some other time. Tell your mother I said goodbye."

"Okay, later."

I stood on the doorstep until Kervyn got into his car and drove away with his girlfriend. Then I made my way to the kitchen.

"How do you feel?" my mother asked me, stirring the pot of chicken.

"Dis is da best day of my life," I said, overwhelmed.

I returned to my bedroom feeling like I was wanted, appreciated, and loved. After sixteen years on this planet, I had finally found a male family member who I could look up to for advice. Without knowing who my other brothers were, or what they looked like, I already considered them to be my role models; I just wished they had known me earlier, especially at times when I needed someone to help me with my homework.

They attended the top secondary school on the island and they went on studying in Cuba. Perhaps, if my footsteps were pointed to the same paths as my older brothers', Tobias would have been proud of me; maybe I would have gotten his attention; maybe then he wouldn't have been ashamed of his youngest son.

From the moment I met Kervyn, he treated me like a real brother—not like Tobias's secret child on the side. Most weekends, my newly found brother picked me up in his green Mitsubishi Lancer (the same car he taught me how to drive) for evening activities. And from then on, whenever I was on my way to the sports complex for basketball practice, I would drop by his work place in the government building, just to say hi. Because of Kervyn, I had an opportunity to meet the rest of my older brothers: Segun, Chidi, and Chima. I was only able to build a closer relationship with Kervyn and Segun; they were the ones who showed they cared by keeping in touch.

Entrepot Secondary School Champions, 2000

Denver Joseph, Jermeel Pierre,
Ed Desir, Myself and Coach

Second Quarter

Taking the Lead

Chapter 13

On to the Next One

January 2002, school reopened for its second term. My CXC was now less than six months away, which meant I was on my graduation home stretch. And just when I decided to ease down on playing basketball at The Summit to focus on my studies, I received an invitational letter that made me reconsider. The letter read:

> Dear Arnold Henry, you are invited to the Saint Lucia National Sports Awards. You are nominated for Junior Male Basketball Player of the year 2001. The award ceremony will be held at the National Cultural Center at 7:00 p.m. You are allowed to bring one guest.

Out of all the good players on the island, why was I the one chosen for this prestigious awarded?

"Mummy, read dis," I insisted.

"What's that?"

"Please, jus' read it," I grinned, then pleaded.

"Okay, bring me my glasses." For every word she browsed, I noticed a smile building. "That is great news. I am so proud of you."

"So you comin' with me?" I asked.

"Mario, you don't have anyone else to come with you?" I arched my eyebrows.

"Like who?"

"Like a girlfriend?"

"You know I don't have a girlfriend."

"I'm just joking with you." She handed me back the letter. "I will come if my leg feels good."

On the night of the National Sports Awards, although my mother was still in pain, she was able to accompany me by leaning on my arm. She looked stunning with her long orange dress and low heel shoes. Since we weren't able to afford a suit for me, I wore a maroon, long-sleeved, button-up shirt, a black pair of dress pants, and my black pair of basketball sneakers (the same sneakers that were sent down by my godmother from New York which I used to go to school, play basketball, and attend church services). My afro was dabbed down low to make me look more presentable for the live television broadcast of the ceremony.

The award ceremony began and I was seated amongst all the national nominated athletes. In the front row were the very important people, including the prime minter of Saint Lucia. I noticed my father working his camera from the bottom of the stage.

Eventually, I walked across the stage to accept my award. As I received it, Tobias snapped a photo, and my mother bawled, "That's my boy!"

The glass trophy I held in my hands symbolized Gros Piton and Petit Piton—two volcanic spires located on the outskirts of two west coast towns. The towering twin peaks that thrust directly from the sea are one of the most magnificent and impressive natural features in the world, and a UNESCO World Heritage Site.

Seeing my name engraved on the trophy, I decided I would never stop playing basketball. The awards for National Sportsman and Sportswoman of the year for 2001 were given to male cricketer Darren Sammy, and female high jumper Levern Spencer. These were the only two awards with monetary values; if I had known about them, I would have worked extra hard. *My family could have made good use of that thousand dollar prize award.*

My taste for pursuing track and field as a sport career became bitter. The national award made me believe that basketball was more prosperous.

The day that Mrs. St. Marthe announced the 2002 Carifta team, I had given up all hope of being a successful shot put athlete. Still, when my name wasn't called from the list she held in her hands, it was the first time I cried over track and field. I was the only one from last year's team who wasn't chosen.

Mrs. St. Marthe noticed tears running down my face. She explained, "I'm sorry Arnold…you are now 17-years old which makes you a senior. It's true that you received the gold in shot put at the Inter-Secondary School Track and Field Meet but your distance didn't make the qualifying mark." I couldn't look her in the eyes. She rubbed my back. "Just keep on working hard…there's always next year."

Later, I realized that Mrs. Marthe was absolutely right; though her decision hurt, truthfully, I wasn't ready to compete against regional under-20 shot put throwers. Five years of shot put experience was flushed down the drain.

I had one option left: *if Ed Desir could get a full American basketball scholarship, then why couldn't I?*

With limited resources, I investigated my island for answers on how Ed did it. Occasionally, at The Summit, I questioned a few older basketball acquaintances. "You know anyting about gettin' a full basketball scholarship to play in America?" Instead of receiving beneficial information, I was just told a bunch of stories about successful Saint Lucian recipients of US basketball scholarships and their odysseys.

One person told me, "There was a feller who got a basketball scholarship but he was deported back to Saint Lucia for the use of illegal drugs." I thought, *what a shame, he must be the stupidest person to pass up a rare opportunity like that.*

Someone else told me that there were two brothers playing college basketball in America.

After evaluation, I decided that it was actually possible for a Saint Lucian to play basketball in America. I just needed to figure out how they did it, and work hard, and pray for a miracle.

Meanwhile, my CXC was more important. Even if I didn't get a basketball scholarship, I had always wanted to go to a college to study computers—with hopes that someday I could have a professional career as a computer specialist or technician.

Chapter 14

College?

It always made my mother happy whenever I brought home good grades, trophies, medals, or good news; but on my graduation day, she glowed as if she was attending her prom night.

The class of 2002 graduation took place at the National Cultural Center. My mother, Marvin, and Marva were in the building as my supporting cast. It was the last time I wore the blue and gray uniform colors, as well as the last time I was in the same room with all my classmates and teachers.

During the ceremony, as we recited our graduation song, "I will get there" by Boyz II Men, I reminisced over my years at Entrepot Secondary School—five solid years of sports and academic commitment and dedication. For my efforts, I was rewarded three trophies: Athlete of the Year, Basketball Player of the Year, and Sportsman of the Year.

I had a future ahead of me and day by day, I worried about how I could make my American basketball dream come true.

The day I received my CXC results, I realized that there was a sure alternative to my basketball life—college. I passed all seven subject exams I attempted: Technical Drawing, Principles of Business, Integrated Science, Physics, Information Technology, Mathematics, and English; passing five CXC subjects was an important admittance requirement for our local two-year college.

A few months before receiving the results, Dudley and I had applied to the Division of Technical Education and Management Studies at SALCC (Sir Arthur Lewis Community College). As best friends, we both decided to study Computer Maintenance and Systems Engineering. With our fairly good CXC results, we were accepted to the college's two-year program. Kendell, who had better CXC results than both Dudley and I, decided to skip college.

I was so excited; I felt my life was on a positive route. All I needed was financial support for the local college tuition fee of $500.00 which seemed like one million dollars to my unemployed mother.

One summer day, I sat on our doorstep in front of my home, cooling down from an evening of playing basketball at The Summit. I was just in time to eavesdrop on one of my mother's rare phone conversations. I heard her say, "Toby, you have any money to help me send Mario to college?" A few seconds later, she responded, "It's about

$500.00." Another few seconds later she shouted, "Okay, okay, whatever, bye...bye!" The sound of the receiver slamming startled me so much that I didn't even realize Rosalie stood beside me.

"Hey Rosalie."

"Hey Mario."

Rosalie called loudly to get my mother's attention, knocking on the front door. She had just arrived from work to pick up Kobie.

"Good evening," my mother sighed as she greeted Rosalie. "Come in uh." My mother looked down with big eyes as she acknowledged my presence. In a surprised tone she said, "Hey Mario, I didn't know you were back from the court. Come; let me give you some money. I need a tin of milk."

I answered, "Okay," but wondered why she couldn't ask Marvin or Marva?

When I received the two dollars, I pretended like I was on my way to the convenience shop. Instead, I did a three-sixty and stooped down on the doorstep next to our home's opened glass louvers to continue eavesdropping—this time to my mother and Rosalie's conversation.

"I cannot believe Toby," my mother wept.

"Why, what happened?" Rosalie asked.

"You mean to tell me, Toby cannot even help me pay for his own son's college fees," my mother complained to Rosalie. "I leave the bastard deh!"

Oh no, I won't be going to college, registered in the back of my mind. I had never heard my mother so upset with Tobias.

"He wanted me to have an abortion when I was pregnant with Mario," she said.

Was I a mistake? I wondered. I slowly started walking to the shop, not caring if my mother saw me leaving. I felt like my heart had dropped down to my toes. My eyes were so filled with tears that every step I took, they fell on my shirt. It was obvious that I wasn't wanted by Tobias. But actually hearing it in my mother's voice was painful.

I took longer than usual to return home from the shop because I needed the extra time to dry off my tears. Rosalie and Kobie had already gone to their home. As soon as I handed my mother the tin of milk I whispered to her, "Mummy, so I not going to college?" Her eyebrows converged.

"Where you get that from?" she asked.

"Uh, uh, nowhere...I jus'...jus' askin' you," I stammered. Her eyebrows diverged.

"Of course you still going to college. Why would you think that?"

"No reason," I replied.

"How about getting a job?" she suggested.

"Um, no Mummy. I wanna go college! Dudley going you know!" I immediately wished I had not made that statement.

"I can't afford it! I can't afford it!" she shouted back in frustration. Feeling ashamed, I silently crept to my room.

"Wha' happen?" Marvin asked.

"Leave me alone!" I shouted, crawling to my lower bunk-bed.

I was so worried about being unable to experience the college life that I prayed to God for his love, blessings, and guidance.

The following days, everything was in a state of urgency. The college's fee deadline was approaching and I really thought my mother's mind was made up that I had to go to work.

One day she caught me by surprise as I returned from playing basketball. "Here's the money you need for your college. Please do not make me regret it," my mother said. I gave her a big smile and a tight hug.

She did what was needed to obtain the money by borrowing, begging, or skipping priorities such as phone bills, water bills, or light bills. I wondered if it was the money she had been saving for her leg surgery. My mother always talked about an operation, but I highly doubted she had a hidden stash of money—it was almost impossible for her to save one penny a fortnight when Rosalie paid her. I believed she probably borrowed the money from Rosalie or somehow convinced Tobias. For something as important as school, she always found a way.

In early August, I was selected once more to represent Saint Lucia at the Windward Islands Secondary Schools Games. The competition was supposed to be held on the island of Saint Vincent but, due to their financial issues, Saint Lucia had to host the games. Despite the late notice and limited time for preparation, athletes from Grenada, Dominica, and Saint Vincent were still able to fly in to participate.

For our accommodations, we were supplied with twin-size mattresses to be used in the classrooms of the Castries Comprehensive Secondary School. Some athletes used the school's desks or chairs to set up a bed, while others just laid their mattress on the dusty concrete floors. Each island was separated throughout the school's campus but we weren't too far from each other. Male and female showers were built for this special occasion and we were fed at least three meals a day.

The basketball, volleyball, netball, and football games were held at our usual grounds—Vigie Multi-Purpose Sports Complex—about a ten minutes' drive from the school. The track and field event was located in the southern town of Vieux Fort at our newly built national multi-use stadium—known today as George Odlum Stadium. That year was the first time any athlete ran or competed on a synthetic surface (rather than grass) in Saint Lucia.

Just like in 2001, it was a week of sportsmanship, competitiveness, teamwork, team spirit, sweat, and laughter. It was my first opportunity to shine in front of my home crowd; though our Saint Lucian team wasn't as powerful as the previous year's team—a few students had graduated from either secondary school or college which meant that they were no longer eligible to participate.

By the end of the games, the total scores were tallied and Saint Lucia had to settle for a disappointing second place. Even though it was a team sport, I put some blame on myself for our loss—that was one way I motivated myself to work harder.

For the rest of the summer, there was nothing I could do except make a ridiculous number of visits to The Summit. I wanted to improve my basketball game more than ever. As a result, I walked up the Entrepot hill twice a day—early morning and later each evening, at least until my college opened.

Chapter 15

Sir Arthur Lewis Community College

September 2002 was the stepping stone for the next big phase in my life—the college life. My new school was situated at the peak of mountain Morne Fortune, a historic mountain that overlooks the Castries Harbor. Morne Fortune, occasionally known as "Hill of Good Luck," was a prime battleground between the French and the British over ownership of Saint Lucia during the 18th century.

The community college was named after the late Sir William Arthur Lewis to honor his contributions in the field of economic development. He was a Saint Lucian economist who won the Nobel Prize in Economics in 1979, at the same time becoming the first Black person to win a Nobel Prize in a category other than Peace. With such a prominent figure buried on my college campus, I felt the need to honor the deceased by taking my studies seriously.

I was back to my regular school routine. As always, by the time my mother woke me to commence my weekdays, Lucius was gone and Marvin and Marva were already on their way to school. My mother would be home all day until she had to pick up Kobie from pre-school.

College life was a bit more flexible about things, including my class schedules. My college's department didn't enforced school uniforms, therefore, I got my hair braided at least twice a week and wore a pair of jeans and a plain polo shirt. Every day I ensured I presented myself to the public with a fresh demeanor. I had developed a fashion sense after my first day at secondary school where I had learned that first impressions live forever. This time, no one could make fun of the way I dressed.

Every morning, before I kissed my mother goodbye on her cheeks, she handed me ten dollars to cover my meals and public transportation. She was the number one reason why college meant so much to me—I wanted that education so that I could become financially stable—especially to restore every dime my mother spent on me. If she could sacrifice the savings for her leg surgery, then she deserved to live the rest of her life happy and work-free.

It would have cost me two bus fare payments to arrive at my destination so I saved one dollar and twenty-five cents whenever I took the twenty minute walk from Bishop's Gap to my college bus-stop in town and vice versa.

Most of the time, Dudley and I made plans to walk down the Marchand Road to our college's bus-stand; it was the safest way due to increased crime in our area. We acted like blood brothers who were ready to protect each other from the young, violent gang members.

The bus ride to college wasn't more than 15 minutes. To indicate a bus stop, I would say, "Driver, I stoppin' deh." One of the better public basketball courts on the island was only a few feet away from where I got off the bus. In fact, all buildings on-campus were within a 10 minute walk radius which made it easy for me to adjust to my new surroundings. I immediately fell in love with college life.

It was refreshing to see many familiar faces from my previous school, as well as a few basketball foes from around the island; it was expected as there weren't many options for local colleges. Sir Arthur Lewis Community College was like a combination of the entire island's secondary schools' alumni. In fact, I never met a foreign student at college. We were obviously all locals and my fellow students were incredibly sociable. Plus, the women were beautiful and remarkably intelligent.

Dudley and I soon became friends with our down-south classmates, Ali, Raijive, and Omowale, who all attended Vieux Fort Comprehensive Secondary School. We all had some of the same interests—we studied the same major, took the same courses, and had previously played in the secondary schools basketball competition. Dudley and I were the taller ones in our new circle of friends. During school hours, we ate lunch at the same time, studied, and played basketball together. Besides the cafeteria, our usual hangout was on the isolated and peaceful sheltered bleachers near the basketball court.

To show our commitment to our favorite sport, anytime we had a free period between our classes, Dudley, Ali, Raijive, Omowale, and I would join other players on the nearby court. We didn't care that we were in our school attire or about playing under the blazing hot sun.

When we returned to a scheduled class period we smelled funky and perspired. The initial feeling of sweat dripping down my body made me lack focus in the classrooms as my professors lectured. Eventually we would cool down; our lectures were held in our first ever air-conditioned classrooms.

On a daily basis, I realized that basketball was in my system and it was very hard for me to ignore the game even when I was trying to focus only on my education. In my classes, instead of jotting down notes, sometimes I would sketch myself playing in America on an indoor, wooden basketball court. After class, instead of revising my notes, more than 90 percent of the time, I was found on the sundrenched basketball court.

The court's easy access only built up my urge to play over and over again throughout the day. *Besides*, I thought, *playing during the day relieves my academic stress.* But I learned a quick lesson: by midterm I was having a little trouble keeping up good grades in my courses, especially Calculus and others that I never heard of until college. It was evident that I couldn't escape the game so I created a balance—I made a sacrifice to study throughout the day and to only play on evenings and weekends. My new protocol caused my quiz and exam percentages to steadily increase.

I was now in control of my life on-campus but there was one person I still wanted to have a stronger connection with—my sperm-donor father. Ironically, being at college emphasized the situation. On a weekly basis, I was physically closer to Tobias than ever before; his work place was located near campus. I took the opportunity to visit him as much as possible.

The first time that I entered the HTS television studios I didn't know what to say to the secretary. "My fada dere?" The question accidently slipped out of my mouth.

"Excuse me?" she said. I looked quickly, hoping she didn't catch what I said.

"Tobias dere?" I corrected myself.

I wanted to establish a family-like bond so bad that I was referring to him as my father when he hadn't given me any reasons to. When we finally caught up, we mainly spoke about my performance inside the classroom. As always, it was nearly impossible to have more than a minute-long conversation. Every moment felt like I was being introduced to a new person; I found it difficult to engage in conversation with a statue.

I didn't want much. I thought that one single, meaningful "I love you" could make-up for the 17 years of lost time between us. Hearing these three words come out of his mouth would have at least made me feel like I wasn't a waste of his sperm. All my attempts to kindle a family between us were failures. At least I had enough chances to interact with him to determine that there was no point. I realized that I never really needed this man in my life; I was doing fine with just my mother.

My college phase was life-changing. Basketball and education wasn't everything. I felt the need to find my first girlfriend. I'd been rejected so many times in the past that I had always felt like my chances to hook-up with a college girl were impossible. Until one day, during our college's three-on-three basketball tournament, I spotted a young lady amongst three others, behind the court's fence. She was innocent looking, sweet, light-skinned, and breath-takingly beautiful. My eyes couldn't resist staring her down. I instantly got a boost to play much better than I was already playing.

A few baskets later, I became aware that these four girls only rooted for Ali, Raijive, and Omowale—who Dudley and I had collaborated with to enter the tournament. I did more impressive moves and still no one from their group mentioned my name.

After a competitive day of basketball, our five-man team remained the undisputed champions of the 3-on-3 tournament. I was announced as the most valuable player, but truthfully, I couldn't have done it without the team chemistry we displayed during our games.

As Ali, Dudley, Raijive, Omowale, and I walked off the court, I couldn't help myself but question my teammates about the girls. "Oye, you know dem girls over dere?"

"Yeah mun, dey went to our school," Raijive answered.

"Wha's dat light skin girl name?" I asked them.

"Suean," Ali answered first. "You like to see her mun?"

I took another glance before answering. "Boy, she looking good ih," I replied confidently.

"Well look her right dere, go talk to de girl, nuh," Ali suggested.

"Eh mind dat, I go talk to her," I said bravely. When we finally caught up with the four girls who waited for us at the exit, I fled without a word.

"Oye Arnold, where you going?" Omowale teased me while Raijive, Ali and Dudley laughed.

Without looking back, I shouted before hopping on the bus, "I goin' home gason!"

For the next few days at school, Ali pressured me to initiate a conversation with Suean. He became so annoying that I decided never to tell Ali any of my secrets ever again. But I had a lot to thank him for—at some point, I was motivated to engage in conversation with Suean.

From our very first conversation, Suean and I made an instant connection. She was the only girl who I pursued at college. Then she became the person I spoke to most on a daily basis. I was even focusing more on her than my schoolwork or basketball. At home, we would speak for hours over the phone. I even expressed my feelings towards her in love notes. This was the first time I felt affection from a girl. It felt like we were dating for years when it had only been weeks. I had never gotten so close to anyone in such a short period of time. I felt like my world was complete.

On Monday, November 16, 2003, Suean had a birthday. As her boyfriend, it was a perfect opportunity for me to show my appreciation for our strong and loving relationship. I didn't want to do anything too extreme so I asked Dudley and Ali for assistance. I'd made early plans. In order for me to afford her birthday gift, I had to miss out on my lunch at the school for a couple of days. When I had enough money, Dudley, Ali, and I roamed the stores in Castries, in search of some items.

At the end of my shopping, I bought a birthday card, a bracelet, a teddy bear, and a cylinder-shaped case filled with Cadbury chocolate. I also bought a fancy gift bag and placed everything inside. Dudley and Ali were positive she would love it. I just hoped that she would at least appreciate the idea.

On the Friday before Suean's birthday, I awaited her arrival at our usual hangout area. I stood outside the cafeteria and held the gift bag behind my back as she approached. As the distance between us decreased, I realized that she wasn't in the best of moods. I wondered if she forgot it was her special day? When I saw her face I knew something was wrong. "Wham to you?" I asked, trying to give her a hug; our uncomfortable embrace was shortened by her quick step backwards. We stood face to face. She held back her tears and I was confused as ever.

"I can't be with you anymore," she said. My heart skipped a beat.

"Huh…wha'…uh…why," I stuttered.

"I just can't do it," she replied carefully. My eyebrows connected. I was now attempting to hold back tears.

"Bu'…buh…why?"

"My father found one of the letters you wrote for me. He said that he sent me to college to study so he doesn't want me to have a boyfriend."

"Serious ting?" I asked, but didn't need an answer. Before the tears came running down my face, I quickly handed her the present and rushed to the restroom around the corner. I locked the door behind me and shed a cup full of tears.

The next days at school were depressing. I finally understood what artist's love lyrics meant when they sang about having sleepless nights and being unable to eat. It was hard for me to see her on-campus without thoughts of fixing things between us. I had to distance myself from everyone and everything. All our friends who thought that we were the cutest couple on-campus were seeking answers.

When all was said and done, I still had my friends to help me through my first relationship breakup. And as always, the game of basketball was my one true psychologist. It helped to get my mind off everything.

Every evening, right after my last class period, I noticed that there was an ongoing basketball function on the college's court. There was an open invitation for anyone at the college, including the public. The sessions were conducted by Mathew Raphael, also known as Fudge. I remembered him as one of the referees who officiated my secondary school basketball games. His sessions seemed constructive so Ali, Dudley, and I participated every night at six. Omowale and Raijive went home because they lived down south and had to catch the Vieux Fort bus before it was too late.

I enjoyed the way Fudge conducted his sessions. I believed he did it out of the goodness of his heart and to provide a means for basketball players to improve their skills. For the first hour, he focused on basketball developmental skills with various offensive and defensive drills. The following hour or two we scrimmaged. There was nothing too complicated or difficult. Fudge was one of those coaches who was easygoing—it took a lot for him to get mad at anyone. Basketball with him and everyone else involved, was fun and competitive.

One night, after an intense session, Dudley, Ali, and I were cooling down as Fudge prepared to exit the court. "Oye Fudge, you know anyting on how I can get a basketball scholarship, foreign?" I asked.

"Boy, I doh really know nutting about dat uh." As I frowned, I thought, *at least it was worth a try.*

Ali interrupted my thoughts. "Arnold, you trying to leave mun in Saint Lucia or wha'?"

"Well, from times I wanna play in America gason."

"Oh...wait," Fudge said. I sensed hope in his voice. "You heard of Yogi Leo?"

"Who?" I asked.

"He played college basketball in North Carolina. He played professionally overseas too. But he eh playing no more."

"Uh huh," I murmured, interested to hear the rest of Fudge's story. We all listened as he continued.

"Yogi grew up in Saint Lucia. He livin' in Charlotte, North Carolina now. He is one of my good friends from times." Fudge looked up into the stars as if he was trying to recollect something. "To me he said he was coming to Saint Lucia really soon with his wife for vacation."

"When…when?" I asked.

"Um, I'm not too sure. I go have to get back to you on dat. I will give him a call tonight. I go ask him information about dat scholarship for you too," Fudge said.

I thought, *just what I need—a foreign connection.*

Dudley, Ali, and I walked down the hill to the nearest bus-stop. "One ting Arnold, eh forget bout us in Lucia when you get a basketball scholarship, eh," Ali joked.

"Yeah," Dudley agreed.

"Nah mun," I replied. "But gason, who tell you I go get dat scholarship. Fudge jus' tell me he know a mun dat could help me out."

Ali didn't look worried. He encouraged me. "Oye Arnold, by de time de mun see how you playin', he mus' be impress with you."

"Yeah mun, I agree with Ali," said Dudley.

For some reason, Ali and Dudley weren't even interested in pursuing the same American hoop dream as me, even though they were basketball players too. I was flattered by their support.

Dudley and Ali went home but I didn't. I caught the bus near the college to downtown, then I walked up the Marchand Road, then up the Entrepot Hill to The Summit where I joined the rest of my friends, Kendell, Java, Bobdole, and Kern who were playing 4-on-4 half-court games.

By the time I got to The Summit it was 10 in the evening. We weren't always able to play there at that late hour. Our local electricity provider, Lucelec, locked up the nearby box with the access to the main power switch. Lucelec did this after the players in the community failed to pay the overdue light bills of thousands of dollars. They had given us plenty of warning. The older players made plenty of attempts to collect one dollar every time someone used the court, but we weren't able to afford it because most of us were only students. I became so frustrated with the sunset ruining our evening basketball games that I'd kicked opened and broke the box. We kept the secret amongst ourselves and were able to enjoy playing basketball after sunset.

Chapter 16

The Phone Call

It was a week before my eighteenth birthday when I met my second girlfriend, Margaritte Louis, in junior college. During our first encounter at the college's cafeteria, I was impressed first with her height, then her beauty—she stood about five foot eleven with a slim physique and a body that resembled a runway model. Margaritte's long, black, curly hair revealed that she was mixed, Indian and Black.

My intimate relationship with Margaritte was a bit different from my previous one with Suean. I was 17-years old while Margaritte was 25. She was already an established school teacher who was attending the teacher's college department to further her education.

From the moment I met Margaritte, we spent almost every day together; not only at the college, but also numerous nights at her rented home. She lived alone; about five minutes' drive from our college. It was my first time spending nights at my girlfriend's home. My mother approved of it after she met Margaritte in person.

Margaritte had a son, but he was never around when I was at her home. He lived with his grandmother. Margaritte only wanted to be with me behind closed doors. She hid me from her baby's daddy, her family, and, most of all, her friends. Her actions made me lack trust in our relationship. I never felt that strong, loving connection from Margaritte, but for some reason, I kept on staying; it must have been our strong sexual chemistry.

One thing I liked about Margaritte was that she was heavily involved in and supportive of my sports. When our college hosted a housing system basketball tournament, she attended and cheered me on. And if she ever missed any of my games, she always wanted to know the full details of my performance.

At Sir Arthur Lewis Community College, I represented the yellow house. Levern Spencer, one of my sports inspirations, represented the same house. In fact, the majority of the top athletes I competed against at secondary school tournaments were part of the yellow house. There was no way that the other three houses could have challenged us.

Throughout the school year, I contributed to my house by participating in basketball and track and field events. For the house basketball competition, my team and I were the champs; for track and field, I received two gold medals in shot put and discus.

Arnold Henry

Before the school year ended, Sir Arthur Lewis Community College held an awards ceremony and dinner for all the outstanding athletes. I was awarded trophies for most valuable player for the 3-on-3 basketball tournament, most valuable player for the house basketball tournament, and Sportsman of the Year.

When I returned home that night, my mother pointed out that my trophy collection overcrowded her three-level television stand. "Just now I have to buy you your own trophy case, my boy," my mother said jokingly.

Marvin had two trophies which he had received for running marathons when he was younger. One day, he said, "I go get more trophies dan you."

"In your dreams," I said. The only way Marvin could have been able to outnumber my trophies was if he started running long distance races again. He was a great runner for his age, but he didn't have the discipline to commit to the sport.

While Marvin was strategizing a way to outnumber my trophies, I sought opportunities to add to my collection. Fudge was preparing a team of elite players at my college for an upcoming men's basketball league. The league involved several teams from around the island. We were the only school team in the competition so we were simply known as "Combined Schools".

I was eighteen and this was my first time competing against men. To prepare for the tournament, Fudge continued hosting basketball practices after classes.

One night at practice, while my teammates and I awaited Fudge's arrival, I noticed a Black man and a Caucasian lady sitting in the nearby sheltered bleachers. It was rare to see a Caucasian. They were seated comfortably with no apparent worries so I suspected that they were either anticipating our practice session or meeting someone.

Ali was curious. "Arnold, who's dem people over dere?" he asked.

"Um, boi I eh even know dem people uh. Dey mus' be lost," I replied.

A few minutes later, Fudge arrived at practice. The stranger left the lady and walked towards Fudge. Instantly, I muttered, *could dis be…could dis be Yogi?*

Fudge blew his whistle to indicate his arrival. We formed a huddle around him and the stranger. "Dis is one of my good friends, Yogi Leo. I know him my whole life. He left Saint Lucia some years ago after receiving a full basketball scholarship to Queens College in North Carolina," Fudge said. He then pointed to the Caucasian lady who was still sitting on the bleachers. "He on vacation with his wife."

My heart pounded faster. I was delighted and overwhelmed to know that Yogi made it to our practice. Fudge really knew a former USA college basketball player.

I couldn't stop staring at Yogi; he was not like the basketball players I played with. Even though I was a couple of centimeters taller than him, I had never come across any player as broad as he was.

Basketball practice commenced with warm-up drills and then Fudge split us into groups of five for a full-court basketball game. Yogi was geared up and he came to play. As we prepared I thought, *I am not going to let this opportunity pass me by.*

During the game, Yogi played the same position as me so I defended him on the low post. It seemed like Fudge intentionally selected Yogi and I to be on opposite teams. It was difficult to defend him on the post because of his size and strength, but I tried my best to keep up my I'm-never-going-to-back-down attitude.

As usual, my mouth was sealed and I allowed my skills to do all the talking. After our friendly scrimmage, Yogi approached me as Ali and Dudley were convincing me that this was one of my best practices. I shook Yogi's hand and greeted him like he was the owner of a basketball franchise. "Good evening Sir," I said.

"Nah man...call me Yogi," he advised. Yogi sounded more American than Saint Lucian.

"Okay si...I mean, okay Yogi." I could hear Ali and Dudley giggling in the background.

"Good game brother...I will definitely be coming to the Complex to watch your basketball game on Saturday," Yogi said.

"Okay...thanks...see you dere," I replied calmly, but in my mind I wanted to scream like a little girl. I was surprised that Yogi was taking time off his vacation to come to my game. I was now convinced that I had just had an awesome practice.

Apart from Ali and Dudley, Margaritte and my family were the only ones who knew of our conversation. I felt like I needed to be humble about the situation until I received greater news, like an official offer and signed documents from an American coach.

Saturday evening, I arrived at my basketball game two hours early. Yogi was already there with his wife watching an earlier game in progress. I sat next to him seeking words of inspiration. The tone in his voice was very welcoming which made it easy for me to talk to him. He spoke briefly about his transition and adjustment from the Saint Lucian culture to the United States' customs. He also spoke about his basketball experiences. That day, the most important advice I picked up from him was what basketball gave him: a free education, a job as a professional athlete, and, most importantly, a wife and a life he was thankful for.

After Yogi and I talked, I became highly motivated to perform beyond my usual standards during the game. I was determined to leave everything I had on the court—my blood, sweat, and tears. I had at least 30-plus points, 10-plus rebounds and 5-plus blocks along with six slam dunks that night.

After we won the matchup, I was desperate to hear Yogi's remarks. I approached him in the bleachers where he remained seated with his wife. "Good game," Yogi said with a grin. I sighed and then smiled with relief after hearing those words.

Yogi wasted no time. "Write down your number and email address and I will contact my old college coach when I get back to the US. You should expect a phone call or an email from Coach Bruce Kreutzer within a week," he said. I quickly asked someone for a pen, neatly jotted down the information, and handed it to him. "If everything goes well, I will be seeing you soon," Yogi concluded.

For the following days, I stayed away from visiting Margaritte in order to be at home as much as possible—just in case the American coach called. The second semester of my school year had already ended so there was no need to attend the college except for 6:00 p.m. basketball practice.

It felt like I waited for an eternity. Every time the house phone rang, I was quick to answer it. I've never in my life anticipated a phone call so much. I had a few long nights—nightmares of being unable to answer a ringing phone.

What if Yogi lost the piece of paper with my information? Was it just a nicety so that he wouldn't hurt my feelings? Did he remember me?

After two weeks of waiting for a phone call, I decided that I was not destined to play basketball in the United States. I thought, *what a waste of time anticipating a call I will never get.*

For a moment, I felt betrayed—*Yogi wasn't a man of his word,* I thought. Eventually I got over it and moved on with my life. I had just finished a successful first year in college and I had one more year to complete my associate degree. But first, one long summer was ahead of me.

"Arnold!" my mother shouted on a Saturday evening.

"Huh? *Arnold?*" I grumbled.

"Arnold…," she hollered again, but this time, the tone in her voice sounded like a tease—the same tone she used whenever a female called the house asking for me. She never called me Arnold unless it was one of my school friends at the front door or on the phone. Before she called my name again, I rose from my bed where I had been lying, doing absolutely nothing.

"Telephone."

"Oh, it mus' be Dudley or Ali trying to tell me let's go to da Summit," I muttered. "Oye, wham to you deh gason?"

"Hello...Arnold Henry?" said an unrecognizable, deep, American voice.

I cleared my throat. "Ye...yeah?"

"This is Coach Bruce Kreutzer—"

The receiver of the phone was no longer on my ear as I started dancing and rejoicing while screaming, "Yes! Yes! Yes!" (I was careful to keep my hand over the mouthpiece). Marvin and Marva, who were seated in the living room watching television, stared at me as if they had just seen a monkey. I took a deep breath then unblocked the mouth piece of the phone's receiver. "I beg your pardon Sir," I said, trying to imitate an American accent.

"Coach Bruce Kreutzer calling from North Carolina." I knew exactly what he said the first time—hearing it twice reassured me that I hadn't fallen asleep while lounging on my bed.

"Hey, Coach Kreutzer, what a pleasant surprise."

"Yogi told me a lot of great stuff about you."

Oh thank you so much Yogi, I thought, briefly gazing at the ceiling.

"I would love for you to play for me." Chills crawled up my skins. *Bingo,* I thought.

"That's my dream Coach...that's my dreams," I cried.

"Here's where we are at—the head basketball coach of Queens College has just resigned. So as the assistant coach, I've tried to pick up where he left off. Unfortunately, the job was handed to a new coaching staff. I am now in the process of starting a new Post Graduate Men's Basketball program located in Woodstock, Virginia. How does that sound?"

I thought, *are you kidding me? Anything would do.* "Sounds great to me, Coach," I responded.

There was a long pause. "It is a military school—Massanutten Military Academy." There was a slight awkward moment but Coach Kreutzer chuckled and broke the silence. He asked, "Is that alright with you?"

Without hesitation, I answered, "Yes, of course. I have a question though."

"Sure."

"Will that be a full basketball scholarship?"

I would have to deny the offer immediately if I had to pay.

"Oh yes. And you will have an opportunity to get another basketball scholarship too, from a four year college, if you do well here.

Thank God, I thought.

"I have your email address here with me. I will be sending you an email shortly with the scholarship information and requirements," he continued.

"Cool...cool...thank you so much for this opportunity, Coach."

After I hung up, I shouted, "Mummy, you eh go believe dis!"

"What Mario?"

"I did it...I got a basketball scholarship!" I folded my arms around her neck, holding back tears.

"For true?" she whispered. I looked straight into her eyes.

"For true!"

Chapter 17

I Will Get There...Somehow!

Massanutten Military Academy—a military school? I didn't know what to expect; but who cared? All I was concerned about was being able to play basketball in America. I had researched and found out that Massanutten Military Academy was like a post high-school that prepared students for college. I thought, *perfect, just what I need.*

For as much as I loved my country, it felt like the time for my departure was right—I was disgusted with the number of crimes happening in my communities. Gang wars were life threatening to innocent bystanders; bullets ended lives early for many of our youth. Young teens' minds were corrupted with violence, drugs, and weapons. I wanted no part of it. But a few days after I accepted the scholarship offer, conflicts infiltrated my group of friends. We had created rivals on our own streets and I got a dose of reality after I was arrested for an alleged assault on one of our foes. Apparently the victim gave my name to the officers.

My mother cried when the Marchand Police came to pick me up from our home. For her to see me handcuffed, made me feel like a big disappointment. I couldn't look her in the eyes.

Luckily, an eyewitness spoke on my behalf and told the officers that I had only separated the physical fight which had occurred between Kendell and Java and one of our enemies. No charges were filed against me. Those four hours I spent locked up behind bars were moments I never wanted to live again. I wondered how anyone could handle life in prison. I knew that I wouldn't be able to sit in a cell as the real world passed me by—there was too much to live for. Being in prison would also give me a bad reputation and could really affect my future, especially having a police record when applying for a US visa.

It was time for me to leave the past behind—my family, my friends, Margaritte, my college—to focus on my dreams of a basketball career.

Coach Kreutzer sent me the information for my scholarship. It covered my tuition, room, and board for a year while attending Massanutten Military Academy, but I needed to pay for my health insurance. Coach also explained in the emails that I had to apply and pay for my own US student visa.

The required documents for the student visa were mailed to my local post office. These documents included a letter and an I-20—a hard copy proof of my sponsorship and acceptance to Massanutten Military Academy. Supposedly, these signed hard copies guaranteed me access to the United States.

I had all the paperwork I needed, but there were still the financial issues. This was the most difficult part of the process to overcome.

Time was limited. We were in the sunny month of July; only one more month until I needed to be in Virginia. My mother and I had to act quickly.

To sum it all up, I needed: one round trip airplane ticket to the United States Embassy located in Bridgetown, Barbados; 100 US dollars for the fee for my student visa; a one-way airplane ticket to Virginia; and approximately 500 US dollars for my health insurance fees. Roughly, it was a cost of over 2000 Eastern Caribbean dollars. And that didn't include unexpected costs.

It was impossible for my mother to come up with even $100 EC in one month. Out of desperation, my mother and I decided to roam the busy streets of the downtown area to beg for financial aid. Even though she struggled to walk on her bad leg, there was nothing that would have stopped her from giving it a try. We first visited the Minister of Education, Human Resource Development, Youth and Sports— Honorable Mario Michel. Since I had already represented Saint Lucia on many occasions, it was my mother's idea to seek assistance from the minister.

I left my mother at the front door of his department and walked into his office unannounced after I told his secretary that it was an emergency. I was sure that it wouldn't be a problem for the government to help me out.

"Arnold Henry," I greeted him as I shook his hands and looked him in the eye with a big smile.

"Oh yeah." He acted as if my name rang a bell. "The athlete and basketball player, right?"

"Yes Sir."

"What can I do for you?"

"I'm sorry to bother you buh I jus' wanna inform you of my accomplishment." He continued signing the documents on his desk. "I jus' receive a full basketball scholarship for one year to a military school in de states."

"Congratulations." He flipped through another page.

"I was wonderin' if it possible you can sponsor me a plane ticket to de States. It's really urgent."

"When you suppose to be there?"

"Next month," I replied. He stopped and looked me in the eye.

"To tell you the truth, I don't think I'm able to assist you. It's just not enough time to come up with the money." His reply made it very difficult for me to swallow.

"Okay, thanks den."

While I exited his office, I kept on thinking, *wow, the government of Saint Lucia has no money, no links, no connections? Nothing?* I never thought that I would have been turned down by the government.

"Dats it. Let's go home now," I said to my mother.

"What happened?"

"He said dat he cah help me Mummy."

"Don't worry my boy. We are going to find someone. Have faith."

My mother knew a lot of business people who worked in nearby buildings. We spent the entire day walking from office to office, disturbing workers and begging for assistance. It was surprising to witness the number of people she knew. Every time we walked into an office, I felt so embarrassed to know what my mother was about to do. She was now in the position of the vagrants who she'd always give a dollar coin, back when she had a steady job. Now my mother was the one begging for money.

She wanted me to stay behind as she had one-on-one conversations with her friends. Eventually, I overheard a conversation.

"My oldest son, Mario, he just got a basketball scholarship to America. The only thing is—I need to get him there. It is costing me so much because I have to buy a plane ticket for him to go get his visa in Barbados and another plane ticket to go to America. And he needs to be at the school by next month." The expression on my mother's face was saddening. "If you have anything…anything to help me out, I will really appreciate it."

The government may have turned me down, but by the end of the day, a few of my mother's friends promised to assist me. Margaritte was generous enough to share some of her money too.

I visited my oldest brother, Kervyn, at his office as well. Back then, he was the kindest person I knew. Running a conversation with him was so easy. He didn't have any problems assisting me. In fact, he was so proud of my achievement that he handed me $300 US; more money than I had expected. "Someday you can pay me back," Kervyn said.

Tobias had even come through for me—he bought me a round-trip plane ticket to Barbados. He must have gotten a free ticket from LIAT Airlines—the airline he used to travel for regional sporting purposes.

I wasted no time. I caught a 6:00 a.m. flight to Barbados—a 30 minute plane ride—to apply for my US student visa. Upon my arrival, I took a taxi to the US Embassy. I handed the taxi-driver 30 Barbadian dollars.

I arrived at the embassy about 8:00 in the morning. To my surprise, the lines were as long as lines at a theme park. I waited with people from several islands of the Caribbean. Thank God we stood under clear blue skies because if it rained we would have been soaked in the unsheltered waiting area.

Before I went through the security checkpoint at the main door, I rechecked my yellow folder to ensure that I had all my required documents: my Saint Lucian passport, the copy of my I-20, two passport size photos, the US student visa forms, the letter of acceptance from the school, and 100 US dollars.

Going through security reminded me of an airport—metal detectors, removal of belt and shoes. There were even more seated people inside than people standing outside. The inside was so quiet that you could hear every whisper and flipped paper. I sat down waiting for the number I was given to be announced.

I briefly stared at the clock, 10:00 a.m. The silence made me apprehensive. Everyone's worried faces made me question myself. What if I was denied the visa? What if I was missing something? I heard rumors of applicants being denied their visas after paying—with no refund. I was denied a visitor visa in 2000 when my mother tried to apply for me. I prayed that situation wouldn't be repeated.

My number was called and I walked up to a booth where I faced a Caucasian male dressed in a shirt and tie. We were separated by a bullet-proof glass window. I handed him all my documents. After a brief evaluation, he asked, "I see you received a full basketball scholarship, huh?"

I tried to wipe the sweat off my face and replied, "Yes Sir."

"Congratulations."

The process was short and simple. I thought, *that's it?* He kept my passport and suggested that I return after 2:00 p.m. to pick it up. For a moment, I felt relieved, but I still wondered, *was I approved for the student visa?* I had no idea and I was too nervous to ask.

I arrived back in Saint Lucia the same evening. My mother awaited me in the airport parking lot with a taxi. When I first looked at her from the distance, she was all smiles, but the closer I got to her, the more that smile faded.

"What happened Mario? Did you get it?"

I looked down at the ground, shook my head, and said, "I doh know."

"What! What you mean you don't know?"

I pulled my passport from my back pocket. "Look, open it."

"Hold on. Let me put on my glasses," she said. "Boy! Don't be playing games like that with me."

I raised my head. "Wha'? I got it?"

"You didn't know?"

"I wanted us to open it together." We both laughed.

"They only gave you the visa for one year," my mother stated.

"Wha' dat mean?"

"Well, it will be expiring next year."

"Oh Mummy, doh worry. I go get anada scholarship from a college."

"One thing, if you don't get another scholarship, you better try to stay in America, eh. Saint Lucia has nothing."

"I go try my hardes' Mummy…And remember, de coach say if I do well, a four year college go give me anada basketball scholarship."

"As long as you know what you doing my boy."

"Trus' me Mummy, I know."

With a copy of my student visa stamped into my Saint Lucian passport, I was now prepared to go to America. But there was just one more problem we needed to surmount—purchasing my plane ticket to fly to Virginia. The money we had gathered from my mother's friends, Kervyn, and Margaritte was just enough for my school's health insurance.

Two weeks until my expected departure day and I hadn't booked a flight.

Just when my mother and I had run out of solutions, I remembered my long-time friend, Jonathan Hall, who once lived in Saint Lucia but moved to the city of Philadelphia. Before he left the island, he told me to holler at him if I ever needed anything.

I sent Jonathan an email explaining my dilemma. Before I ended the message, I wrote, "…Anyways, I was really hoping you can help me pay for my plane ticket. It would mean so much to my mother and me. Thanking you in advance."

The next day, I read Jonathan's response. He replied with a better idea of his own: because he was already working for US Airways— something I knew nothing about—he would give me an airline ticket instead of the money.

Coach Kreutzer was the first one to hear my good news—I was now ready to come to America. "Hey Coach, I will be seeing you on August 31," I said.

My future looked bright.

Chapter 18

Farewell Saint Lucia

Before I left for America, I represented Saint Lucia one final time at the 2003 Windward Islands Secondary School Games.

That year, the games were hosted on the island of Dominica. And again, for the third year in a row, I was selected for the track and field and basketball events. By the end of the games, Saint Lucia had regained the first place title.

The hardest part of leaving Saint Lucia was saying goodbye to my family, my friends, my schoolmates, Margaritte, and the island that was my home for 18 years. The easiest part was getting away from my broken home, to never have to experience tension with Lucius again.

I was one step closer to fulfilling my basketball dream; to being able to tell my mother there was no need for her to work anymore; to showing Tobias that I never needed him to be my father.

For my last few days, I had to balance spending time with my friends, Margaritte, and my family. My last encounter with Margaritte was in her bedroom where we discussed our future plans. "I eh wanna be with no American girl. I go wait for you," I told her that night.

We both swore that we wouldn't see anyone else.

My closest friends—Kendell, Java, Bobdole, Kern, Dudley, and Ali were thrilled about my scholarship. "One ting, when you make it, I go want a free NBA jersey eh," they said to me.

I also had to leave the two-year brotherly-love relationship I'd built with Kervyn. He wanted the best for me. And as for Tobias, I found an ounce of strength to call him to say goodbye. I assumed that he was happy about my disappearance.

It seemed that the most disappointed by my departure was my track and field coach, Noup. Through his eyes, I was a quitter. But I knew I wasn't. The sport of basketball was about to give me a once in a lifetime opportunity. And being six foot five, weighing only 195lbs, it would have taken me too long to reach my full potential as a shot put and discus thrower. I loved throwing shot put and discus and appreciated Noup's efforts, but I couldn't let my hoop dreams slip away.

It took me about three days to prepare for my departure. I packed all my belongings in one suitcase, including my most memorable family and sports portraits, and the VHS cassettes of my secondary school basketball games. I had my hair braided one last time by my friend, Sabrina, and my barber shaped-up and trimmed my facial hair.

HANGING ON TO MY DREAMS

By noon, on the last day of August 2003, my mother, Marvin, Marva, and Kobie were all aboard Rosalie's green Suzuki Jeep on our way to the island's only international airport—Hewanorra International Airport, located in Vieux-Fort, the second largest town on the island. The 50-minute drive along the coastline from the north to the south, gave me a brief glimpse of the calm, clear, deep blue seas that I was about to leave behind.

We arrived at the airport two hours prior to my flight. As I prepared to check-in to the security area, I noticed the worried expression on my mother's face. It would be my first time away from her for more than a month.

"My boy, I cannot even give you a few US dollars for your pocket change. I'm so sorry," my mother cried out.

"Mummy, eh worry about me. I jus' wanted to make it up dere and you did your job," I said.

"Take care of yourself and please stay out of trouble. Make sure you reply to all my letters eh. I will continue praying for you," she said. And as I reached to hug my mother, she whispered a warning. "One thing Mario, be careful with these American girls eh. You remember what just happened to Kobe Bryant?" My mother, who hardly knew anything about basketball, knew the NBA superstar for two reasons: His name sounded the same as Rosalie's child, and, Kobe Bryant had just been charged in connection with an alleged sexual assault complaint.

I hugged her tighter before responding. "Okay Mummy. I go be too focus for dem tings to happen to me."

One last look at my mother's disturbing ankle furthered my motivation to strive for success in America.

The plane was 90 percent filled with Caucasian tourists. I felt like I was airborne in America. They all wore their tropical T-shirts with their cargo shorts.

"I had an incredible vacation. I love Saint Lucia," I overheard a nearby passenger mention.

"Me too. I loved the Sulphur Springs, the pitons, and the beaches."

"Beautiful."

"I know…I will definitely be back."

Their conversations were making me homesick already. To distract myself, I took out my green notepad from my backpack, and decided to keep a journal of my odyssey. I knew that this was about to be a life changing experience which very few Saint Lucians would ever get to experience—so by documenting it on paper, I would at least recollect some events to share later in life.

It took eighteen years of my life for me to finally step foot on the land of opportunity. Upon exiting the aircraft, I took in a deep breath then released, pretending like I had just smelled a fresh, freedom breeze. The Philadelphia Airport was enormous compared to what I had seen. Everything around me seemed technologically advanced. Being around such diverse people—Asians, Indians, Caucasians, Blacks...—was also unexpected.

I followed a US Immigration sign. At the front of the line, I met an officer who asked for my documents. The officer, with a gun placed into a holster buckled to his waist, made me feel very uneasy. I kept quiet and ensured my every move was cautious. He showed no emotion. It felt even scarier when he snapped my mug-shot and scanned my finger-prints. *I must be arrested,* I thought.

My eyes followed his every movement—which included the signing of some papers; typing in some information on the computer; opening and stamping my passport; then stapling a piece of paper near my student visa. He gave me back my I-20, letter of acceptance, and my passport. And just like that, I was following a sign that read, Luggage/Pick-Up.

A hand clasped my shoulder.

"Hey buddy, how was your flight?"

I held the left side of my chest. "Yo, Jonathan, oh my God, you scare me." He pretended like he never heard me and steadily increased his walking pace. "Why we rushin'?" I asked. He kept his eyes in the direction up ahead.

"Boy, if you don't hurry up, you going to miss your next flight."

"Wha' about my bag?"

"Don't worry. You will pick it up when you reach Washington, D.C."

"Oh, irie den."

I must have seen Jonathan for about five minutes and I was already on another flight, on my way to Dulles Airport.

Chapter 19

A Military Life

The only thing on my mind was a plate of my mother's delicious Sunday food—stewed chicken submerged in a portion of brown saucy gravy; baked macaroni and cheese pie; slices of fried ripe plantains; pieces of breadfruit, yam, green-fig and sweet potatoes; a chunk of coleslaw, potato-salad, and lentils; and a cup of local juice. Then naptime on my lower bunk-bed for a few hours. But instead, I was picking up my bag from the Dulles Airport carousel. When I made it out the exit door, a mature Caucasian man, who held a piece of cardboard with my name printed on it, chauffeured me to Massanutten Military Academy.

In the backseat of his car, I tilted my head back, and drifted to sleep.

After two hours, I awoke at my final destination in Woodstock, Virginia. I wondered, *two hour ride in a car? I thought we were in a different country.*

The driver had pulled in front of a tall brick building near a light-pole. It was hard to see through the darkness but it seemed like only trees and bushes surrounded the area.

I briefly gazed at my watch with my half-opened eyes and realized that it was already two hours past my usual midnight bedtime. The driver kindly assisted me with my bag, and then directed me inside the dark building. After he dismissed himself, I met up with a short, young Caucasian male who was dressed up like the American soldiers I'd seen in the movies. My initial thought: *why is this young guy up so late, wearing a uniform as if he was at an Independence parade?* Nevertheless, I greeted him with a smile and a handshake. He returned a straight face and almost squashed the bones in my hand.

"Colonel Reis," he said. I wondered, *who names their child, Colonel?* He wrote my name down in a big black book, making my arrival official.

The seriousness expressed on Colonel Reis's face made me feel unwelcome. He immediately showered me with on-campus rules. He pointed to my head; my jeans and polo shirt; my watch and silver chains, then stated, "You need to cut your hair, shave your facial hair, no civilian clothing, and no jewelry. Do you understand?"

I thought, *oh my God, Coach Kreutzer never told me about these rules.*

Feeling like I had no other options, I answered, "Um, yeah."

"Yes Sir," Colonel Reis demanded.

I had sleep in my eyes; it was so early in the morning and this dude, who appeared to be younger than me, was trying to discipline me. I rolled my eyes. "Yes, Sir...I go do it when I get a chance."

"No! You need to get it done this morning."

"Okay man." Colonel Reis gave me a vicious look. "Sorry...sorry...I mean Sir."

Colonel Reis assisted me with my bag and directed me up three levels to my bedroom. The various flights of stairs were spooky—the only light was from the outside light-pole that shone through the glass windows; the building felt chilly due to the air-conditioner unit; there were older men dressed in camouflage army suits who acted like night security guards; and the sounds of people snoring echoed through the hallway walls.

When I got to my room and spotted an empty slot on top of the bunk-bed, I ignored my already asleep roommate, dropped my bags, and fell to sleep almost before they could land on the shiny tiled floor.

I was having the best sleep of my life when someone in my dreamland blasted a bugle in my ears. My mind was telling me that I should get up, but my body felt dead. A few minutes later, the same signal was broadcast through a bugle. It felt like someone was playing games with me. I jumped out of my bed searching for the culprit who woke me up, but I only found my roommate wide awake and dressed the same way I'd seen Colonel Reis about two hours ago. He just sat there motionless.

"Wha' goin' on?" I asked.

"What?" asked my roommate as we finally made eye contact.

"What's...going...on?" I repeated, but this time I pronounced my words clearly.

"Oh! We gotta get ready dawg."

"Ready?"

"Yeah dawg. We got breakfast."

I thought, *I'm awake at 5:45 a.m. for breakfast? And I thought my mother was bad.*

I soon came back to my senses and realized that I was at a military school. I introduced myself to my roommate who appeared to be about six foot two, African American. He replied, "Antoine Mayhand."

"Well Antoine, I'm goin' back to bed. I tired."

"We have to go dawg," Antoine advised me.

Feeling like I had no other option, I lagged along.

HANGING ON TO MY DREAMS

It was chaotic outside our bedroom. There were more guys dressed up like Antoine and they all sprinted in the same direction. For some reason, my appearance kind of slowed down the motion in the hallway. Everyone stared at me as if they had just seen an alien—I couldn't tell if they stared at the color of my skin, my height, or my casual clothes.

The bugle sound went off one more time; I started to believe that we needed to pick up our pace. I jogged my way outside, through the front entrance of the building, and to an organized gathering of possibly every student on-campus; everyone dressed alike with an awkward shaped hat, the same gray colored shirt tucked into long gray pants, and black polished dress shoes. About 99 percent of the assembly seemed younger than I was. Everything seemed bigger than in Saint Lucia—the pavement, the roads, the buildings, the trees, the houses...well, everything felt bigger, except for the majority of the students. I remembered Coach Kreutzer mentioning that this military academy was also a middle school and high school; no wonder everyone seemed younger than me.

Most students stood in a formation which was divided up into five groups; each included a leader who conducted organization and roll-calls within their group. The students were predominantly Caucasian with a few more Asians than Blacks. I noticed only one female formation.

I followed Antoine into a group of about twelve males, three of them Caucasian, who all seemed to be more my age. I assumed that they were my teammates since we towered over the rest of the students.

"Stand at ease," Antoine whispered in my ear.

"Stan' at wha'?" I asked.

"Just do everything I do dawg." I adjusted my position by shifting my feet shoulder width apart, placed my hands behind my back, and looked straight ahead. For a moment, I felt like I was about to be handcuffed by a police officer.

Facing the center of our formation, about 30 meters away, was Colonel Reis. With the colonel were three other males and a female. I thought, *wait a minute, Colonel isn't his first name; he must have the highest rank at this school which makes him our leader.*

My thoughts reminded me of my new environment—a military school.

Colonel Reis shouted, "Company!" (I later learned that *Company* referred to the formations, and that each had a unique name: Alpha, Bravo, Charlie, Delta, and Golf—I was part of Golf Company).

"Company!" The platoon leaders repeated the orders, passing on Colonel Reis's commands.

95

"Attention!" instructed by Colonel Reis.

"Spit shine from head to toe," roared the entire formation, (well, except for me), instantly everyone stood at attention by bringing their feet together and placing their hands to their sides. The unexpected chant and swift adjustments made my heart skip a beat. Everyone stood still, making no movement, again, except for me. I followed procedures a few seconds later. I immediately learned that standing at attention was less relaxing than standing at ease.

Colonel Reis shouted once more, "Company!"

"Company!" repeated our captain.

"Right Face!" Everyone maneuvered to the right to face an American flag, held by two students and attached to a rope at the bottom of a white pole.

"Present arms!" Everyone placed their right hand just near their right eye, better known as a salute. The same bugle sound aired through the speakers. I wondered why the people who lived in the nearby houses hadn't busted a gunshot in the air as a sign of warning for us to keep the noise level down.

While the music played, the American flag was raised. I felt like I was transformed into an American soldier despite still being dressed like a civilian. When the flag reached the peak of the pole, the music stopped and Colonel Reis shouted, "Order arms!" Everyone brought their hand back to their side. Colonel Reis and his associates walked to the very front of the formation then shouted, "Forward march!" The entire formation started marching forward with the captain calling instructional steps in a musical manner. "Left, right, left, right left..."

Despite my lack of energy, I tried to assimilate. I did my best to save myself the embarrassment of someone shouting in my face, "Get in step," or, "Stay in step!" But I mostly chanted, "Left, right, sorry...left, right...sorry." All the dust from underneath my black basketball sneakers was transferred to my mate's black dress shoes. We halted outside the Mess Hall, or Mess I, in an orderly manner, and then group by group, marched inside the building in single file.

Inside, we stood at attention and waited for orders. Once everyone was at their designated table and chair, a prayer was recited. Then we were instructed to stand at ease until everyone at our table had gotten their meals.

What did I get myself into? I definitely wasn't expecting military life for high school students to have so many rules. Since my teammates and I were all new to the academy, we were considered cadets. And as a cadet, my independent privileges were even more limited than other students with higher rankings.

For instance, while seated at the table, our backs weren't allowed to touch the back of the chair—we remained seated at attention with our head facing straight forward, not even our eyes were allowed to move. We were only allowed to eat our food in square meals: basically, we raised our food from our plate or our drinks with our hands vertically then brought the food or drinks to our mouth horizontally, making imaginary right angles to eat. We weren't allowed to talk.

After our meals, if we needed to return to our rooms, we weren't allowed to leave on our own; there were no exceptions. Instead, we reformed our formation and marched as a unit whenever our leaders found it appropriate to lead us back. I reminded myself that basketball was the reason for coming to America in the first place, and tried to maintain a positive attitude throughout the military experience.

Back at the dorms, I had a better chance to introduce myself to the rest of my teammates. We all lived on the same floor, sharing the same community bathrooms and toilets down the same hallway.

Two of my teammates were from the Bahamas, one was from Morocco, and one was from Canada. The others were from Washington, DC, and various cities in the states of Pennsylvania, Maryland, North Carolina, and Ohio. One was a local. A few of my teammates proclaimed that, since they were from the streets of Washington, DC, they were the toughest humans on this planet.

It was still minutes before seven in the morning—the usual time my mother would wake me up for school. As I attempted to catch up on my missed sleep, Antoine explained our daily morning inspections and advised me that our rooms needed to be clean with our beds made and everything squared away. At these times, my mother would have been proud to see me sweep the floors, dust the furniture, make my bed, and tidy up my chest of drawers.

It was orientation week, and since I was a latecomer, it was my duty to catch up with the rest of my teammates. Being in my casual clothing with my hair extending down my back and my facial hair masking my true identity made me feel like I didn't belong on-campus. I needed to get myself together before I ended up in a confrontation with Colonel Reis.

Everything we needed was right on the school's campus. I thought, *no wonder it's called a boarding school.* My teammates suggested that I get a haircut from the school's barbershop. When I heard the school's barber was a woman, I ignored his suggestion. It was my first time hearing of a female barber. Luckily, one of my teammates had his own hair-clippers. The cutting of my four-year-old braids was sort of an icebreaker—everyone wanted to witness my haircut from an afro to a bald head. And as they all watched, we exchanged personal stories and bonded. It reminded me of a real barbershop at home.

Antoine, who lived a two hour drive from the school, asked, "So where is Sent Loo...Sent Loosh—" I had to interrupt him to save him from the embarrassment.

"You mean, Saint Lucia?"

"Yeah, where is that joint?" asked Aaron while he cut my hair.

"It in de Caribbean...part of de West Indies...nex' to Barbados," I replied.

"Man, what did you say? I can't understand a word you're saying," Antoine remarked harshly.

I ignored his tone and repeated slowly, "It's in the Ca-rib-be-an."

"Oh the Car-rib-bean," Antoine corrected me as if his pronunciation was more reasonable. Everyone's laughter became very annoying; I wasn't sure if they were laughing at me or with me. Either way, I tried to hide my irritation behind a smile.

It was only day one and I was already feeling like it was high school all over again.

After I received an orthodox fade-haircut from Aaron, I borrowed a razor and some shaving cream from Antoine and diligently removed all my facial hair.

Later, I made a visit to the school's tailor who took my measurements and immediately handed me all my necessary military uniforms and sporting gear. I deposited my 500 US dollars for health insurance at the health center. Finally, I picked up my books at the school's bookstore.

All this running around the school's campus made me feel like I was sleep-walking. I had no time to rest. In fact, no one was allowed in their rooms during the day, especially students having the rank of a cadet. To break free from the cadet prison, there was a test given to all cadets in the campus chapel throughout orientation week. I was determined to get a perfect score because I was frustrated with not being able to eat like a normal person.

For studying purposes, all cadets were given a yellow handbook which documented all the school's rules and regulations. Then we were tested. With my first attempt at the multiple choice and fill in the blank exam I scored a total of 98 percent, moving my rank to Private First Class.

We were told that we'd be honored sometime during the week at Mess II, which would open up some more freedom for me, such as the elimination of eating square meals at Mess I, II, and III.

At 1800 hours, we assembled at the same location for the third and final formation, in preparation for dinner, or Mess III. During that time, the bugle call was broadcast and we saluted the lowering of the American flag.

The first evening after Mess III, Coach Kreutzer visited me for the first time. Everyone called him, "Coach K," which was much easier for me to pronounce; I had been worried I would call him Coach Chrysler.

Even though I was exhausted, I stepped outside my room to show respect to our head coach who had made it possible for me to fulfill my dreams. I faced a mature Caucasian man—white hair the same color as his mustache and a callused, tan face. He was about four inches shorter than I was.

"Arnold, nice of you to join us," Coach K joked as if I was late on purpose.

"Thank you Coach," I said. He stretched his arm out for a handshake, which I returned, but he let it lead to a tight hug. And for the first time since my arrival, I felt less homesick. He advised me that the basketball floor was being refinished and that we would be able to start our practice sessions by the next week.

"Coach, it go be my first time playin' on an indoor court," I said.

Coach K laughed. "Well, your jump-shot will not be blown by the wind, that's for sure."

Thoughts of playing on a better surface crossed my mind as I remembered when I fell on The Summit's gravel like a baseball player sliding to his home base; it had left scars on the palms of my hands and right knee.

I daydreamed of my new-found indoor court, thinking, *less pain on my knees; no more bruises on my knees, hand, and elbow; no more pouring rain interrupting our games; no more fetching loose balls down the road while dodging traffic; no more depending on the government to build a better court with a smooth surface, better rims, and a fence.*

Later that night, my teammates and I met the final addition to our team—our assistant coach, Coach Phillip. He was about the same height and skin color as our head coach but Coach Phillip was much younger, in his mid-thirties.

Unlike Coach K, Coach Phillip lived on the same floor and hallway as us; he could tell Coach K of any misconduct by his basketball players.

Coach Phillip was a very decent man and a good motivational speaker. From our very first conversation, he started to teach me. "Arnold, I guarantee you will become a better basketball player before

99

you leave here. I played for Coach K during my college years and he is the best in the business."

Coach Phillip was the type of person who would be in your face expressing his love for the game through his own personal experiences as a college player. His words made me eager to start immediately.

At ten minutes to 2200 hours, the sound of the bugle echoed in the hallways for the final time, indicating preparation for a strictly enforced lights-out. I was told it was customary to stand at attention as the bugle recited a tune that sounded like something played at a military funeral.

Chapter 20

Bugle Call

I wanted to rip apart the speakers that played the bugle sounds, especially during the early morning hours. Waking up became the hardest part of my day. In fact, being in America for the first time in my life became the most difficult experience I'd ever had. Each day felt like it would never end.

My weekdays involved the same boring daily routine: wake-up calls and breakfast at 0545 hours; at 0700 hours we handled our chores on the floor, and in our bedrooms, as well as community services; at 0800 hours, I attended my four classes: ESL (English as a Second Language), SAT/ACT preparatory class, Algebra I and LET (a military course). Lunch was at 1145; individual basketball work-outs, drills and weightlifting were at 1330; by 1600 hours, I went to the library for a mandatory study session. My last meal of the day was at 1800 hours; and finally, from 1930 hours to 2130 hours I had basketball practice which gave me 30 minutes to shower and be in bed before lights out at 2200 hours. Before I closed my eyes for the night, I wrote in my diary.

It was our duty to ensure that we were dressed appropriately at every formation. Each night I took the time to prepare—*Spit shine from head to toe!*—for the three daily formations—morning, noon, and evening—by shaving my face, ironing my military uniform, and literally spit-shining my shoes with saliva and black shoe polish. Every day, I felt like I represented Golf Company in a presentable manner. And whenever I was in uniform, I felt like a respected young man. I envisioned my mother boasting to her friends, "Look at my boy. He looks so handsome." I wished she was able to see me survive on my own.

Boredom existed throughout my weekdays—we weren't allowed to roam the streets of Woodstock, go to the movies, or visit malls. Weekends, Friday evenings through Sunday evenings, were the only times students could be excused from campus, and only if you were in good standing. If a student violated the academy's rules, they were punished with a number of penalizing hours according to the severity of their offense. And to work off these hours, there was a scheduled time where violators met up with a disciplinary officer to either do marching drills with a rifle or to do community service around campus. Believe me, there was nothing fun about either one of those options.

Arnold Henry

There were no breaks in my schedule. The highlights of my days were at basketball workouts and practices, away from all the military procedures. It was just me, my teammates and coaches inside the closed gym; outsiders weren't allowed to enter. Why should I complain? After all, that was my number one reason for coming to America—to learn basketball.

The very first time I stepped foot on the wooden, shiny floors of the indoor basketball court, it was love at first sight. It was everything that I imagined from the images I'd caught on television—a smooth surface, a safer free fall, and a more appealing look. I literally laid down on the court for a minute. I know my teammates must have thought that I was crazy, but I was enjoying the moment of playing basketball in America.

From the beginning, some of my teammates treated me like I didn't belong in their country. And the more comfortable we got with each other, the worse it became.

The most disrespectful phrases included:

"Speak English!"

"Where you live, everyone dresses with leaves and no one wears shoes!"

"Go back to your country on your banana boat!"

Everyone said these things just to create laughter. But their jokes sparked a fuse in me. I tried my best to keep my anger and rage within me. I didn't want to Hulk-out on them. Being the tallest on the team and the strongest in the weight-room, I felt like I could have easily made an example out of any of them. But being the only Saint Lucian on-campus, I also felt outnumbered.

I didn't dare tell my coaches about my problems because my teammates always preached, "Snitches get stitches."

If I couldn't speak English, then how come everyone in Saint Lucia was able to understand me? To them, my accent may have been heavy, but I was trying my best to pronounce my words. I wanted to punch someone in the face. But that would have only dismissed me from the school—which could also lead to deportation.

To render happy thoughts, I constantly reminded myself again and again, *I came to America for a better life for myself and my family.* Thoughts of my mother made me stronger and gave me the will and the strength to hang on to my dreams.

During our first practice sessions, many times I overheard bad conversations about me. "This nigga sucks!" Their harsh words were slowly looming over my self-confidence. I thought, *maybe Coach K and Coach Phillip might think I suck too.* It was depressing because it seemed like Coach shouted my name the most. And it wasn't for anything good.

Learning the new style of play, or rather the American basketball system, was too much for my basketball I.Q. to handle all at once. I felt like I was learning the game all over again. Most of my teammates were accustomed to that style of play; for me, it was like playing American football—I wouldn't have a clue what to do if I was put on a field.

It all reminded me of my first unsuccessful basketball tryouts at Entrepot Secondary School. Luckily, my experiences with previous failures were more reasons for me to push harder; to keep moving forward, closer to all my dreams.

To some extent, my teammates were probably accurate about my performance—I just didn't like the way they handled it. They made me feel worthless and unappreciated. I admit to having some terrible practices from day one. For some reason, I was having trouble catching the basketball, as if before every practice, I chucked my hands in a bowl of butter. I frequently, but unintentionally, did the opposite of what my coaches instructed. And I took forever to learn our game-plays.

After a week or two I realized that I needed to be more focused during practices. So, after every Mess III, I displayed my game-face. It was my way of being focused. And day by day, week by week, my mistakes became less frequent. I felt like I became more coachable. At a certain point, after an intense practice session, I remember Coach Phillip saying, "That was really impressive Arnold. I could hug you right now." He shared these kind words when I joined in running full-court-sprints with my teammates who were being punished for missing their classes. Though some of them felt I was being sycophantic, I felt the extra work was much needed.

There was still much that needed attention, including my shooting skills, free-throw percentage, post moves, and my defensive tactics; therefore, every opportunity for extra work, I was present. Later down the line, after a few successful practices, I was respected by everyone; the jokes about me dropped down to a minimum.

To me, basketball in America was focused around organization. To prepare for a game, we needed a plan which featured both offensive and defensive plays. (In Saint Lucia, the only offensive plays I knew were pass-pass-pass, screen-screen-screen until someone attained an opportunity to score). I was now executing plays successfully. My increasing knowledge of the game made me realize that the point guards I watched on television weren't throwing up gang signs, they were actually hand signaling an offensive game play designed by their coaches.

Defensively, many of the plays sounded familiar. One problem my coaches noticed about me was my defensive stance—rather than standing straight with my arms down, I needed to squat with arms spread widely, parallel to the floor, all the time.

At one point, we were given new uniforms. I worried that by the end of the school year I would be handed a large bill of all my expenses so I asked Coach, "I gettin' bill for dat? I doh have no money for dat Coach."

"No, Arnold. It's free. Our post-graduate basketball program is sponsored by Nike. That's your practice uniform."

I was confused, yet ecstatic. I couldn't believe I'd just received a free pair of Nike basketball sneakers, a pair of Nike socks, and a matching Nike training jersey and shorts. Never in my life had I received so much free name brand gear all at once—it felt like a blessing from God.

As the leaves of the trees slowly vanished, so did the warmth. The unfamiliar climate meant that I needed warm clothes. Since the school provided all our uniforms and gear, purchasing winter clothes wasn't necessary. We were obligated to wear what was provided to us, on their timeline. I felt like I was walking inside a refrigerator, but the authorities didn't find it necessary to covered up with our school's jacket, scarf, beanie, or gloves, so I had to suffer in the winter winds. The military's lack of consideration for island boys like me, made it clear that there were no exceptions—everyone was treated equally.

One chilly Sunday morning, I woke up with a terrible headache and a high temperature. I felt like a bucket of ice-cold water was thrown onto my bed. This was the first time, in a very long time, that I'd fallen sick. I didn't even know how to take care of myself since my mother was no longer around.

I didn't want to miss out on Mess I, so I approached formation with my body covered in winter gear from head to toe. But even what I wore was unable to keep me warm. When I stepped outside the building, I felt goose bumps creeping all over my skin and my lips trembled.

Colonel Reis shouted, "Henry! Why are you out of uniform?"

"Sir, I really sick!" I answered.

"Change into today's uniform and hustle back for formation," he demanded.

I went back to my room, feeling indecisive as to whether or not I wanted to continue my stay at this school.

I looked out one of the hallway's windows. The last bugle sounded and I heard Colonel Reis shout, "Forward March!" The entire formation was already on their way to Mess. I thought, *what's the point. I'm staying in my room to get some rest.* So I crawled back in bed.

Even though I had just slept for eight hours, I felt exhausted. Colonel Reis's actions made me frustrated as well. I continued to think, *why didn't he understand I'm sick? Why no one respects me in this country?* Feeling a bit discouraged by the lack of consideration by others, I remembered once more that I just needed to hang on to my dream—with or without anyone's assistance.

I made an effort to visit the health center; all the nurse gave me were some tablets. I thought, *what a waste of my $500.00.* At home, my mother would have known exactly how to treat me. Her remedies never changed: two tablets of Sudafed, bush tea medicine, and a bowl of chicken noodle soup taken daily throughout the week until recovery was complete.

At the military school, I stayed in my room and slept the entire day. If no one understood I was sick, I would just ignored them. Even though faking a sickness was probably the best way to exempt me from any military procedures, I thought, w*hy would I lie about being sick? Especially on the same day as a basketball practice.*

My teammates warned me that the authorities had questioned my absence. "You didn' tell dem I sick?" I asked, barely able to move my lips.

"Yeah, we did but they don't seem to care."

"Well, jus' tell Coach I cah make it to practice dis evenin'."

Right before lights out, I borrowed a pack of Ramen Chicken Noodle Soup from Antoine, and tucked myself into bed.

The sounds of the bugle woke me the following day. Again, I heard Colonel Reis shout, "Forward March!" Even though I had not eaten a healthy meal in the last 36 hours, I missed formation and Mess I for a second time. I felt the need to rest as much as possible, to be fully recovered, so that I would be able to function during my classes and basketball practice.

Shortly, an officer slammed opened my bedroom door so hard that its impact startled me awake. I stared, confused at the mid-thirties, nerdy Caucasian man.

"Why weren't you at formation?" he demanded.

"Sir, I feeling really sick," I muttered, hoping he could hear my voice.

"You need to get off the bed now and head over to Mess I," he insisted. He waited for me to get up. "Henry!"

"Yes Sir," I answered on the verge of tears.

"Henry, get off the bed or I will be forced to remove you." His last statement triggered an outburst of raw emotions.

"I'm fuckin' sick! Wha' da fuck wrong wit you! Leave me da fuck alone, you inconsiderate bastard!"

Seconds later, I wished the Americans didn't understand my broken English. For my behavior, I was given a total of 25 hours for disrespecting an officer.

For 60 minutes before my classes in the morning and then again before basketball practice in the evening, I marched back and forth holding a rifle in one arm, rhyming to military tunes. *This is no ordinary school...I'm in a damn boot camp,* I thought. *This is harder than I thought.*

Chapter 21

Much Needed Motivation

Finally, early in October, I received my first letter from my mother. It was much needed since I had not heard from anyone in Saint Lucia. My mother wrote three pages. Every word and sentence felt as if she was reaching out to me; like I extended my arms and she held on to my hands saying hang in there my boy. In the midst of admiring how much I'd been missed by everyone, my eyes teared-up when I read, "After we dropped you off at the airport, Marvin was crying on our way back home." I'd never seen my younger brother express heart-felt emotion towards me.

About three weeks later, I was free at last from my daily marching drills with the rifle, and community service of raking leaves and cleaning bathrooms. My 25 hours were complete and I was allowed to leave campus during the weekends—just in time to tag along with Coach K on a road trip to North Carolina. I considered it to be a perfect get-away from all my teammates, colleagues, the military academy, the tight, uncomfortable uniforms, and most of all, that annoying bugle. Since we never had basketball practice on Friday and Saturday, most of my teammates' families came to pick them up for the weekends.

From Shenandoah County, or what I called *boot camp territory,* to Charlotte, North Carolina was about a five hour drive. While Coach K did all the driving, I looked out the window, expecting to see skyscrapers, flashy lights and billboards, or strip-long malls. Instead, I noticed lakes, cows and sheep, road-signs advertising motels, restaurants, gas-stations, and a highway that I'd thought led to nowhere. I had my first dose of the real America; well a small fraction of it, until I fell into a deep sleep, only to open my eyes to Yogi's two-storey residence.

"Boy, you look like you ready for a war," Yogi joked as Coach K drove off.

"Oye, I so ready to take off dat uniform," I said as we walked into his home. Yogi and his wife welcomed me. Their invitation had reduced my homesickness. I was thankful for the escape.

For the few days that I had off from school, I looked up to Yogi as a big brother, a mentor, my personal advisor. It was a great opportunity to be with a Saint Lucian like me, and someone who had college basketball experience. His guidance was exactly what I needed to survive the American basketball lifestyle. It felt like God had sent me an angel. I could have listened to Yogi all night, but my body needed the rest more.

I slept for 12 hours straight—the best sleep I'd had in America and my first ever on a queen-size bed with warm comforters and fluffy pillows.

Yogi had predicted that I would sleep-in. When I finally rose, we had some breakfast and headed straight to the gym.

"Boy, it seems like you have been hitting the gym hard," Yogi claimed as I stripped out of my T-shirt to my practice jersey. "You getting big eh." *If you think I'm big, what you think about yourself,* I thought. To me, Yogi was the world's strongest man.

"Yeah, I de strongest on my team," I bragged. "Coach recorded our personal best in the weight room and I bench-press 300 pounds."

"How much you weigh now?" he asked.

"210 pounds."

"Keep it up my man."

We started with some upper-body weightlifting. While I played follow-the-leader on some of Yogi's exercises, he continued to inspire me with speeches. We talked briefly between sets.

"I played against Ben Wallace in college...he was also my teammate during an all-star game."

"NBA superstar, Ben Wallace?" I asked with disbelief.

"Yeah my man."

"I tink I wanna play jus' like him, you know, grab rebounds jus' like him."

"Well if you stay focused, you can be as good," he assured me. I thought, *I must have a lot of potential then.* If Yogi, former college and professional basketball player, had seen a star in me, I felt like I was destined for greatness.

When we were done weightlifting we moved to the basketball court. Yogi focused on developing my offensive skills through a series of shooting and post-move drills. Some of the moves I had already learned from Coach K and Coach Phillip but some were new to me. Yogi even noted some of my deficiencies. "My man, when you shoot the ball, you want to follow through all the way," he said as he demonstrated a flicking movement with his shooting hand. "When you're taking the ball to the basket, be more explosive, go up stronger, and you want your shoulders parallel to the backboard, that way it makes it more difficult for defenders." I listened some more.

"There are three ways to defeat your defender: Quickness—by using a series of fast moves and speed, you can quickly establish a position to score or get around your defenders. Power—you can use your strength to go right through his body; just watch out for lowering and powering your shoulders into his chest because you can be charged with an offensive foul. Explosiveness—playing the game from above the rim by out jumping your defenders." I learned from the master.

Back at Yogi's house, we watched a few recorded VHS cassettes of his college basketball games. As I paid close attention to the television, I saw Yogi's love for the game—he had a winner's mentality—displaying the heart of a champion. He looked like a beast amongst humans. I was inspired to know that someone of my Caribbean island background represented the game with so much passion.

I had a few college related questions that needed answers; watching Yogi's college games made me worried about my own future.

"So Yogi, wha' next for me after Massanutten Military Academy?" I asked.

"You want to aim for a NCAA (National Collegiate Athletics Association) Division I basketball program," Yogi suggested.

"Wha' you mean by NCAA Division I?"

"You ever seen the college basketball games played on ESPN, CBS or ABC?"

"Uh, yeah," I replied as I thought of the only two I remembered— Duke and the University of North Carolina.

"Well those are NCAA Division I colleges or universities," he stated. "It's the highest level of college basketball played here in America. You have a good shot at playing that level."

"So wha' Division you played at Queens College?" I asked.

"NCAA Division II," Yogi answered. "I don't think there's any Saint Lucian who has played NCAA Division I…I'm not too sure."

"So, dat means it hard to play on that level?"

"My man, always believe you can achieve the impossible." Yogi was so positive that I could play basketball at the Division I level that he printed a list of every NCAA Division I basketball program in America. "Familiarize yourself with these schools," he told me.

According to my diary, the two night escape at Yogi's home in Charlotte, North Carolina ended on Sunday afternoon, October 26, 2003. I wished I was able to extend my stay, but I had mandatory classes and basketball practice the following Monday, plus my very first American basketball game was only four days away.

Before Coach K came to pick me up, Yogi gave me a gift: an official NBA VHS cassette titled, *Sir Charles*.

Chapter 22

My First Experiences

Sir Charles—a documentary covering the life and basketball career of NBA superstar, Charles Barkley. I watched the video just before my first American basketball game. And I'm glad I did, because it was inspiring and motivating. It displayed Barkley as a hard worker who never gave up, even after numerous failures.

To me, failure isn't failing the first, second or third time—it is when you give up easily after your first try; that's when you've failed!

A few hours before my 7:00 p.m. game on Thursday, October 30, 2003, I received a surprised phone call from Margaritte. She called to say, "Good luck Arnold." Because I'd only heard from her once since I'd been in America, I thought, *at least she remembered my first game.*

In our home locker-room, as I mentally prepared myself for the game, I reread the second letter I'd received from my mother. It reminded me that even though she wasn't in America, I was still in her heart. If my mother had only written a simple, "I love and miss you my boy," instead of four pages, that would have been enough encouragement for me to live by.

"Basketball is 90 percent mental; 10 percent physical," Coach K always preached. It made sense to me because I felt that I needed to recap and mentally execute everything I'd learned from day one.

A few minutes before tip-off, feeling prepared to execute Coach K's game-plan against our very first opponent, I reflected on my improvements in basketball since arriving in America: I was better at my defensive and open-court awareness; I sprinted back on both ends of the floor; with a combination of new techniques, I was an offensive threat for defenders; being outspoken on defense unified my team to execute better defense; the swim move was effective, which was a defensive strategy that allowed me to get around my opponents by a variation of arm movements and foot work; bending my knees, staying low, wide, and firm with my eyes on the rim prepared me to grab more rebounds after executing a box-out maneuver in front of my opponents; smarter decisions and better timing gave me an edge to be a better shot blocker; rapidly moving my feet and extending my arms wide, allowed me to stay in front of the offensive players and decreased my number of fouls; and finally, I remembered to place my hand in front of the shooter's face anytime he put up a shot. Coach K and Coach Phillip had a great impact on my progression.

I remained seated in our locker-room, and I felt prepared for my first American basketball game. I was in the best shape of my life. All I needed was to remain focused. But as soon as my teammates, coaches, and I rushed onto the basketball court to commence the first 20 minutes of action, my stomach turned upside-down. My mind broke down with nervousness. Our gym was packed with a rowdy audience of students, faculty, and alumni wearing their military attire. The environment looked foreign—I didn't feel like it was a home game—being surrounded on the basketball court felt like a battlefield. I imagined that all our supporters were against me, as if they all held a gun, screaming, *if you lose this game, you are a dead man.* I had to keep reminding myself, *it is just a military academy...it is just a school...I won't get shot for my mistakes...I won't.*

At six foot seven, 210 pounds, I was the starting center; in fact, I was an undersized post-player. I might have been one of the tallest in Saint Lucia, but the players in America made me look like a toddler amongst grown men.

To keep my spot on my team's starting-five, I had to prove to everyone that I deserved it—game one was the perfect opportunity. Not only that, but the entire school had very high expectations of us.

Ten minutes into the game, the butterflies in my stomach were moving as fast as hummingbirds. My butter-fingers era had welcomed me back—whenever my teammates passed me the basketball in the painted area, I would fumble and allowed a few turnovers. Even though we were in complete control of the game from the first whistle, I felt like I was the rotten apple on the team—my contributions were useless. And to make it worse, early foul trouble allowed me to ride the bench for the rest of the first half.

I thought, *you wanted to play basketball in America for so long...so badly...Mummy struggled so much...this is your time to shine...this is the moment you have been waiting for...you are in control of your dream!*

Despite being scoreless in the first half, Coach K still reselected me to be part of the starting-five for the second half of the game. I proceeded with a different mentality.

The sounds of our supporters were barred with my focus-force-field—in other words, I was now able to concentrate on our game-plan. After a brief breakdown of the play-by-play strategies and a few encouraging words from our coaches, I was finally in my comfort zone. America was my new home basketball court.

Feeling more relaxed, I started the second half with three back-to-back slam dunks that equaled six points. I remember that the crowd was so hyped it cheered and stomped. I even noticed a student doing a Michael Jackson moonwalk on the sidelines. It was military school gone wild and I loved every moment of it.

The team chemistry we displayed on the court felt like family-love which was amazing given our differences off the court. We all understood that teamwork wins games—my teammates were winners. By the time the referee blew the final whistle, we had captured our very first victory against Christendom College—the final score: 100-77. The only statistic that I recorded in my diary was scoring 16 points.

Since our men's post-graduate basketball program was a new addition to the school, there was some pressure on Coach K to deliver success for Massanutten Military Academy. On my way to the locker-room, I noticed the happy face on our school's president. We represented the school well and left everyone with highlights to brag about. Overall, Coach K and Coach Phillip were satisfied with our victory. But there were a few errors that needed correcting. For us to perform better as a team, our coaches felt it would take more practices, as well as more official games, to which I was agreeable since I felt the same way about my performance.

One game was all it took for me to gain on-court respect from my teammates. I'd even gotten some great feedback from students who had attended the game that night. I began to feel accepted in their environment, even though it had to come through a basketball game. There was still one problem though—my three teammates from Washington, DC.

The situation escalated on November 1, 2003, on a Saturday evening after our second scheduled basketball game. It was a weekend night, so lights-out was programmed for midnight. Given that we never had much to do for entertainment, we either watched cable television programs or played videogames in a dark storage room on our floor. On that particular night, we took turns challenging each other whilst playing NBA 2k3 for PlayStation 2. Since it was a two-player basketball videogame, our only rules were that winners faced the next challenger who yelled *Next* while the losers had to pass on the videogame-controller to that person.

As Antoine picked up the controller, I shouted, "Next!" and waited for the next loser. There's no fun waiting at least 30 to 40 minutes for a game, and, being unfamiliar with that video game, I was likely to lose, but I patiently waited.

After an intense match-up with name-calling and harsh remarks, Antoine lost. "Next!" I said, to reassure everyone that I called it first. Antoine didn't want to give up the controller. "Yo, my turn dawg," I said. He acted deaf. "Can I get the controller?" Again, no response; his eyes were glued to the television. With everyone giggling at the situation, I felt disrespected. I snatched the controller out of Antoine's hands then proceeded to challenge the winner. In a split second, Antoine grabbed me in a chokehold. Being five inches taller and 10 pounds heavier than him with a longer arm reach, I could have landed a jab to his eye. But I did nothing.

Then Joey Butler, our starting point guard said, "Punch dat nigga, Antoine!"

I grabbed Antoine's hand and shoved it away. As I started to walk to my room, with emotions ready to explode, Antoine connected punches to the back of my head and to my side near my ribs. I continued walking towards the exit-door. In my room, I sat down behind the door, crying quietly. "Punch dat nigga, Antoine," repeated in the back of my mind over and over again. *Why Joey hates me? I thought we were teammates.*

I decided that I needed to confront Joey. I walked two doors down the hallway into his room and found him on his bottom bunk-bed. His roommate and hometown buddy, Darnell Mack, was on the upper bunk-bed looking surprised at my entrance.

"So I hear you tell Antoine to punch me," I said.

"Boy, if you don't get your ass out my room," he replied with a smile on his face. Joey obviously wasn't taking me seriously so I kicked his mattress, nearly missing his face.

"Well, do someting!" I shouted. Darnell and Joey jumped out of their bed and attacked me, as if they'd waited for that moment from day one. I tried to defend myself by giving them my back, closing my eyes, ducking down, and covering my face with my arms to prevent their combo-punches. My crouching position had left them with no other choice but to punch me on the back of my head and neck. When the blows became increasingly painful, I swung my elbow wildly up in the air, with no intended target, but hoping I would strike at least one of them.

I opened my eyes then my mouth dropped. Blood gushed down Darnell's lips, chin, and body. The blood squirted from his upper lip. Joey just stood there in shock; I was in shock too. I slowly backpedaled to the hallway, staring down Darnell and Joey.

Another second later, everyone on our floor rushed in to witness a bloody scenario—even Coach Phillip and Colonel Reis were present. In fact, the entire Golf Company was at the scene.

"I'm gonna kill that nigga...I swear to God...this nigga made me bleed...I'm gonna kill him," Darnell finally said in a rage, at the same time trying to fight off the people who held him back. Scared for my life, I ran to a nearby room and locked the door. I paced back and forth, grasping my forehead, afraid of the consequences of my violent actions.

I'm going to get kicked out of school, I kept on repeating in my head.

After all the commotion died down, I heard a knock on the door. "Who dat?" I asked.

"Antoine."

"Wha' you want?"

"Open up, I just wanna talk to you." I slowly opened, took a peek, and allowed him to enter when I realized he was alone. "Dawg, I'm sorry for earlier…I don't wanna go to bed and have to worry about you attacking me while I'm sleeping," Antoine pleaded.

"Aight dawg, it's all good," I claimed, and as we exchanged a hug, I felt like we had rekindled our friendship.

Moments later, Coach K was at the door. My heart raced expecting the worst. "Arnold, I don't know how I'm going to get you out of this one," Coach K admitted. My head felt so heavy that I didn't dare look him in his eyes. "You might be going home Arnold." To me, it sounded like Coach had made a final decision. *This is the end,* I thought.

"Let me hear what Joey and Darnell have to say," Coach K said. I remained alone in my room; contemplating my wrong doings. How do I resolve this issue? All I wanted was some respect.

Coach K returned five minutes later and quoted words from Joey and Darnell. "Whatever problems we have, it can be worked out."

I sighed. *Thank you God, thank you.*

"Arnold, this is your last chance…anymore problems and it's back to Saint Lucia for you."

"Coach, dis will never happen again," I promised.

"Get a goodnight sleep. Make sure that you apologize to Darnell and Joey tomorrow."

"Okay Coach, I will."

Before I slept, I wondered, *why Joey and Darnell did not encourage my dismissal? Maybe, as basketball players, they did not want to be responsible for destroying my dreams. Maybe they didn't want to destroy the team's hopes of success. Maybe they felt guilty.*

Whatever their reasons, I'd learned a lesson that day. Resorting to violence might obliterate my future and career. After that incident, my Washington teammates stopped hectoring me.

Chapter 23

A Cold Town

It wasn't until late November when we were permitted to wear our winter gear (beanie, scarf, jacket, and gloves). All the fuss that the authorities had made about me breeching the uniform rules due to my sickness was not necessary—I'd realized that there was no difference by wearing the winter gear they'd provided; I was still as cold as being butt-naked. *Why did it feel like I was the only one complaining? Most likely, I was the only one who had never experienced winter.*

To cope with the climate, Coach K bought me a pair of Long Johns, or thermal underwear. The under garments barely helped. And to make it worse, our daily routine never changed; we still had to wake up early on weekday mornings, the coldest part of our day.

At formations, it was quite impossible for me to stand at attention without feeling like the blood pumping through my system was frozen. Also, there was a painful, prickling sensation on my fingertips and the edge of my nose and ears as if someone was gripping pliers to them. I was no longer living on a two-season (wet and dry) tropical island.

On an ordinary bitter, dull, December weekday afternoon, Golf Company was assembling for our routine formation to head back to the barracks from Mess II. The instant I strode through the exit door of the cafeteria, I detected droplets of frozen rain liquefying on my shoes, but the ground was still dry. I raised my eyebrows and thought, *it can't be.* I looked up in the sky to confirm my assumption. *It is…it is snowing.* Ignoring my captain's orders, I tilted my head backwards, spread my arms wide and opened my mouth to catch the flakes, while rotating my body in a circular motion. There was nothing to be impressed about; it only tasted like ice-cold-raindrops. "Henry!" shouted my captain. I was caught in the moment.

"Yes, Sir," I responded.

"Why aren't you standing at attention?" I pointed to the skies.

"The snow, the snow, Sir, the snow is fallin'," I replied hoping that was a perfect excuse. My answered only generated an outburst of laughter.

"That's your first time seeing snow?"

"Um, yeah…Sir," I answered. *I'm from Saint Lucia…like duh!*

Later that night, after two hours of practice, I stepped outside the gym in amazement. The snow had accumulated to my knees. "Oh my God," was my initial reaction. Then I immediately bundled up a portion and pressed it into a ball of snow which I kept in my bedroom's mini-refrigerator for a very long time. While some of my teammates laughed at my childish behavior, others who were actually spontaneous taught me how to make a snowman and a snow-angel. When I started feeling numbness in some of my body parts, I ran into the building.

The winter weather in the town of Woodstock wasn't the only cold occurrence I'd stumbled upon. Up to that point in time, I'd always viewed the world as one human race—we're just all sinful human beings who came out in different shapes, sizes, and skin colors. Growing up amongst different cultures, backgrounds, and origins, my friends and I had plenty of confrontations with each other, but we'd learned from our mistakes and tried to forgive each other. And I believed those who failed to comply by our heavenly Father's wishes would not be granted everlasting life. But on two separate occasions, roaming the streets of the small town of Woodstock, I felt like an unwanted alien. There were still too many cold-hearted people on this planet.

One Friday evening, a couple of my teammates and I decided to take a walk and visit the local stores and businesses. We were well dressed in our military attire; one way to identify us as students of Massanutten Military Academy. My teammates usually used their off-campus time to go to the movies, the skating rink, Chinese restaurants, or convenience stores. I never had the money to go, but on that particular night I felt like I needed the walk, so I tagged along.

The population of Woodstock was just about 4,000 people, but it really felt like walking through a ghost town. On our way to the convenience store, we'd caught up with a few of our high school students who were also headed in the same direction.

Out of nowhere, a white car sped by, swerving on the narrow streets, nearly making contact with us even though we all strolled on the sidewalk. Everyone thought it was drunk teenagers being silly. Seconds later, we realized they had different motives. One of the four male occupants (who all appeared to be Caucasian), poked his head out the window and yelled, "Get out of our town! All you Niggers!"

Some of my schoolmates tried running down the speeding car; they cursed and shouted, "Come back here! "Why don't you fucking come here?" But no human could have caught that accelerating car. The racist young teenagers had left everyone with a sickening, disgusted feeling. And to make the matter worse, we couldn't teach them a lesson by providing an ass whooping.

"Wha' happen…why dem people actin' like dat?" I asked.

"Because they damn racists," someone else responded.

"Racism still exists?" I said softly, hoping no one heard me.

"Yeah dawg," replied a schoolmate.

"I hate this town…this is a fuckin' racist town!" someone yelled.

It was after that "Nigger" statement that I realized everyone with me that day just happened to be black. Usually, out of the three Caucasians on our team, at least one always walked with us. Back then, the only knowledge I had of the "N" word was through the movies on the black television station (BET). I used to take notes on the cruelties black people faced in early societies: slavery and segregation. Saint Lucia was predominately black, so I never had the desire to study more on racism. But being in America, I felt I needed to learn as much as possible before I started to believe that the color of my skin was an issue in the eyes of every Caucasian there. Apparently, it was just a few of them who still expressed their ignorance.

The second racist encounter occurred when Darnell and I walked into a local convenience store attempting to purchase some boxes of Ramen Chicken Noodle Soup for our nightly meals. As soon as we walked into the building, we felt an unwelcoming energy from both the customers and cashiers—as if we'd just invaded a stranger's private home. We ignored the awkward tension and proceeded to walk down the aisles. Since we were new to the store, it took us a while to find our items. Eyes followed our every move. It was becoming way too creepy. "Darnell, look I find some noodles dere," I pointed out.

I stooped to the bottom shelf and grabbed one packet for myself. And by the time I stood back up, I realized all eyes in the store were staring us down, as if we were about to steal something. We both felt so uncomfortable that we replaced the soup and left.

"Dawg, you saw dem people looking at us?" I asked Darnell.

"Yeah man, they acting like niggas about to steal something."

"Dis is so weird," I said. Our conversation was interrupted by the man who we'd noticed behind the counter.

"Go…go…go away; you're too close…go, across the streets," screeched the elderly Caucasian cashier.

"Huh?" I muttered, looking at that man like he was high on some illegal substance. Darnell and I weren't even that close—we stood on the sidewalk about 20 meters from the store. His attitude made me feel like I was just flushed down the filthy bowl of a crappy toilet. We didn't want any trouble so we complied. While crossing the street, still in disbelief, I asked Darnell, "Did you do someting to dem people?"

"No dawg! You don't get it? They're racist!"

I was having a hard time understanding how grown people could be so ignorant. I never thought I would experience racism in the 21st Century. I now looked at America differently.

Chapter 24

Away

Tuesday, December 9, 2003—by that date our men's post-graduate basketball program had already played about 12 different teams, with most of our matchups being away games and the majority of opponents from actual colleges. This was brilliant because we got the opportunity to experience advanced competition playing at the college level, without actually attending a college.

Playing basketball games away from home was the only time we were considered to be free from our military demeanors, although each time away from Woodstock didn't last more than 24 hours. We always travelled on the school's small bus and then we'd returned following the conclusion of our game. The long bus trips were sometimes aggravating; that was another situation that I had to get use to—I'd never had to travel to a basketball game being seated for 3 to 5 hours.

December 13, 2003 was the only time we actually stayed out-of-town overnight. We stayed at the Red Roof Inn on Chapel Hill Boulevard, Durham, North Carolina, near our next opponent, The University of North Carolina at Chapel Hill (UNC, the legendary Tar Heels). The day I noticed that they were on our agenda, I did a double take and wondered if this was the same college Michael Jordan attended?

"Hey Coach, are we really playin' against da UNC Tar Heels?" I asked.

"No, Arnold. We will be playing their junior-varsity team," Coach K verified.

"Huh? Junior-varsity?"

"We will be playing the same school, at the same place, but it is not the same team we are used to seeing on television…the junior-varsity team plays at a lower collegiate level."

Even though we weren't about to play against the regular UNC Tar Heels, I was still overjoyed to be stepping on the same ground as my basketball idol.

The day we arrived in Durham, we headed straight for Chapel Hill. Our game wasn't scheduled until 5:30 p.m. the following day. We had some time to kill, so with Coach K's connections, he had set up a memorable field trip for us—at least it was for me.

That year, we'd been to a few colleges and universities, but nothing was quite as big as UNC's campus. We took a mini tour inside the multi-purpose arena which was named after Michael Jordan's UNC head coach, Dean E. Smith. The arena was the home of the North Carolina at Chapel Hill Tar Heels men's basketball team.

Being inside the Dean Smith Center, or the Dean Dome, felt like walking through a hall of fame. There were imprinted names on picture plaques all over the walls of the building from familiar people such as NBA superstars, Vince Carter, Rasheed Wallace, Antawn Jamison, Jerry Stackhouse, and of course, hall-of-famer Michael Jordan. I felt like that was already enough motivation for any UNC athlete to push themselves to the limit at every practice, scrimmage, or official game. That was the type of environment I wanted for my future—to be playing in the footsteps and spirits of basketball icons, hoping one day I could achieve and outdo their successes.

At the same time we were in the building, we walked into the upper-deck seating section of the main home court, to an in-progress practice session of the UNC men's senior basketball team. I saw a few recognizable faces of coaches and players on the center court; the arena of over 20,000 seats was colored with white and baby-blue and their championship banners and famous player jerseys hung from the ceiling. This was paradise for basketball players.

Coach K informed us that we were invited to their practice which was usually closed to the public. As a team, we sat down quietly and observed one of the best NCAA Division I teams in the nation; possibly the best basketball program of all time. I believe the entire experience constructed a stronger bond between us.

UNC Tarheels had already won all seven games since their season began. I knew that because, back then, they were the only school I followed. Head Coach Roy Williams, and his star players, Sean May and Rashad McCants, were amongst the names and faces I remembered.

Watching the UNC players at practice was like viewing a gathering of professional business men in suits at a conference meeting, disguised in white and baby-blue uniforms and sneakers, discussing profitable strategies and plans to defeat their competitors. From my point of view, there weren't any weaklings, and the team displayed a well-organized structure, working towards one common goal—victory. They meant business.

Roy Williams exchanged a few inspiring words with our team after he was through conducting his practice. I cannot recall his exact words, but his presence alone was enough inspiration for me.

That moment had brought me to think about my own potential as a NCAA Division I basketball player. Wasn't I good enough? Why hadn't one college contacted me? Some of my teammates were already getting attention (phone calls, letters and visits) from NCAA Division I coaches. I tried to stay positive, knowing that the season was far from over. Like Coach K always said, "You must always play your best because you never know who's watching you in the crowd." I applied Coach K's quote to every single practice and game.

The next day, we faced the junior-varsity team and won the game by four points.

Massanutten Military Academy, 2003

Third Quarter

Double Team

Chapter 25

Conquering the United States Education System

With the start of a new year in the US, and still feeling alienated from my American hometown, I pledged to honor my 2004 New Year's resolution: to attain an outstanding SAT/ACT test score and to somehow achieve a full basketball scholarship to any school willing to accept me. At that desperate point in time, I would have been happy if the worst college program in the history of America had offered me a full ride—I just couldn't return to Saint Lucia as a disappointment. Even though I was the only starter on my team who wasn't in the college spotlight, I had shut the envy out of my eyes and patiently waited for my time to shine.

In the past I'd always come up with unachievable resolutions like becoming a billionaire by inventing a time machine. This time I put some thought into my goals so that I could maintain focus on continuing to pursue my college basketball dreams—again, that was my number one reason for coming to America in the first place.

One important lesson I learned about the American educational system was this: students are admitted into a four-year college based on their test performance and, as a result, low test scores might prevent an individual from succeeding with the college admissions process. In my uncomplicated mind, all I needed was to score a total of 100-percent on these types of entrance aptitude test (SAT or ACT)—attempting a perfect score was my simplest method to eliminate America's educational complexities.

To help stay on the right track, from my very first military school day, I sat attentively in the front row, taking down important elements and useful notes from my teachers, especially during my preparatory class for the college entrance exams. Also, through my studies, I found the American educational system to be easier than Saint Lucia's system, so I was familiar with a lot of the material being taught.

I sat in a room filled with schoolmates on February 7, 2004 to write my ACT exams. I'd assembled all the confidence and knowledge I needed to overcome one of the most nerve-wracking exams of all time. My preparation helped me breeze through the test. I realized that I could be the best basketball player in the world, but I wouldn't be able to achieve my hoop dreams if I was the dumbest.

A few weeks later, Coach K called me into his office. I assumed that I was in some type of trouble since that had been the only time authority ever wanted to have a one-on-one conversation with me.

"Hey Arnold, I have some news for you," Coach K said. "Your results for the ACT came in today." My heart felt as if it was bouncing back and forth between my back and chest.

"How I do?" I asked anxiously.

"Well, let's just say you are at the top of Massanutten Military Academy…"

"Serious ting?" I asked in disbelief.

"Yeah Arnold…your scores are really impressive," Coach responded while chuckling. He then handed me the sheet of paper with my results. I had a cumulative score of 24—I really didn't understand the scoring scale, but I guessed that was excellent according to Coach's expression.

"With that ACT score, together with your outstanding high school transcript and CXC results you'll be able to be accepted to many well-known colleges across America," Coach K said.

My achievements in academics had definitely lifted tons of stress off my shoulders, but I was still missing a basketball scholarship offer from any college before my one year F-1 US student visa expired. Yet, it was beyond my control—college coaches see potential and when they do, they pursue, then persuade these future star or role players to sign to their schools. For me, it was still a struggle to prove myself on the court; I didn't even know if there were college coaches at our games; it didn't stop me from trying. Every day I reminded myself, *your limits are somewhere up there, waiting for you to reach beyond infinity.*

By the end of February, the last official whistle was blown, ending my first American basketball season. As a team, we had finished the season with an overall record of 19 wins and 7 losses. My only stats I recorded in my diary that season were an average of ten points and nine rebounds per game. Desperate times were calling for desperate measures—meaning, in less than three months I needed to find a college or else it would have been hello Saint Lucia and goodbye American college hoop dreams.

Chapter 26

Recruit

Have you ever waited hour after hour at a bus-stop, not knowing whether or not you've already missed the last bus? If you miss that bus, how do you plan to reach your destination? What are your other means of transportation? What's your backup plan? Have you already thought about a plan A, B, C, or even D? Who are you going to turn to? Who's willing to pick you up?

Luckily, basketball wasn't just a career I had planned to pursue, or a fortuitous event playing in America; basketball was like the air that I breathed and the blood in my veins that led to my heart. My love for the game had enabled me to hang on to my dream a little longer. The season had ended so the only thing left to do was to attend post-season workouts, and even though attending classes was irrelevant for me at that point (knowing that my grades were up to standard for college admittance), I still attended and participated. And I still complied with the school's military protocols.

Feeling like I had no one locally to turn to, I sought guidance and words of wisdom from my mother. A phone conversation had calmed my worries, but her advice wasn't sufficient.

"Mummy I doh know if I go get anada basketball scholarship," I wept over the phone.

"Well Mario, if that's the case, you should just stay in the states and start a new life."

"Buh Mummy if I stay I go be dere illegally."

"I know, but you know how hard it was to get a US visa…remember in 2000 they denied your US visitor visa?

"Yeah…buh—"

"But nothing…you should just go to New York and stay by Aunty Monica. Or go stay by Olvin or Jermal and Jovan."

"Yeah Mummy, maybe you right."

"Things getting hard in Saint Lucia my boy…plus there's so much crime happening these days. I want the best for you."

"Okay Mummy, I go keep you updated."

"I lit up a candle for you and I will continue to pray for you."

"Thanks Mummy. I love and miss you."

The following days, college basketball coaches flocked our on-campus gym during our postseason workouts. It felt like we were part of a famous car show, auditioning for the best buyers or the highest bidders. There were head and assistant coaches from all over the nation: The University of Pennsylvania, Wright State University, University of Georgia, Boston University, College of Holy Cross, and Miami University—to name a few. Even though they came to the building unannounced, or without warning, I was beyond ready for the opportunity. I just didn't understand their reasons for being interested in players so late in the school-year. But later Coach K said that most college programs were finishing up their 2003-2004 regular basketball season.

As we prepared to put on a show for these coaches, I mentally prepared myself to execute my game plan as the hardest working basketball player on the court. I'd looked upon these coaches who stood on the sidelines, scrutinizing our every move, as my pearly white gates to glory. It was time to convince them that I was ready to play on the next level—my time was limited, therefore, it was now or never.

We began to battle and it seemed as if we demonstrated to these coaches who would outlast their opponents if it came down to 12 rounds in a boxing match. And although we were teammates, we fought hard against each other and displayed no mercy. Coach K couldn't convince any of the college coaches that we were ready for the next level; we had to prove it ourselves.

Every once in a while, I would peak out the corner of my eye to see if anyone was showing interest in me. It was easy to see that the majority of these coaches were really intrigued by a few of my other teammates.

As soon as we were released from practice, college coaches raced towards us, seeking our attention as if they were the fans and we were the superstars about to board our tour-bus. Limping towards me was a six foot, chubby, Caucasian male in his mid-twenties. His smile assured me that he was about to approach me. I blinked twice to make sure that I wasn't trapped in a dream. But this was no dream.

"Hey, Arnold Henry. I'm Coach Jeffery Rush, assistant coach for the University of Vermont."

I thought, *wow he knows my name.*

I exchanged a hand shake and responded, imitating an American accent, "Nice to meet you Coach."

"I heard you're from an island in the Caribbean, Saint Lucia, right?"

"Yeah Coach," I answered.

"How you liking the weather?"

"Ugh, it is cold." At least he found that funny.

I limited myself in conversation with Coach Rush, which may have come off as being reserved, but I tried to avoid displaying arrogance. Honestly, deep down, fireworks were exploding across my mind, rejoicing in that moment. "I really enjoyed what I saw today. I believe you would be a good addition to our program," Coach Rush said. I didn't want to seem desperate so I continued to listen to everything he had to say. Coach Rush gave me a brief history of Vermont as a state and as a college. From our conversation it seemed like their basketball program was doing great. "The University of Vermont (UVM) is a NCAA Division I program…part of the America East Conference," Coach Rush continued.

Division I? My heart raced.

"We just won our America East Conference Tournament and got selected to compete in the National Tournament. If you get a chance, tune in next week to watch our first round matchup against the University of Connecticut, Huskies (UConn)."

While Coach Rush was informing me about UVM's recent achievements, I felt like I just hit the jackpot. *NCAA Division I…National Tournament?* The rest was Coach Rush wasting his breath. I was more than interested.

"How about you use a visit to check out the UVM campus?"

How Coach Rush expect me to pay for that trip? But before I showed my ignorance, he continued, "We will cover all your travelling arrangements, accommodations, and meals."

"Serious ting?" I asked. I'm sure he figured out that I was new to this.

After my meeting with Coach Rush, two other college coaches showed their interest in me. They were from College of Holy Cross and Boston University, which was also in the same conference as the University of Vermont. I had informed them that I was really interested in UVM but they warned me to at least visit their campus before I made any decisions to sign. I agreed since I didn't want to put all my eggs in one basket. UVM was the better team since they were the conference champions and the only team from that conference competing in the national tournament.

Out of all my teammates, I left the gym with the biggest smile. A few of them were approached by even bigger NCAA Division I schools, yet they were curious to know who I spoke to.

"Dat was Vermont," I boasted.

"You going to freeze your butt off…If you think Virginia is cold…wait til you get up there," someone teased me.

"Dawg, you tink I care about dat?"

Chapter 27

The Visit

On my way to Dulles Airport, I kept on having flashbacks of the night I watched the live NCAA Division I National Tournament elimination game between the University of Vermont (Catamounts) and University of Connecticut (Huskies), which aired on CBS. I pictured myself wearing their uniform, playing that game in front of thousands of fans as if I was already part of the team.

My family, friends, and even the people of Saint Lucia would be so proud to see their own playing basketball on an established television network. The only other Saint-Lucian-born I remembered being on a major television network was Joseph Marcell, best known as Geoffrey Barbara Butler on the sitcom, *The Fresh Prince of Bel-Air*, starring Will Smith.

On the evening of March 18, 2004, I acted like a fan, as well as a basketball-analyst, as I watched that game on television, observing their style of play and their attitudes on the court and, at the same time, cheered them on. I kept having flashbacks about the game because I was about to meet my possible future teammates and coaches—the same ones who I'd just seen play live on television.

What if they don't like me? What if the coaches decide to change their mind about offering me a full scholarship?

From my research I knew that the University of Vermont had had an exceptional winning basketball season. And even though they got knocked off in that first round matchup, 70-53, it was still impressive to know that they actually played in the national tournament. Every year, out of over 300 NCAA Division I basketball teams, only 65 get to participate (a rule which came into effect on March 13, 2001). That year, 2004, UConn went on winning each game they played in every round and was crowned the national champion by the end of the tournament.

I glanced briefly at Coach K who was driving me to the airport. I reminisced about the first day I shook his hand, our first practice session, our first official basketball game, our last game, all the good laughs and the bad times, up to the point when I was almost sent back to Saint Lucia for fighting with my teammates. Coach K had given me a second chance and I'd proved to him that I could make him proud.

It was a two hour drive to the airport. Coach K couldn't resist asking what was going through my mind. "Arnold, you know this will be a great school for you," Coach K said while he stared at the road.

"Oh yeah?" I muttered.

"Yup, it's a Division I program...they made the national tournament last year and this year...yes, I think you will love it there."

Coach K's role in assisting me to make decisions about my future colleges had reminded me of a father directing his son. I'd only seen these types of father-son-relationships in movies. Before I entered the airport Coach K asked, "So you think you gonna commit to Vermont?" I wasn't sure how to answer his question.

"I doh know Coach...I go see how tings go."

"Well I hope it goes well, Arnold...oh, one more thing, be sure to ask the head coach how much longer he plans to be at Vermont."

A direct two and a half hour flight got me to Burlington, Vermont. I was picked up by Coach Rush as planned. From the moment I walked through the exit door of the Burlington Airport, I shivered as the cold winds blew through my thin casual outfit (short-sleeve polo shirt and blue jeans). I thought we were already in spring judging from the warmth I was experiencing in Virginia. But I guess there was a delay in Vermont's receiving the spring-season-memo.

"We actually have warm beautiful weather today," Coach Rush bragged.

I reminded myself that I would need jackets...plenty of big, warm, winter jackets, if I was to live there.

Driving through the inner metropolitan area, and looking in the distance, I could see what the license plates meant by the Green Mountain State. Chunks of snow were still piled up on the roadside as if it snowed a few days ago. Nevertheless, I was thrilled to be in what appeared to be a neat, laidback city.

Coach Rush handed me an itinerary—a thirty-six hour timeline of places I needed to be during my visit. Then he dropped me off in the dorm-room of Kyle Cieplicki, a redshirt freshman player on the team. Kyle showed his hospitality by providing me lodging in his room for my short stay. He also expressed a friendly demeanor from our very first conversation.

"I heard you from Saint Lucia, right?" Kyle asked.

"Oh yeah, I am."

"I know of some brothers from Saint Lucia."

"Dey live here?" I asked enthusiastically.

"Yeah, I think so...but I don't have any contact information for them though," Kyle replied.

I thought, *a Saint Lucian, living in a cold state like Vermont? What were they thinking?* But then again, I was in no position to criticize.

Kyle and I had a few minutes to chill until I was picked up by Coach Rush who showed me around the campus, and for every path we walked, he provided me with information about everything on that site. Then later, he introduced me to the rest of the coaching staff.

When I first met Tom Brennan (UVM's head basketball coach) during an evening dinner at a local restaurant, I thought that he would never stop cracking jokes. It was hard to imagine him having any dull moments in his life—not once did I see this mature Caucasian man with anything other than a smile. Coach Brennan conversed with such high energy that his partial gray hair could have fooled me. We briefly introduced ourselves then he said to me, "I hope you will commit to our program by the end of your visit…we have a great program here…I am proud of my boys…they are good guys…you will love them."

I just nodded and smiled as he spoke because I found it difficult to communicate with him. This man was just aired on a live television network so, in my eyes, he was an A-list celebrity.

Out of the five coaches, there was only one black assistant named Pat Filien. Jesse Agel was the associate head coach and Jack Phelan was the other assistant coach. Later on, I met with the strength and conditioning coach, Chris Poulin, at his very own personal gym. While I thought having Coach K and Coach Phillip was too many coaches on one team, it was actually a dream come true to be this close to NCAA Division I coaches.

For the rest of my time at UVM, Coach Rush continued his tasks as my tour guide; it was a regular school day on-campus. The campus was so big that it was best to travel via the on-campus shuttle. It was very refreshing to witness students wearing casual clothes, making their own decisions and enjoying college life. There must have been over 90 percent Caucasians there; it was very hard to see any Black students which made me wonder if there might be the possibility that I'd experience racism like I did in Woodstock, Virginia. It did seem like a friendly, studious environment.

Like Coach Rush promised, I was introduced to a few of the faculty, advisors, and staff whose services would benefit my academic progression in the classroom. Next we walked through the inside of the university's gymnasium, the Roy L. Patrick Gymnasium: a multipurpose sports arena, equipped with a full fitness center, recreational basketball courts, racquet-ball courts, swimming pools, an indoor track, and classrooms. If I had been alone, it would have been easy to get lost inside this enormous place. We stopped momentarily on the center court where UVM played their home games; there was seating for over 3,200 people.

"One day this court will belong to you," Coach Rush said to me as we watched the banners that reflected UVM's achievement over the years. I smiled to show my gratitude.

After receiving a glimpse of life on-campus, I was put to the test in a scrimmage game with some of the players from UVM's men's basketball team. They were taller and bigger in person than they appeared on television. Since only six of us showed up, we played a 3-on-3 matchup. My objective was to convince these senior players that I deserved to be there; there was no time for nervousness or excuses.

Playing 3-on-3 on one-half of the court was a breeze but to play it full-court wasn't the norm; for me, it was strenuous. Never in my life had I experienced such a physical challenge. What made it worse was that I defended Taylor Coppenrath, one of the best NCAA Division I scorers in the nation. He stood about six foot nine with a very wide body frame and must have weighed tons because I had a difficult time pushing him around. Despite that, I believed I still played up to their expectations.

Before I went back to Woodstock, I was brought into Coach Brennan's office for a one-on-one debriefing of my visit. Coach Brennan was very brief with me. "You had a chance to visit the campus," he said. How did you like it?"

"I really enjoyed it Coach," I replied softly.

"You played with our guys and they had some good things to say about you…we trust our guys…and we believe you can help us achieve our goals." It felt good to hear those kind words from the head coach and the players. He continued, "So will you be joining us?" I sighed then stared at the ceiling due to the sudden question. Then I looked at Coach Rush who sat quietly to my side before my eyes fell back on Coach Brennan.

"How long you plan on coaching here?"

As if he expected that question, he replied instantly. "You don't have to worry about that…we will see that you graduate from Vermont."

I believed Coach Brennan meant it so I committed to UVM on the spot. "Yes Coach, I'm ready."

"Great!" Coach Brennan's excitement broke the silence and smiles showered across the room. "We will start processing your paperwork immediately and get you to officially sign your scholarship documents later this week."

Arnold Henry

"Okay Coach, thank you for da opportunity."

During my visit, it didn't take a wild college party to persuade me to commit, nor did it take any hot-sexy-college-chicks to seduce me; from the moment I'd arrived in Burlington, my purpose was to get acquainted with the learning environment and to meet the men's basketball program. I felt welcome. It was a successful trip which made it easy to decide that UVM was the best situation for me.

Sitting aboard the aircraft on my way back to Virginia, I reflected on the past 19 years of my life and everything up to my verbal commitment to the University of Vermont. My life finally felt complete and I was pumped-up for my future. Right then, nothing could have wiped the smile off my face.

Chapter 28

The Signing

"Mummy! Mummy!" I screamed through the phone's receiver.

"What's going on?" my mother yelled back.

"I got a scholarship to the University of Vermont ih!"

"For true? For how long this time?" she asked.

"It's a four year school, Mummy."

"Argh, congrats my boy!"

"Yeah, so I go see you in Saint Lucia soon—"

"But why you need to come down if you already get a scholarship? You know I cannot afford a plane ticket?"

"I need to renew my visa in Barbados. But when I go to renew it, I tink dey go give it to me for four years dis time instead of one. And doh worry about de plane ticket. When I go to New York City, I go ask Aunty Monica, some friends, and my godmother for help."

Since I made a verbal commitment to UVM there was no need for me to remain on the campus of Massanutten Military Academy. A few of my teammates felt the same way so, in mid-April, the numbers on my basketball team began decreasing due to players' commitments to other colleges or universities. By the time I left the school, only five of us had made it to NCAA Division I basketball programs, a few got offers to NCAA Division II programs, and the others were still searching.

I was certain that I was never returning so I packed up all my belongings. And, even though I was happy to regain my freedom, I knew deep down I'd gained more than I came with, despite the strictness. With my accomplishments and new knowledge as a basketball player and as an individual, I thanked and said my goodbyes to everyone who contributed towards me feeling like a changed man.

On the day Joey was leaving, I took a ride with his father to Washington, D.C. to catch a Greyhound bus to New York City—it was the most affordable form of transportation. I could have saved money and flown straight to Saint Lucia, but I wasn't returning home after only making a verbal commitment with UVM. I still needed to sign my scholarship and the documents for the renewal of my US student visa; it was best to visit my childhood best friends, Olvin, Jermal, and Jovan for a week or two.

My first impression of New York City was, *whoa, I'm definitely not in Virginia anymore.* I was picked up from the Penn Station by

Olvin who had the same impression of me as I had of his city—taller and bigger.

"Oye, you really get tall and big eh." We gave each other a tight hug.

"Wassup son?" I asked, mocking his accent.

"You not even in America for one year and you already yanking?"

"Gason, papicho you tryin' to take me for?" I jokingly said with my strong Saint Lucian accent, (Meaning: "Boy, are you trying to make fun of me?").

Since he lived in Brooklyn with his family, it was a heavy-traffic drive from the borough of Manhattan. The scenery was what I expected from the images I'd seen in the movies: skyscrapers, flashy billboards, overcrowded diverse population, underground trains, yellow cabs, and the Statue of Liberty. I finally felt like I was living in the real America.

For the remainder of my time in the city, I stayed with Olvin's kind, loving family who all lived in the same three-storey brick apartment building. It seemed as if all the houses on the block were similar. And not too far away lived Jermal, Jovan, and their mother. It was as if our old neighborhood had reformed in a modernized world.

The cultural aspect of New York City reminded me of life in the Caribbean. There were Caribbean communities, foods, music, dancehalls, and barbershops.

On the days when Olvin and his family went on with their regular lives, I reconnected and chatted with a few friends from Saint Lucia via MSN, explored the city, visited some family and friends throughout the boroughs, and played basketball in the park. I was just enjoying my time being free from the military school, all the while patiently waiting for Coach Rush to return my phone calls or emails. The delay of my scholarship signing had me a bit worried. I thought that there must have been a change of plans. It would have made me look like a liar because I'd already passed on the news to almost all my family and friends in America and Saint Lucia.

A week later, Coach Rush called. "Hey Arnold, sorry I haven't been in touch. We were out of town recruiting other players," he said.

"Oh, I was so worried Coach Rush. I was calling other coaches already," I said.

"Oh no Arnold, we are still interested. It's just that the admission's office was still processing your high school transcript, CXC results, and ACT test scores."

"Oh okay."

"So this week I will send the scholarship papers and documents through overnight mail."

Coach Rush had given me his word, but I didn't want to get my hopes up until I'd seen all the necessary documents in front of my face.

Two nights later, I received my $36,000.00 worth of scholarship and other documents. All I needed was to confirm my commitment with my signature to seal the deal. As I read through the information on the paper, I reflected on a statement that a sports personnel and former sports anchor from Saint Lucia had said to me a day ago while we chatted on MSN. "You know, if you sign to the University of Vermont, you will be the first Saint Lucian ever to play NCAA Division I basketball as a freshman."

Knowing I would be the first one brought more meaning to the scholarship signing. After I'd scribbled my signature, there was a sense of relief and victory that streamed through my system. It was official—I was now a Catamount and a NCAA Division I basketball player from Saint Lucia.

Following my signing, an article was released on UVM's website and sent out for other associated collegiate sites. The article described me as, "an outstanding leaper and a solid rebounder."

Coach Brennan was quoted as saying, "We are thrilled to have Arnold join our program. We feel that his athleticism and tenacity will bring a great deal to our team."

Chapter 29

Before I Leave For Possibly Four Years

With the assistance and sponsorships from family and friends living in New York City, I had enough money to book a one-way plane ticket to Saint Lucia, with enough for other travel arrangements.

Back on my tropical homeland I felt as if I had been gone for decades. My body acted like frozen meat thawing in the Caribbean heat. I was pleased to be surrounded by everything my mother had to offer—her love, her ever-ready support, her mouth-watering food, and her earsplitting laughter—I'd missed it all. And judging from how she glowed at the airport when she first saw my new appearance, I assumed that she was even prouder than me. She complimented my shaved head and face for the entire drive home. I, too, had something to praise her for—she had lost a fair amount of weight and her bruised-up ankle was doing much better than before. It was not quite fully recovered, she still struggled slightly with her mobility.

Home looked the same except for some damage in the roof that allowed mice to constantly get in and run on the ceilings. The wooden floor creaked even louder. *I can't wait to buy Mummy a new home.*

Tobias had heard of my scholarship news and he contacted me on my second day home. He wanted to congratulate me on my recent successes. I wanted to inform him of his hypocritical behavior, but it was best to let the deadbeat-father rest in peace.

Lucius seemed a different man; he suddenly knew how to smile on a regular basis. There was no telling what was on his mind to trigger such never-before-seen acts. Nevertheless, that didn't change anything between us. Our relationship was more distant than ever. He didn't even compliment me on my achievement. I still greeted him, "Good morning Daddy," because these words still made my mother happy.

There weren't any major changes with my younger siblings. The only addition I noticed was a rubber basketball in my bedroom.

"Whose ball?" I curiously asked Marvin.

"Mine gason," he replied.

"Seriously? You play basketball now? Since when?"

"I does go on de Summit with de fellas and Mummy does pay for my weekend basketball lessons."

"Oh dats really cool. Well I will teach you some moves as I'm here."

The first time I took Marvin for a practice session on the Summit, many of my acquaintances asked me some of the same questions. "Gason, I eh see you long time...where you was hiding?"

Then they commented on the 20 pounds of muscles I had put on. "Oye you really get big eh."

They even made fun of my shaved head. "Haha, de mun cut his hair!"

And then they teased me about my new dialect. "I cah believe de mun already yanking." It was all in love though; just being around my friends again was the best welcome-home present.

The first time I saw my younger brother play basketball, I saw the potential in his game. He'd picked it up quickly. Marvin was no longer the little brother wandering close to Da Yard—being 16-years old, he was old enough to handle business on his own. Since he was now playing basketball, he had developed a closer relationship with my friends, Dudley, Kendell, Java, and Hakeem. It felt good to know that he wasn't following the wrong crowd.

After the first few days of being back, all of my closest friends knew of my arrival—even my brother, Kervyn knew. There was just one more special person I had to surprise—Margaritte. I was longing for her companionship. On my end, promises were never broken.

"Surprise!" I shouted as I stood holding a gift at the front door of Margaritte's home.

"Wha...what, you doing here? Oh my God," she stammered as she placed one hand on her chest and the other across her lips. I spread my arms to initiate a hug and a kiss, but her slow reactions made me wonder if I should have called first. I felt even more unwelcome when she only gave me a hug and sealed my puckered lips with her cheek. I walked into her house feeling like I was better off standing outside.

I was introduced to a male stranger. "Thee...this is Arnold," Margaritte stuttered to him. Then he fled to the spare bedroom, which left Margaritte and I alone in the living room.

"Dats your roommate?"

"Yes," she nervously answered as we sat on opposite ends of the couch. I couldn't find the words to describe how much I'd missed her, so I just handed her the gift I'd bought for her in New York City. She shoved it aside and claimed that she would open it later. "When you came back?" she asked.

"A few days ago."

"Wha' happen? Why you here?"

"I just com' dong to renew my visa in Barbados."

"So what, you get another scholarship?"

"Yeah, da University of Vermont."

"Oh wow, congrats. I always knew you would make it," she bragged. "How long you back for?"

"Jus' three weeks," I replied.

Frustrated with Margaritte's behavior, I stood up, gently held on to her hand and tried to proceed to the bedroom.

Maybe some action would ease up the tension, I thought. She snapped back her hand.

"Wha' happen?" I asked furiously.

"My roommate deh," she whispered. I sighed heavily then sat back down.

The awkwardness and silence in the room was broken by the sounds of the ringing cell phone in her pocket. She quickly jumped up and ran into her bedroom; seconds later, I heard her whispering in her room. Before she returned to the living room, I left through the front door and never looked back.

I shed some tears on my way back home. I believed that she had returned to her baby's daddy. Who knows? All I knew was that my heart was shattered.

As always, playing basketball and training eliminated most of the loneliness and depression in my life. And so every day at 5 in the morning, I jogged long-distance and developed my skills on the court. I even took Marvin with me a few times. It was my duty as the big brother to set the standards and lead the way. America had increased my knowledge of the game so I passed on all the lessons to him, and like a sponge, Marvin was ready and eager to soak them all in. I remember telling him, "In America, everyone is good, but not everybody is great, so you still have a chance to be as good as, or even better than any of them."

The second time around, it was easier to organize and arrange my travels back to America because the media had given me some island-wide-exposure through television, the newspapers, and radio. The articles and interviews resulted in a helping hand from a local hotel which covered my airline fees to Burlington, Vermont. Shortly after my return flight from Barbados, I was on my way to living the actual dream.

Chapter 30

Stay Out of Trouble

Coach Rush picked me up from the Burlington Airport, and then dropped me off at one of the university's residential campuses— Redstone Campus. It was his idea for my early return; it was for my own benefit. He introduced me to the Summer Enrichment Scholarship Program, or SESP, a program for a select number of colored and bi/multi-racial incoming first-year students which included participation in fun activities, six college credit courses, and a paid part-time job. Being from a Caribbean island, I was one of the chosen few to be selected to the program sponsored annually by ALANA (African, Latino(a), Asian and Native Americans). The rest of the students in the program lived in America but had backgrounds from other countries; Argentina, Portugal, Africa, Puerto Rico, and the Dominican Republic were just a few.

Upon my arrival, I was introduced to the mentors of the program, upperclassmen and fellow minorities (juniors and seniors) from the university. They escorted me to my double-occupancy dormitory which was to be my accommodation for the duration of the one-month summer program. I met my roommate, a chubby, African-American young man with Jamaican background who resided in New York, New York. From our very first conversation we bonded, although, it was obvious that he hadn't come out of the closet. In Saint Lucia, if any of my friends had seen me associating with a homosexual, then I would be considered gay as well; after all, homosexual acts were illegal in my country and could lead to imprisonment if convicted. At first, I felt uncomfortable closing my eyes to fall asleep, but I quickly learned to accept the rules of the new culture I now lived in. Besides, the University of Vermont documented equal opportunity policies for all sexual orientations, and any form of discrimination was taken as a serious offense.

When I met the rest of the SESP students, I discovered some lesbians who were open with their sexual preferences amongst our group. They were also lesbians from the women's basketball team. Being from a place where the majority of the people were homophobic, this was definitely an environment I had to come to grips with.

During my first week, I met with Keith Smith and Beverly Colston, a gentle, kindhearted African-American man and woman who were responsible for my acceptance to their program. Keith and

Beverly were also the coordinator and director of SESP. I thought of them as our college parents; they were the type of people who spoke with great words of encouragement and inspiration. Whenever anyone violated the program's rules, Keith or Beverly were the ones who counseled us about the importance of obedience.

There were a few SESP rules and regulations we had to abide by—though not as many as Massanutten Military Academy. I often learned the rules after I'd violated them.

During a small weekend gathering of SESP students at the ALANA student center, Tiffany Smith, a red-skinned girl, and I decided to secretly excuse ourselves from our group to head back to the dormitory for our own private time.

Tiffany was attracted to me from day one—she screamed, "Wow," the day she caught me topless in my room. The twinkle in her eyes, scrutinizing my upper body, felt everlasting. Ever since that day, we'd been getting acquainted during small conversations after a long day in the classroom and workplace.

On that particular weekend night, we had decided to initiate some sparks. We wasted no time from the moment we made contact with my twin-size bed. Wet, long, and passionate kisses were swapped while the sensations of our hands sensually aroused and stirred up the steam in my room.

As I begun to unbutton her trousers, Tiffany asked, "You gotta condom?"

"Yeah, of course," I replied.

I jumped out of my bed, excited for my first college action. I looked in my drawers, picked up a condom and as soon I proceeded to stimulate my desires, a loud bang on the door interrupted us. Tiffany quickly dressed and jetted underneath my bed. The knock on the door became louder.

I opened the door enough to face the two mentors who stood at it. "Where's Tiffany?" they asked aggressively.

"Uh, I doh know," I answered.

"We saw the two of y'all leave so I know she's with you." While thinking of my next line, unexpectedly, Tiffany grabbed the door, opened it widely, and walked out. I tried to sell it off with a surprised expression.

"Oh, dere she is." They weren't buying it.

What's the big deal, I thought.

The following day, Keith called me into his office. "Arnold, it has been brought to my attention that you and a female were locked up in your room," he said.

"Yeah, but I didn't know about dat rule," I pleaded.

"The rules are there for a reason, Arnold. Now, if I hear anything again, I will be forced to make your coaches aware of your behavior."

With eyes wide I replied, "Okay, okay."

I was disappointed in myself. From that point on, my attitude changed; I was no longer the socializing type. And to stay away from getting myself in any further dilemmas, I decided to stop seeing Tiffany and focus on my weekly routine: my two classes (Pre-Calculus and Psychology), my part-time job on-campus, and basketball workouts. I also pretended like I lived in this world all by myself—it might have come off as standoffish to everyone, but it worked for me. Sometimes, like in this case, my solutions created more problems.

An incident took place while walking next to a circle of friends on our way to the ALANA center for a free movie night. I was by my lonesome, just listening to their conversations, when a female from their group seemed bothered by my quietness. "Oh you too good to interact with us?" she said. I didn't even know her name. Apparently she had made friends with the rest of the mentees, but still, I felt she had no right to talk to me with such an annoying tone. So, I just ignored her question. She continued, "You must think that you're special." Again, I just kept on walking. She snatched my white Yankee baseball cap off my head.

"Give me my cap back," I said.

"No, come take it," she demanded. Her bossiness and stubbornness agitated the thin line that separated my good intentions from my bad ones.

"Give me my forkin' cap back," I said.

"Come get it!" she replied again. I approached her to snatch my cap out her hand but it became childish to a point where I was snatching air; every time I tried to grab my cap, she pulled it away.

"Give me my cap back, bitch!" I shouted.

"Who you calling bitch!"

"I doh want no trouble. Jus' give me my cap back," I said. She walked off and threw my white cap in the wet green grass.

"Wat da fuck?! Girl, you betta pay me back for my cap," I yelled after I'd seen the green streaks all over it.

The following day, Keith called me into his office so that I could tell my version of the story. I couldn't believe that she snitched when she was the instigator. I was in trouble due to my use of inappropriate language. That's when I realized that in a college environment, there's no such thing as freedom of speech. I had to apologize to the woman, but in the end, she gave me the money to purchase a new baseball cap.

After I was lectured by Keith, I had to visit Coach Brennan at his office.

Oh no! I'm going to get kicked off the team, was my initial thought.

"I just cannot have that kind of behavior in this program," Coach Brennan yelled at me as I stood embarrassed in front of his office desk.

"I'm sorry Coach. I promise it eh go never happen again," I stammered.

"You're damn right it won't happen again!" He looked at me with a life-threatening stare. "We never see you in the office. You never come to say hi. Our doors are always open for our guys. You can always come talk to us if something is bothering you."

This was news. I never thought I had the option to walk into a NCAA Division I coach's office whenever I wanted.

NCAA Division I coaches are too busy to see players, I thought. Maybe, their off-court-presence just wasn't my comfort zone, or maybe that was my way of displaying my respect for them. I just never paid visits to my coaches. And now that I knew I could, I still didn't bother to take Coach Brennan up on his offer. I felt like it wouldn't have been a good idea since I was already on bad standings with the university. Any problems of mine, I'd rather keep hidden.

Chapter 31

Lonely

It was a very hot, humid summer in Burlington, Vermont, but my loneliness made the days and nights seem dark and cold. Nothing could compare to life on a wet-and-dry volcanic island. I missed basketball at The Summit, playing against the northeast trade winds in front of a hyped Saint Lucian crowd; hanging with my friends, sharing laughs and chatting in our own Kwéyòl dialect; forever missing my mother and the tastes of our local home-made meals and juices; the holidays and activities that made up our heritage and culture. I missed the role of big brother; and the tropical sweetness of my hometown; I missed the simple beauty of Saint Lucia.

A few of my teammates who lived off-campus came to exercise at the university's gym. I grew a friendship with Germain Mopa Nijla—the first Black teammate I met. We had more things in common: we were both foreign students and had the same interests studying computer science, but Germain was entering his senior year. He was from Cameroon and still spoke with his heavy African accent. Germain and I would meet at the gym for weightlifting and shooting drills. That was the only time I didn't feel everyone was against me. I thought that making more friends would just lead to more bad events. I should have appreciated the diversity amongst my peers from the Summer Enrichment Scholarship Program because, judging from experiences in Virginia, once the school year began, it would be even more difficult to make white friends.

On the other hand, I developed a friendlier relationship with Danielle Sabourin, also a returning student-athlete and a born-Canadian on the women's basketball team. Her actions over the summer really defined a true friend and she came around when I needed someone the most.

During the last week of SESP, we were informed that we had to pack up everything and leave the premises before a certain date. All the other students were ecstatic to be returning to their homes. They lived in the states of California, New York, Massachusetts, Maine, and Vermont. It was only about three weeks until the commencement of the 2004-2005 school year, so I didn't find it necessary to fly back to Saint Lucia, plus I wasn't able to afford a plane ticket. Embarrassed about my homelessness and inability to afford travel arrangements, I planned to secretly remain in my SESP assigned room.

By the last Saturday evening of July, I was the only one on the floors of the residential hall. I had said farewell to my roommate, and lied about flying to New York City to visit my aunt. My room was my hideout as everyone emptied the building. I was fortunate that the mentors didn't inspect the closet in my room that Saturday morning.

The university had shut down completely for the weekend. I mean, I was literally the only one living on this massive campus. I was so bored that I felt like pulling out the hairs of my afro. My stomach growled seeking its usual daily meals. With the $500.00 check I had earned from my part-time job, I could have at least done some shopping, but I was afraid that the doors to the building would lock behind me and then I would really have been homeless.

When I felt like jumping out the window from the fourth floor of the building, I thought about my mother; I sensed her spirit in my room, begging, *hang in there my boy. Things will get better one day.*

I finally found the courage to pick up my cell-phone and dial Danielle. "I do not have anywhere to go," I cried out, and in the back of my mind thinking, *my shelter shouldn't be anyone's responsibility but my own.*

"Where are you A?" she asked.

"In da dorms on Redstone Campus," I replied.

"Who's there with you?"

"No one. Da program finish. I'm dere by myself."

"That's insane. Have you eaten?"

"No."

In less than 15 minutes, Danielle was at the door with a bag of food and drinks. "Is everything okay?"

"I doh know," I said. "I'm feeling so homesick right now. I miss my Mummy."

"Aw, I understand what you mean, you know. I went through the same thing my freshman year, eh. Once school starts, things will be better. You're handsome, you won't have any problems meeting people."

Danielle's presence and kind words reduced the prickling sensation in my heart; I'd only met her for a few days yet her kindness showered me with love. The next day, she also checked up on me and brought me more food.

Early Monday morning, I was startled awake by the sounds of keys jingling and the movement of the doorknob. I could have sworn I was in a horror film.

Who could this be? I wondered. It couldn't be Danielle because she would need a card to swipe for entrance to the building's main doors. And I know I shut the doors after she left, otherwise the alarm would go off throughout the night if the doors were open for too long. In less than two seconds I found a stranger at my bedroom's door; a Caucasian lady with a bucket and a broom in her hand. "I thought everyone left," she said.

"Uh, yeah," I muttered nervously.

"What you still doing here?"

"Um, I doh know," I shrugged.

"You need to get out. We have to clean this building," she said harshly.

Fearful, I had no choice but to call Danielle. She advised me to call Germain because he might have some empty rooms in his off-campus apartment. "Yo G, I was wonderin' if I could stay by your place until school starts," I asked.

"Oh not a problem Arnold," he said.

I packed all my belongings and was soon in Germain's car on my way to his apartment on South Willard Street, only five-minutes away.

During my time spent at his apartment, Germain treated me like a little brother. A mattress to rest my body was already too much to ask, but he showed even more hospitality and when he ate, I ate—when he cooked, he cooked for two. We spent the rest of our summer days working out in the gym and partying on the weekends. That was the type of unrelated-brotherly-love that helped decrease my loneliness and depression.

Chapter 32

Freshman Year
Fall Semester

The long awaited American college life was finally at my front door—I opened the door widely and welcomed it with a big smile. As an international student, I was permitted early arrival, so I must have been the first student walking through the Harris-Millis dormitory, located on Athletics Campus. I was advised that most incoming first-year student-athletes lived on that particular campus because of the closeness to the gym.

The residence hall of Harris-Millis was made up of two 4-storey buildings and a basement. When entering the building you could go straight, left or right; straight ahead led to the main office, a wide open-space lobby, mailboxes, a big screen TV, a piano, a pool table, couches and tables. The hallways to the left led to Millis and the right led to Harris.

This is the life; the real college life, I thought.

Due to late processing of my room application, I had to settle for two roommates rather than one. When I entered my room on the third floor, I realized that it was more spacious than my double occupancy room on Redstone Campus—this only meant that there was room for an extra piece of furniture with three beds, three desks, and three closets. There wasn't much room to move around. Having to live with one stranger for an entire school-year had already been annoying, but having two was even more exasperating, especially when neither was on my basketball team.

Early Sunday morning, one day before the commencement of the first day of classes, I woke to the sounds of dragging furniture, banging on the walls, and loud voices. I quickly looked through my bedroom's windows to see chaos. Students, both males and females, were moving into the dormitories like ants carrying food. It seemed as if they brought their entire house to school: couches, futons, skis, snowboards, bicycles, small fridges, tables…anything one could think of. I was just glad that my early arrival avoided that crowd and rush.

Eventually I met up with my two roommates, Drew and John, two Caucasian males from Colorado and upstate New York, respectively. After my experiences with racism in Virginia, I'd been cautious in my approach towards white people. I wouldn't dare engage in any conversations until a passable eye contact was established. Despite my racial insecurities, Drew and John made me feel welcome. They were even excited to be rooming with a basketball player.

Later that night, the chaos had settled and the hallways were clear. The only difference was that the school was now full with students and staff—the university was open for business. *You will feel better when school reopens,* Danielle said and she was right. Being in my new room was the most freedom I had had while attending school in America. I was free to eat, sleep, or go to classes, whenever I desired—I was in complete control of my destiny as a student-athlete.

Whenever I felt hungry I could go to the cafeteria located in the basement of the Harris-Millis dormitory—the business hours were 7:00 a.m. to 8:00 p.m. With a swipe of my student identification card, I was able to eat anytime between those hours. Plus, there was $250.00 credited on my card to be used at any UVM store or established local businesses in the area such as Domino's Pizza or the Chinese restaurant.

During my first week, student athletes were scheduled for a mandatory meeting for our upcoming season which welcomed us to the university and our programs and later discussed athletic policies, rules, regulations, and student conduct. One important point made by the hosts of the meeting was that, "It is a privilege and not a right to be a student-athlete." I felt like they spoke directly to me—it was rare indeed to be a collegiate Division I basketball player.

At that same meeting, I was finally able to meet the rest of my team. There were five new faces: four freshmen like me, and a seven-foot junior-transfer from the University of Rhode Island. I also met Tim McCrory, the only African-American player on the team. He was from Mississippi State. Tim spoke with southern country slang, and stood about the same height as me, but he had a smaller build.

A week later, Tim and I discovered that we had much in common: we were both freshmen, studied the same Computer Science major, took some of the same classes, lived in Harris-Millis dorms, and played the same position in basketball. Tim and I became good friends in a short period of time. Not too long after we met we became roommates. Moving in with Tim was one of the smartest decisions I made because both my assigned roommates partied almost every single night. I also saw a pound of weed hidden in John's desk. He was selling it to other students and I wanted no part of it. In my case, getting caught with illegal substances could lead to automatic deportation. Also, with two very disappointing C's in my summer courses, I was determined to achieve A's that semester, in all five courses—English, Geography, Introduction to Computers, Spanish, and Life Skills for Student-Athletes.

On September 11, 2004, I attended my first college house-party, hosted by a few basketball and ice-hockey players. I arrived at the scene and was amazed by the large gathering. I envisioned that it was going to be a fun night. The latest hip-hop and pop music was playing. The line to get in was long, but being a basketball player gave me an easy access pass.

The music was coming from the basement so I followed the sounds down a flight of stairs. I had only taken about three steps when I was approached by my first college crush—five foot eight, long brown hair, Caucasian, with a beautiful smile. I thought, *oh yeah, it doesn't get any better than that.* Our eye contact lasted until I reached the bottom of the stairs where she stood.

"What's up?" she asked. The liquor on her breath was so strong that I could have tasted the vodka.

"Nutting much," I answered as she continued staring into my eyes like we were the only ones at the party. "I remember seein' you in my Geography class."

"I remember seeing you once," she said.

"You wanna go back to my room?" I asked bravely, assuming that was her intention from the moment we engaged in conversation. My question was answered without words; she immediately chugged what was left in her cup, took my hand, and led me out the front door. In no time we were alone in my room. Tim cooperated and allowed me to have private time with my guest for at least an hour.

I didn't know it would be so easy in college, I thought as we cuddled the night away, naked in my bed. "What was your name again?" I jokingly whispered to her after our intense session. After she shared a laugh, she reminded me, "Maggie Wilson."

"Where you from?" I asked while stroking my fingers through her hair.

"Newport, Rhode Island," she answered, slightly slurring, "You?"

"Saint Lucia."

"Where's that?"

"An island in da Caribbean. You live on-campus?"

"Yeah, on Redstone Campus," she replied.

"Oh so you a sophomore?"

"Yeah, it's my second year," she answered.

Eventually we fell asleep, side by side, until the break of dawn.

From that point on, Maggie and I contacted each other every day. We sent daily love messages through Facebook, we spoke over the phone on a nightly basis and even chatted using an instant messaging software.

Chapter 33

Pre-season

On a daily basis, I walked through campus holding my head up high, feeling like the luckiest man in the world. I loved my college environment, my classes, my roommate, my new friends, and my girlfriend. Maggie had really helped to seal my fulfillment and happiness with my college experience. I'd even stopped attending parties. I had everything I needed in my life. Whenever Maggie and I weren't displaying our warm devotion with showers of kisses or incredible love making, I was in basketball workouts, the classroom, or study hall. We did mostly everything together: we ate all our meals together, we studied together, she even waited for me after classes so that we could ride the shuttle back to our rooms together. And when I was at basketball workouts, she would wait in my room for my return.

The pre-season commenced with a workout led by our strength and conditioning coach, Chris Poulin. It started at 6 o'clock in the morning. Due to NCAA Division I rules, we weren't allowed to practice as a team with our head or assistant coaches until the official practice date. For the first two days of pre-season, Chris recorded our speed, endurance, and strength using his own personal drills as a means of keeping track of our progress.

There were five senior players left on the team, three of whom I looked up to: T.J. Sorrentine, Taylor Coppenrath, and Germain Mopa Njila. T.J. was our starting point guard and the leader of the pack. He set the trend for all of us. Taylor stood six foot nine and was our starting power forward and scoring leader. He had an awkward looking jump-shot, but it worked for him; he was amongst the top scorers in the nation averaging about 24 points per game the previous season. With Germain's tenacious defense, it was quite easy to determine that he was the hardest worker. These three guys' enthusiasm motivated me to become a better player, and I was willing to learn from them.

Every night, Tim and I went to bed early, about 10:00 p.m., looking forward to Chris's early morning workouts. Our nearby dorm-mates were considerate enough to keep their noise levels down around that time. Having my first encounter with a strength and conditioning coach, I showed my respect for his impressive techniques by pushing myself. His assignment was to prepare us by getting us physically strong and fit for our official practices and, obviously, for our upcoming season. Chris's sessions were so intense that while we were doing a drill to build agility, one of my teammates tripped over the out-of-bounds lines, fell flat on his face, and broke his front tooth. On a different occasion, I caught a few freshmen puking. That's the type of energy we brought to the gym—all or nothing. I also had my moments when I felt like giving up, but I was able to get through the drills.

When we were free from classes, Tim and I met with our assistant coach, Pat Filien, for an hour of individual workouts. Coach Filien prepared us for the highest level of collegiate basketball by assisting us with advanced basketball maneuvers that improved our offensive and defensive awareness. In the evenings, the rest of the team met up for full-court basketball scrimmages; it was a violation for coaches to monitor or be present while we played as a team.

In October, the NBA team, the Boston Celtics had one week of training camp at our gymnasium. I was delighted when I heard the news. As basketball players of the university, we had special privileges to attend their closed practices. With my busy schedule, I was only able to witness one out of the five Celtics' practice sessions. These were the superstars that I dreamed of becoming one day. I looked up to every single NBA player for their ongoing accomplishments. I had the opportunity to speak with Al Jefferson who was just selected by the Celtics (15th overall pick) in the first round of the 2004 draft. While he put up some midrange jump-shots, I rebounded for him then slowly started a conversation. "How does it feel to be in the NBA?" I asked him.

"Oh man, it's the best feeling in the world," he replied.

"So you got drafted straight outta high school, right?"

"Yeah man, I felt like it was my time," he answered. I envied Al Jefferson.

Out of the rest of the Boston Celtics team and coaching staff, I only recognized Head Coach Doc Rivers and three other players: Paul Pierce, Ricky Davis, and Gary Payton. Their personalities really stood out: Gary Payton was talkative and funny; Paul Pierce was humble and let his game do all the talking; Ricky Davis could have jumped out of the gym with his athleticism.

As I browsed the faces of these giant NBA players, I saw nothing but smiles. Why would they be depressed? They were getting paid millions for the sport that they loved. I wanted to do that too.

Chapter 34

Regrets

Despite the fact that my love for Maggie grew stronger day by day, occasionally, it seemed like we were becoming more distant. Early on, when she said, "I love you too Arnold," the words felt believable as I gazed into her hazel eyes.

But as time went by I noticed Maggie sometimes seemed bored when she was around me. I figured that my lifestyle wasn't appealing to her anymore—I was so caught up with school and basketball that I didn't really have time to party with her. It seemed like our relationship had stolen her true identity as a party girl. In my opinion, she had an alcohol problem. She would consume so much alcohol that she smelled like a liquor store the following morning and wasn't able to recall events that took place that night. As Maggie's boyfriend, I showed my concern by allowing her to choose between me and partying—she chose partying. For one day, I broke up with her; that one day felt like three months, I was missing her too much. When I loved someone, it was really hard for me to let go, so I begged her to fall back into my arms, which she did.

Originally, I thought that Maggie was the perfect girlfriend. But the more time we spent together, the more I realized that there were issues she needed to resolve, the main one being her drinking problem. Even though rumors circulated on-campus about her getting really wasted and sleeping with possibly all the black men at the school, I ignored the gossip because, behind that cup of vodka, I saw someone who fully supported my dreams.

At times, through the corner of my eye, I noticed a few black female students who showed intense dislike whenever Maggie and I walked on-campus holding hands. *I shouldn't be with a white girl,* I imagined them thinking. But I wasn't born that way; I never had racial preferences in the women I dated. I just needed a companion to love and guide me along the right paths to a successful life. And obviously, I'd try to return the same and more.

Off-court, I tried to spark up fireworks, or rekindle a trusting relationship with Maggie. On-court, I struggled to assimilate to NCAA Division I basketball. Chris's pre-season workouts had concluded. After comparing my starting records with my end results, I'd seen tremendous improvements in my speed, endurance, and strength. It was now time for our head and assistant coaches to do their jobs, which meant official practice had begun.

At last, I started seeing Coach Brennan more often, although Coach Jesse acted more like the head of the entire coaching staff. Coach Brennan just sat around, observed, and once in a while demonstrated a few plays, while Coach Jesse truly led the practices. Coach Rush and Coach Filien acted as motivational speakers on the sidelines.

The first few days of practice, I had a difficult time adjusting to Vermont's basketball systems; the drills required high concentration and time was limited, so transitions between learning plays were done quickly. I watched and learned from the more experienced players, but when it was my turn to demonstrate, I felt like I should have been at a basketball camp for dummies. Everything moved too fast for me; I wasn't able to handle the pressure and intensity which made me feel like dead weight. Most of the time, I was lost. And what made it worse was that the support I needed from my coaches was missing—they made me feel like I didn't belong.

"Are you a fuckin' jackass?" Coach Jesse shouted in my face one time after I messed up an offensive play. The gym briefly became silent. My teammates' shocked faces brought tears to my eyes while goose-bumps crawled up my skin.

"You can do it Arnold," my teammates chanted. I fought back the tears and pushed myself a little harder; but by then, I was too shaken by the verbal abused from Coach Jesse. That day was probably my most devastating practice. Being called a jackass by a coach who I respected, made me question my basketball intelligence.

If I didn't know all the plays, there was no point being part of the basketball squad. Instead of sobbing about my mistakes, I put in extra work by scribbling all the team's offensive and defensive plays on a piece of paper. I then studied it like a final exam. My progress slowly picked up and my improved performance was recognized by my coaches. Coach Brennan officially made me feel welcome when he yelled out, "I knew he'd come around," referring to my hustle play which led to a slam dunk.

Nevertheless, I sensed that Coach Brennan and Coach Jesse showed favoritism towards other players. Even the walk-on (non-scholarship player) received more support from the coaches. Maybe I was over sensitive but I scrutinized the behaviors of them all. Amongst the freshmen, Coach Jesse showed more interest in Ryan and Josh— two players who he personally recruited. Coach Brennan loved his senior players, especially our two stars, T.J. Sorrentine and Taylor

Coppenrath; he treated them like his own sons. Also, my roommate, Tim, known to Vermonters as "Timmy Time" (a nickname given to him by Coach Brennan) received plenty of attention from our head coach. When I heard that Coach Brennan had flown all the way to Mississippi to recruit Tim I had a bad gut feeling. *I guess I wasn't worth his time since he didn't even visit me down at Massanutten Military Academy.* I was the first basketball player who Coach Rush ever recruited to the university. This meant I was fortunate in that I was recruited, but it was also regrettable as being his first was like being the last option on the team.

I found Coach Filien to be the most likeable coach on the team— he was the one I could express my feelings to and he always encouraged me. My trust for Coach Brennan and Coach Jesse slowly faded because I felt neglected.

One day after an intense practice, Head Coach Brennan informed us of a team meeting to be held in our locker-room. I cannot recall his speech, but I do remembered the disparaging remarks he made about music by Lil Jon (a rapper, producer, and disc jockey from Atlanta, Georgia). As we entered the locker-room, we realized the CD player was left running and was blasting the crunk-style of music. "Hey, hey, hey, turn off all that Nigger shit," Coach Brennan yelled, followed by a giggle. A deafening silence took over the room.

My white teammates were surprised but my black teammates and one black coach looked hurt. I wondered who was going to step up to the boss. No one dared question the man in charge. When Coach Brennan realized no one found his joke funny, he acted like he never said anything and went on with his speech.

Later that evening, I asked Tim, "Dawg, wha' you tink about Coach Brennan sayin' Nigger?"

"Man, I was disappointed," Tim said sadly.

During another meeting, this time an "emergency" one, Coach Brennan further lost my respect.

"I'm sorry you had to hear it this way but I want to tell you before y'all hear it from other sources," Coach Brennan said while he paced back and forth in the locker room.

I thought, *oh my God, what is he about to say?*

"I planned to tell y'all at the end of the season because I didn't want it to affect the season outcome, with the media and all that," he continued.

Come on! Say what you have to, and stop beating around the bush.

Finally he got to the point. "This season will be my last year coaching college basketball. I'm going to retire at the end of the season."

I ground my teeth to keep my words in, *this man lied to me. I cannot believe it. He told me he'd be here until I graduate.*

It seemed like it was news to the entire room, except for Coach Jesse, of course, who had a grin on his face. Coach Filien looked like he had just gotten fired and Coach Rush looked like someone had stolen his candy.

Could this be the reason Coach Jesse had been acting so bossy? Was Coach Jesse going to be the next head coach? What would happen to us after Coach Brennan retired?

After hearing the details of our head coach's retirement, the NCAA basketball world became clearer to me. *Coach Brennan never cared about my well-being—he only cared about himself and the five seniors who helped him establish his name in Vermont.* Well, at least that's how everything seemed to me.

Even though my coaches made me regret my decision to come to Vermont, I swallowed my pride and focused on what looked to be the greatest season in the university's basketball history. I concentrated on establishing myself on the team.

I'll worry about my future after the season, I decided.

Chapter 35

Thin Ice

UVM basketball introduced me to a whole new approach in preparation for facing our opponents. First off, there was the *scouting report*—before game day, our coaches had us watch a game film on that particular team, to carefully study their styles, strategies, pros and cons of play, and their players' potential during actual in-game situations. This led to the *game plan*—the information gathered from the scouting report was used to plot our own offensive and defensive tactics, supposedly giving an approach for victory. Also, to prepare for the basketball heavier weights, we had to play two exhibition games against teams that we were most likely to defeat.

On November 6, 2004, we played our first exhibition game on our home-court against Saint Michael's College—a local NCAA Division II basketball program. It was around that time (the season opener) that our fans were introduced to their favorite home college team.

My pre-game routine never changed—I kissed the photo of my mother that I kept in my personal locker, and then said a prayer to my Lord. The sold-out game was scheduled to kick off at 1:00 p.m. sharp. Even if the bleachers were packed with over 3,000 cheerful UVM supporters, Maggie was the only one who I definitely knew came out to support me. Sitting right behind our bench, she was hard to miss.

The singing of the American National Anthem, right before the game, initiated an overwhelming feeling in me. It was a glorious moment. And to top it all, the 2003-2004 team was honored with the American East championship banner for their successes in that conference the previous season—more reasons to feel like the luckiest Saint Lucian ever. I was about to play at the highest level of collegiate basketball in the United States of America—a dream come true, indeed.

I may have been on the team, but by the end of the game, I felt like a reserve fighting for a position on the official roster. From 2001 up to that point in my basketball career, I had never started a season on the bench. Don't get me wrong, the starting seniors deserved their glory, but I felt disappointed when I barely saw four minutes of action that game. Sitting on the bench, my anger rose at Coach Brennan.

Our first exhibition victory against Saint Michael's College ended with the final score of 102-88.

After the game, the support of our fans cheered me up for a few minutes. We remained in the building, signing autographs on apparel and fan-cards. That moment made me feel very special, because both adults and kids pointed out my picture and asked for my signature. But later the heartwarming moments were lost when the team celebrated our first victory in the locker-room with pizza and soda, and my senior teammate, David Hehn, took his jokes too far.

David, the only Canadian on the team, who I'd only ever seen at our practices and games, ferociously hammered the open box of pizza onto my hands while I tried to grab a slice. "This box is for white people only," he said.

As half of the team laughed, I said, "Yo Dawg, wha' da fuck is wrong wit' you?" David continued laughing. Leaving the slice of pizza behind, I bolted out the locker-room before anyone witnessed the tears running down my face.

I was shocked with the behavior of the usually-quiet David, who I had respected so much. *This was probably a joke; David didn't mean it*, I thought. So, I decided not to pursue it. Besides, snitches get stitches, and I didn't want to burn any bridges with my teammates. But I was tired of everyone's verbal abuse, especially their comment, "Learn how to speak English," which seemed to be following me everywhere I went.

On November 10, 2004, we played our second and last exhibition game at home, against Concordia—a University from Montreal, Quebec, Canada. We blew them away: 105-66. Even though we were leading by a large margin, I played only five minutes; enough time to grab an offensive rebound and attempt one field goal. Two games seemed to confirm that my coaches favored all other freshmen players over me. No matter how much extra work I'd put in, nothing seemed to change.

Mid November, temperatures were negative twenty degrees Fahrenheit—I remember it was so cold that the sweat dripping down my facial hairs turned into frost whenever I walked outdoors after practice. I predicted that Vermont's upcoming winter would be much worse than Virginia's. I spent most of my time curled up in bed with Maggie, watching movies. Since Maggie's roommate was never around, I spent most of my evenings in her dorm-room on Redstone Campus.

On November 19, 2004, we faced our first regular season game against the number one team in the nation—Kansas Jayhawks—from the Big 12 Conference. The game was expected to be aired on ESPN Plus. Before leaving campus, I begged Maggie to watch my game on television, which she promised to do.

To me, it was like presidential treatment, being able to travel as a team to other cities via aircraft one day before the game—no more riding the bus back and forth, on the same day as the competition. We were given small allowances for our meals throughout the trip and stayed in luxurious hotels.

The Kansas Jayhawks were rated as the best college team in America that year; therefore, many basketball fans expected us to be defeated badly. On game day, the arena with its capacity of 16, 300 seats looked sold-out 30 minutes before tipoff. Never in my life had I stood in front of so many people. We were about to play on their home-court which was named after basketball's inventor, James Naismith, a Canadian who also founded the University of Kansas's basketball program. Just bouncing the basketball on that court during our warm-ups sent shivers down my spine. I prayed that my coaches would allow me to see more court time.

Our coaching staff had carefully prepared us for the game. As I watched attentively from the bench, I desperately awaited my name to be called. But every minute that went by, I became more dejected. I looked over to the coaches hoping they would recognize that I hadn't played one second—no one seemed to care. Seated at the dead-end of the bench, to get my coaches' attention, I purposely stomped my feet and periodically stood up and down; then I clapped my hands loudly, until hopelessness advised me to sit down. I just wanted to contribute to the team.

What's the point of coming to a college to play basketball if I'm going to sit on the bench for the entire season?

Even though I didn't get an opportunity to play my first official NCAA Division I game, it was still a suspenseful game to watch. My teammates were on the verge of committing a huge upset. The loud, raucous supporters in the arena were silent throughout the last few minutes because the outcome of the game was unpredictable. The referees suddenly favored Kansas—it was very difficult for our five players on the floor to beat their eight (if you added the 3 referees to the Jayhawks' starting-five). A fight to the finish was our only hope, but time was limited; we lost our first game by 7 points:68-61. We gained respect from the basketball nation that evening.

After the game, I immediately tried calling Maggie to complain about my zero minutes of playing time. I called her twice—no answer. This wasn't like her. After a few more tries, she finally picked up. "Wha' happen, everyting okay?" I asked loudly, since there was music playing in the background. "Where are you?"

"I'm drinking and watching the game with some friends," she replied with a happy tone.

"Oh, I was callin' and you didn't pick up…I thought someting was wrong wit' you," I said.

"I'm having so much fun, Arnold. I met someone and we are just alike," she stated.

"Huh, Who?" I curiously asked.

"You don't know him."

Him?

"When you get back, we really need to talk, Arnold."

No man wants to hear his significant other say, "We really need to talk." As soon as I got back to school, I went to Maggie's room expecting the worst.

I knocked. From the moment her bedroom door opened, everything became very awkward. "Hey Arnold, this is Warren," Maggie said.

Feeling embarrassed that another man was seated alone on the futon in my girlfriend's bedroom, I whispered in Maggie's ear, "I wanna talk to you downstairs."

Maggie and I went to the lobby of her dormitory on Redstone Campus. Her facial expression wasn't pleasing—this was the most serious I'd ever seen her. I held her hands. "Maggie, wha' going on?"

"I can't do this anymore," she replied, pulling her hands away from my tight grip.

"Why? Wha' I do?"

"I realized I'm missing out on all the fun with my friends…I am not happy in this relationship."

"Maggie please, you cah do dat to me right now…I only have you," I pleaded.

"I can be there for you but I cannot be what you want me to be. I want to go out and have a good time with my friends and never have to worry about being in a relationship. I want to meet other guys."

"You wanna end everyting for dis guy upstairs?"

"Sorry Arnold."

Going through a breakup was no fun. I tried my best to not contact Maggie. There was no one else whom I trusted or could turn to for relationship guidance. I didn't want to let my male-friends know I was stressing over a girl. I thought they would think that I was a wuss. Attempting to talk to the thousands of other girls on-campus wouldn't help the situation. The more days that went by—the more I needed to see, touch, and feel Maggie. Food was hard to swallow and I couldn't sleep. This only added to my bad performance in both school and basketball.

To make matters worse, Thanksgiving break was only days away. Being on the basketball team, we had to remain on-campus for practice and upcoming games. Tim and I were the only students still living in the dorms. Most of our dorm-mates went home to celebrate the holiday with their family. Maggie also left for home. It was my mission to impress her, to win her back, so I planned something special for her return to school.

My intention was to sweep her off her feet, show her what a great guy I could be. With the assistance of my teammates, Chris and Tim, I shopped for some items at the mall (I worked as the school's mascot at the ice-hockey games to earn the extra money). The ideas that we'd came up with were guaranteed to rekindle our relationship— or so I thought.

Before Maggie left her home in Newport, Rhode Island, I contacted her and lied that I needed her to come over to my room because, "I needed a better closure to our relationship." She kindly agreed. Tim already knew the deal so he excused himself from the room for the night and wished me luck.

The knock on my bedroom door to indicate Maggie's arrival, stirred up my nerves. I took a deep breath, exhaled, and whispered, "Here goes nutting." I opened the door widely.

Maggie walked into my candlelit-room, stepping on petals of red roses while some slow R&B music played in the background from my desktop computer. I patiently waited to see that beautiful smile of hers, and it came about after I offered her a slow dance.

"Arnold, this is so beautiful," she cried out.

"Maggie, I truly love you," I said.

She looked so happy; I sensed her heart was at peace with me. "I love you too, Arnold."

"I missed you so much," I murmured.

After we danced one song, I told her, "Hey, I bought someting for you." I handed her a present—a crystal-like ornament that spun in circles while playing mellow tunes. She immediately initiated a kiss that created a lovemaking masterpiece throughout the entire night. I was convinced that it was the beginning of a brand new relationship. That night, we both agreed it was best to take slow steps this time because we initially got involved too quickly.

On November 26, 2004, as a freshman, I played two minutes against Marist College in my first official NCAA Division I basketball game. I only attempted one field goal. We won the game 90-70. Our overall record was now 1-1.

Two days later we won at home against Iona College, which boosted our record to 2-1. Coach Brennan never substituted me in that game.

December 4, 2004, we played our second away game, this time at American University located in Washington, D.C. We lost that game, 67-64. Again, I didn't see any action. Our team record: 2-2.

December 19, 2004, the University of Vermont men's basketball team had a scheduled home game against Binghamton University. Notice I said, "The University of Vermont men's basketball team," and not, "we" or "me."

Chapter 36

The Right to Remain Silent

December 13, 2004
9:15 p.m.

As we drove off in the police car, I thought about the people of Saint Lucia, my family, my basketball career, and my future. My world was crashing down. *Why did she? How could she?*

The car's siren brought me back to reality. I tried to adjust my sitting position. My long legs made the back seat tight. I stared through the metal cage to spot a sign but nothing looked familiar. Just white everywhere; the snowfall made it very difficult to see.

We arrived at UVM Police Headquarters—a destination I'd never known existed. Officer Sue Roberts and Sergeant Phelps assisted me into the facility. The handcuffs came off and I was stripped of my cell phone, silver chains, earrings, silver watch and ring. My arrest seemed like it was all a misunderstanding so I remained calm.

I was brought to sit in a square room, where officer Roberts asked me some personal information, and then wrote down my answers on a form entitled, "Bail and Custody." After I signed the form, the handcuff went back on and I was left to remain seated in the room by myself. Then I thought, *wait a minute, this isn't right.* I shouted to regain the officer's attention.

"Wha' is goin on? Wha' I'm doing here? I did nuttin'! Please! I did nuttin to her! Please, you have to believe me!" Officer Roberts came rushing inside the room. She advised me to keep the noise down. I asked, "Officer, wha' gonna happen to me?"

"We are waiting for the officer of the Chittenden County Correctional Center to come pick you up," she said.

"For wha'?" I asked.

"I've already told you...you've been charged with domestic assault."

I looked up at Officer Roberts. "You gon' believe her words over me? I promise, I swear to God I didn't do anyting."

Officer Roberts's mind was made up and there was nothing I could have said or done to change it. All I had left in me was to bawl until I ran out of tears.

Another two officers came to get me. In less than 15 minutes I was at the Chittenden County Correctional Center. The handcuffs came off as I entered the building. My mug shot was taken. All ten of my fingerprints were recorded. The officer told me that I was going to be spending the night in a cell and I would be at my arraignment in the morning. He confiscated my black boots then told me I was allowed one phone call.

One phone call? Who was I going to call? I had no one left, I thought. *I will spend my night in jail. Then in the morning, I will go to court, plead my case, the judge will dismiss it then I will head back to my room pretending like nothing ever happened.*

In another state I would have been scared to death to be imprisoned with other criminals, but I was in Vermont so it wasn't that bad. In fact, as soon I walked into the cell, a man immediately asked me if I wanted the bed he sat on. I took his offer after recognizing that it was overly crowded. I never expected jailbirds to be so friendly. They all wanted to know what was my situation, but I remained silent and told them that I didn't want to talk about it.

I lay on the bed, staring at the ceiling. I spent the entire night thinking about what my next days would be like. It was almost impossible to sleep. We had no blankets to keep us warm. Some prisoners slept on the floor, while everyone else talked about their problems with society. I just pretended like I was listening. I had my own problems to figure out.

What did Maggie tell the police? Why would she jeopardize my future? What if the judge didn't believe my story? Would I return to jail? What would my coaches say?

It only took me five minutes to realize that I couldn't live my life behind bars. There was one drunk man in there that just couldn't shut up. He had stitches on his head that ran from the top of his forehead to the back of his head. The cut looked fresh. I thought that he must have gotten into a vehicular accident prior to entering in here. He was creative though. He entertained himself by creating a bouquet of red roses out of toilet-paper. He used his leftover red fruit-punch drink to color the white sheets. When he caught me staring at his creations he taught me how to make one. My own creation of red toilet-tissue made me think, *why do fools fall in love?*

"Arnold, no one can do me like you do," Maggie had said to me in the early morning of December 12, 2004. Even though she wasn't in the right state of mind, I couldn't resist her request to come over. I was afraid that she would replace our strong sexual chemistry with someone else. I had already figured that she was probably out partying because her sentences were sloppy. Only four days had gone by since Maggie had officially broken my heart after she announced our second breakup. She called me at 2:00 a.m. I was stupid for going over to her place because I had to be at basketball practice at 7:00 in the morning. Plus, she had just broken up with me to see other guys, so why would I go over there? But I did.

On Tuesday, December 14, 2004, my arraignment began at 11:00 a.m. I waited in the cell until I was handcuffed once again and taken to the District Court of Vermont.

Since I wasn't knowledgeable about the American justice system, I was given a public defender by the name of Erin Smith—a short, petit, Caucasian woman. She briefly went over my charges and affidavit. She told me that there wasn't much she could do for me since I had already given a sworn statement to the UVM police. "The police didn't read you your Miranda rights?" she asked.

"Um, I doh know wha' dat mean."

"You know, your right to remain silent—"

"Oh, oh, No! Dey never...Dey just walk into the room and asked me what happened, and then they arrested me," I replied.

"When you appear in front the judge, you're going to plead not guilty," Erin advised.

When I finally walked into the courtroom, I appeared in front of Judge Edward J. Cashman. My heart beat faster than an African drummer.

"Arnold Henry versus the State."

"How do you plea for the charges of domestic abuse?" asked Judge Cashman.

"Not guilty," I replied confidently. He began reading the documents he held in his hands.

"So it says here that you are from Saint Lucia, right?"

I replied, "Yes Sir," and thought, *oh no, he is going to deport me.*

"Yesterday was y'all National Day," he continued. With all this commotion I hadn't even remembered my own island's National holiday.

"Oh yeah. Dats true," I said, surprised. I continued without permission. "I didn't do it...I was accused of someting I didn't do, your Honor."

"Well you will get a chance to plead your case at a mandatory pre-trial which will be held January 12, 2005 at 1:00 p.m."

I sighed. "Okay your Honor."

"Since this is a misdemeanor charge and your first offense, I will let you leave today but you must not contact Maggie Wilson in any way or form. You must also stay 100 feet away from her and appear in court whenever asked to."

"Okay your Honor." I was given a pink slip with the title, "Condition of Release," which was more informative. I basically couldn't be around or talk to Maggie anymore. I was also given information for my right to a public defender.

The judge seemed really nice so I thought that it was a done deal. Although he didn't dismiss the case, he allowed me to walk again. But I was wrong about his niceness. Judge Cashman directed a nearby officer. "Can you call the Immigration Department to find out if Mr. Henry needs to be deported from the country?"

"Yes your honor," said the officer. I almost pissed in my pants.

This is it...the end of life in America, I thought. My heart beat so fast that it felt like my whole body vibrated. The officer escorted me to a nearby telephone and dialed the number. I watched and fearfully awaited the results. The officer hung the phone up and redialed the number. He hung up once more.

"I'm getting a busy tone. You are free to leave." I sped out of the courthouse. A sense of relief came upon me as I exited that hell-house. *My nightmare was over. I had nothing else to worry about*—so I thought.

Walking through the cold, bitter winter air, in the downtown area of Burlington, I tried to focus on my final exams as well as the last week of the university's first semester. I headed to the on-campus police headquarters to retrieve my belongings. I immediately checked my cell phone. I had two missed calls from Tim and one from a blocked number. Before leaving, Officer Roberts handed me a yellow sheet of paper with the title, "Trespass Notice," which stated, "Arnold Henry is advised to remain off the following properties, buildings, campus areas: all of Redstone campus to include all residence halls, administrative buildings, roadways and shuttles traveling to Redstone for a period of six months."

"Oh well, I doh have any more reasons goin' to Redstone anyways," I mumbled.

Right before I walked out the door, Officer Roberts said to me, "The athletic director, Robert Corran, wants to see you in his office right now."

I jogged to the Patrick Gymnasium. Five minutes later, I arrived in Mr. Corran's office to find a red-hot faced Coach Brennan already seated at the table—I was astounded.

Mr. Corran advised me to sit down. "Arnold, it has been brought to my attention that you were arrested last night after an incident that took place yesterday with a young lady at this school," stated Mr. Corran.

"Yeah but I didn't do it. I swear."

Coach Brennan exploded. "I don't want you in my program anymore!"

Fuck! Fuck! Fuck! skipped through my mind.

Getting teary, I shouted out, "But Coach I didn't do anyting. I—"

Coach Brennan interrupted me. "Last night, I spoke with the young lady's mother and it wasn't a good feeling! I don't want you in my program anymore!"

So Coach knew of this from yesterday? If so, why didn't he help me? Did he just assume I was guilty?

"Coach, no, I swear," I blubbered as I placed my elbows on the table and covered my eyes with my hands.

Mr. Corran continued, "You are accused of a conduct that violates the UVM student-athlete code of conduct and we have no other choice but to suspend you indefinitely until the case has been resolved."

"I cah believe dis," I looked at them both. "How you gonna just believe her?" I asked.

"I know you hit her. You are an angry man," Coach Brennan yelled.

"Coach you tink I will put myself in dat situation?" He looked away as I tried to make eye contact.

In conclusion Mr. Corran said, "Arnold, during your suspension, you won't be able to participate in any UVM athlete activities or events. You first need to take care of your case then we will be able to deal with your future here as an athlete." I shook my head with disappointment.

"Do you want the incident to remain closed?" asked Mr. Corran.

"I don't want it to be released to the media," I responded. He made me sign a sheet to acknowledge my request.

I tried to dodge all eye contact on my way to my room. Every step of the way felt like I was walking through a hall of shame. Tim wasn't in the room at the moment. I remained indoors.

In the meantime, I searched on the internet for possible clues. I looked for Maggie in my buddy lists on my American Instant Messenger, but she appeared to be offline. I looked on my Facebook profile; we were no longer friends. I went on my school's website to search for the latest news releases—it showed at around 11:25 a.m., an article was written by Bruce Bosley from the office of athletic communication.

"Vermont Suspends Men's Basketball Player Arnold Henry: Burlington, V.T.—Arnold Henry, a freshman forward on the University of Vermont men's basketball team, has been suspended indefinitely from the team for a violation of the Student-Athlete Code of Conduct. A native of Castries, St. Lucia, Henry played in one game during the 2004-05 season, seeing two minutes of action in a 90-70 win over Marist on Nov. 26th."

On the UVM basketball website, I had been scratched off the team's roster, vanished completely—I was even cropped out of the team's group photo, which was taken earlier that year.

Tim and a few other concerned friends came to my room seeking answers. "You straight man?" Tim asked.

"Dawg, I doh even know wha' Maggie tell dem people! I am jus confuse as you. All I know dey say I push her, but dawg I eh do no harm to Maggie. I eh even know why she did dat. Dis shit is crazy," I responded.

"Man, we were about to bail you out but the UVM police said that there was no bail," Tim said.

"Damn, dey lie! I had bail…but I appreciate you tryin'."

My stomach growled from lack of food. On my way to the cafeteria, I was approached by more students. They said they just heard my name on the Channel 3 news. *How was that possible?* I thought I signed an agreement with the athletic department.

"What happened," they asked.

"I doh wanna talk about it," I replied. I was too embarrassed to say anything. Instead of following my initial plans to eat, I returned to my room to avoid more questions about the incident.

My room was my safety zone. I logged back on the internet to search for more answers. I typed in, "Vermont Suspends Arnold Henry," in the Google search engine bar. I couldn't believe what I saw. There were already forums posted on websites with the exact title that I searched for. I noticed a comment. "Saint Lucia can't be very proud of their first freshman Division I scholarship basketball player. I know I'm not."

After browsing through the forum, I remained seated, staring at the computer screen, motionless for the next few hours. I tried calling Coach Rush for assistance, but he never returned any of my calls. My headaches became worse with more worries—I worried about my Geography exam that I missed that day. But mostly I worried about the false accusations reaching the media in St. Lucia, and my mother.

Fourth Quarter

Triple Threat

Chapter 37

I Need a Miracle

My cell-phone rang—a call from an unknown local number.

"Hey, is this Arnold Henry?"

"Yeah, speaking...who dis?"

"Mike Cayole."

"Who?"

"Yeah, my dad's friend told us that a Saint Lucian plays basketball for UVM."

"Wait a minute, you from Saint Lucia?"

"My dad is...his name is Philip. But I lived there for four years when I was younger."

"I remembered one of my teammates telling me that he knew some brothers from Saint Lucia," I said.

"I played basketball for Leon Hess in Saint Lucia," Mike said.

"Hold up...you are White Mike?"

"Yeah," he chuckled.

"What! For real...I remember seeing you play back home. Wow, and you live here?"

"Yeah, with my family. I think you played against my brother two weeks ago. His name is Chris. He plays for Saint Michael's College."

After a long pause, I sighed then mentioned, "Oye, Mike, I'm in trouble."

"What...what happened? The tone in his voice went from excited to concern.

"Well, yesterday I got charge wit domestic violence."

"Damn yo. So what happens now?"

"I doh know dawg. I'm so confuse. Tomorrow I will try talkin' to someone."

"Aight...just call me if you need help with anything."

"Okay, cool...thanks."

On December 15, 2004, at about 8:30 a.m., a note slid underneath my bedroom door. "Arnold, the secretary from the office of the Dean of Students called and said that it's very important you call them back ASAP to set up an appointment with Rob Kelley today," the letter stated.

It was my first time meeting Mr. Kelley, the dean of students; just being in his office scared the living crap out of me. All he wanted was to hear my side of the incident, so I told him. The meeting was very brief, and then shortly, I received a follow-up letter signed by him, which read, "Based on preliminary evidence of your involvement in this incident, I believe your continued presence on-campus poses a threat to the well-being of other students within the University Community, and, on that basis, I am invoking an interim suspension. You must remove yourself from campus within 24 hours of this meeting and should not return to campus without receiving permission from me..."

My heart dropped to my feet and my head spun in circles. Where would I go? What would I do? Who could I call for assistance? Not only did I have to defend myself against the state of Vermont; I also needed to save myself as a student at my university, as well as an athlete. Three different cases needed to be solved. Mr. Kelley's letter had left me with only one option. It stated, "...Accompanying this note is a notification letter, including charges to which you will have an opportunity to respond in a University judicial hearing. Please read the enclosed brochure about the judicial process and refer to the Code of Student Rights and Responsibilities for information regarding judicial proceedings. As outlined in the Code, you will be afforded a hearing within 20 academic days...."

Since I had 24 hours to leave the university's premises, I took that time to finish all my exams. Luckily, I only had two exams during the week of finals. My Spanish exam was taken on time. Given that I missed my Geography exam, I showed my professor the paper that contained the details, date and time of my court appearance. *Thank God*, she was reasonable and allowed me to take it on the spot.

The campus was becoming empty because the fall semester was about to come to an end. I called my new found friend, White Mike, for advice. He told me that he would run it by his father. I prayed that night for heaven's angels to guide me through these tough times.

That same night, at 2:00 a.m. sharp, I was awakened by a phone call from a blocked number. That was the second time a blocked number had called my cell phone in two days.

"Hello? Who dis?" I asked.

"Arnold, Arnold, I am so, so, so sorry. I tried to stop the police. I swear." I recognized Maggie's voice. I figured she was drunk.

"Wha' you want," I asked her nervously. I was expecting her call, so I was using a feature on my cell phone to record the conversation. Even though I was restricted from engaging in conversation with her, I figured it would work to my advantage if I allowed her to plead her case—while recording. "Maggie why you do dis to me? Wha' you tell dem police?"

"Arnold, I didn't report you. It was my mother."

"Wha'?"

"I needed someone to talk to, so I told my mother we got into a fight…and she was concerned so she called the UVM police."

"You need to fix dis!"

"Alright, I will write a letter to your coaches and the school for you," Maggie promised. Midway through the conversation, I heard a voice demanded, "Maggie, who are you talking to?"

"Arnold," Maggie whispered. By the tone of the other female's voice, I assumed that she tried to grab the phone and end the call, but Maggie argued, "No Nicole, I have to do this."

I tried to bring up the letter of apology that Maggie suggested. "So you goin' to write da letter, right?" I asked.

"Yeah but I'm scared to get in trouble. They're going to look at me as a liar—"

"No…no! Do it. It will fix everyting. Dey not goin' tink you a liar."

"Arnold, I don't know," Maggie sobbed.

"Maggie, you doh know? What you mean, you doh know?" I yelled back. "You jus' mess up my whole life and you doh know? Well I jus' want you to know I hate you for wha' you did. I doh ever want anyting to do wit you. I never want to see you again."

"Fine! I take everything back, I take it back! I don't want anything to do with this anymore!" Maggie shouted then hung up.

I then realized that it was a bad idea to tell her that I didn't want to see or hear from her anymore. However, I had sufficient evidence recorded and saved on my phone—which included the incoming call from the blocked number, the time, and date of the call. *Enough evidence to resolve all accusations,* I thought. Though the saved recordings only played Maggie's voice and muted mine, Tim reckoned it would help get me out of trouble.

Feeling relieved, the next day I contacted my public defender and told her about Maggie's phone call and the recorded conversation. She told me that I needed to be careful because I violated the court's wishes, plus it was illegal to record a phone call without the person's consent. I respected, trusted, and obeyed Erin Smith for her legal advice. She recommended that I refrain from contacting Maggie, and also said that she would try to get that letter of apology that Maggie promised.

White Mike and his father, Philip, came to my rescue for off-campus accommodations—right on time too. If they hadn't come through, I had plans to act as a vagrant, living on the streets, and begging for food—at least until my case at the school was resolved and I was allowed back on-campus. But there was a God who answered my prayers. The Cayole family never looked at me as a criminal. In fact, they invited me into their home with open arms.

Chapter 38

Fighting For My Future

On December 15, 2004, I received a letter from Erin with copies of the affidavits. Maggie's sworn statement, written by Officer Roberts, read:

"The defendant, Arnold M. Henry (DOB: 2/11/85), was in the room with Ms. Wilson watching TV. Initially Ms. Wilson said she was comfortable with the defendant in the room but when the defendant tried to kiss her, she discussed wanting to end their relationship so that she could see other guys and it was not fair to him. Ms. Wilson advised that the defendant became angry and that is when he threw her down on the futon in her room. Ms. Wilson suffered a scratch to the right side of her neck and was screaming and crying. When Ms. Wilson screamed for him to get out, the defendant placed his hand over her mouth. Ms. Wilson stated that she knew if she screamed again he would hurt her more. Ms. Wilson advised that she was alone with the defendant in her room and asked him several times to leave and told him that he was scaring her. The defendant held on to her hands and wrists and caused pain during this encounter. Ms. Wilson described the defendant's grip to cause pain to her wrists and rated it a 3 on a scale of 1 to 5 with 5 being the most severe.

Ms. Wilson was eventually allowed to get up from the futon and she walked over toward the door to her room. She then bolted out the door and ran upstairs to a friend's room. The defendant had Ms. Wilson's keys to her room and locked her room door. Ms. Wilson encountered the defendant in the hall a short time later and collected her keys. She had a friend with her and the defendant returned the keys without incident."

My initial thought of Maggie's affidavit was, *what a big fat liar. This is what got me in trouble?* So I guessed it was white woman's words over black man's? I even started to believe that everything was a conspiracy—that Coach Brennan, Maggie's mother and the UVM police were all connected with a plot—*let's get rid of Arnold Henry.*

December 19, 2004, I watched the game at Philip's residence as the University of Vermont men's basketball team defeated Binghamton University, 83-53.

The following day, Philip Cayole and Keith Smith stood at my side as I prepared for my judicial hearing which was held at the university. I was allowed to bring one person inside the room to represent me, so I chose to bring Philip. And although he wasn't allowed to talk, his presence reminded me of a father supporting his son.

I met with Harriet Williams, Assistant Director of Student Ethics and Standards. She conducted the hearing. At first, I was nervous, but when I noticed the color of Ms. Williams's skin, my world lit up—finally, a black person running an office. It made me relax since, at the time, I thought every white person affiliated with the university was against me.

Ms. Williams proceeded. "This hearing will decide if your Interim Suspension will remain in effect or if you will be allowed to return to UVM as a student for the 2005 spring semester."

"Yes ma'am," I answered.

"Were there any witnesses present during the incident?" Ms. Williams asked. "If you have any witnesses they can contact me on the phone to speak on your behalf."

"No ma'am."

Ms. Williams then explained the appeals process. She told me that I would be given the opportunity to present my case and she would make her decision on my future at UVM.

Ms. Williams then asked me if I was responsible or not responsible for the domestic violence charges pending against me. I replied I was not responsible. I was then allowed to tell my side of the story. For better communication, I tried my best to speak proper English.

"On December 8, 2004, Maggie decided to end our relationship. She said that she wanted to see other guys. Although it broke my heart, I moved along. On December 12, 2004, Maggie called me from a party at 2:00 a.m. asking me to come over to her room. I missed her so I went. We made love and I left in the morning for basketball practice—"

"How is this story relevant to the case?" Ms. Williams asked.

"I just want to show you how she is," I said. "On December 13, 2004, Maggie and I were having a conversation on American Instant Messenger around 3:00 in the afternoon. She asked me if I wanted to come over to chill—"

"What does that mean to you?" Ms. Williams asked.

"Just hang out and do something, talk or watch TV," I replied. "I arrived at Maggie's room at 3:45 p.m. and as I entered, she told me that she was leaving to check her laundry. I sat on her futon and watched some music videos on the BET television station. A few minutes later, she returned, and joined me. We initiated a normal conversation which led into a sexual conversation; then we were no longer seated apart. Maggie said that if we had sex she didn't want me to get the idea that we were back together. I told her that it was alright. Before we got started Maggie pulled down the curtains and turned off the lights.

We started with kisses. I took off her clothes. She took off mine. Before engaging in intercourse, she picked up a condom from her desk, and then I put it on. During sex, hearing the sounds of her moaning, I dug deeper.

Suddenly Maggie was in tears. Afraid I might have hurt her, I stopped to ask her what was wrong. She said nothing. Then I asked her if she was sure, and she replied, yes. She then advised me that I should change the condom. Confused about her statement, I asked her why. She told me that she ran out of birth control and that I just needed to change it.

Still confused, I complied with Maggie's offer and quickly changed the condom. We were back in action, but this time, Maggie seemed as if she desperately needed me to ejaculate.

Maggie threw out the condom herself in the garbage. While I was putting on my boxers, Maggie got fully dressed into sweat pants and shirt. She told me that I would have to leave really soon because she was going to the gym. Again, I asked her if everything was okay."

"Why did you think something was wrong?" Ms. Williams asked.

"I asked in regards to her fast pace movements and the slamming of everything that she held in her hands. She replied that, yes, everything was okay. But I wasn't buying it. I told her that if something was wrong I need to know. She said that she was fine.

I thought that if Maggie planned to leave the room upset at me, after sexual intercourse, then I needed to know what was going through her mind.

I tried my best to calm her down. She said that we shouldn't be doing this. I asked her what she meant. We were standing in front of the futon. She shouted in my face that we shouldn't be having sex. I told her I thought that was what she wanted. But she told me that she didn't want me thinking that we were back together. I told her that I knew that it was just sex.

I then tried to gently hug her, but she pushed me. I tried again but I stumbled forward, lost my balance and landed on top of her. She screamed and told me that I should get off her. I asked her what the hell was wrong. She screamed again, asking me to get off her and saying that I was scaring her. I said, okay, and pleaded for her to talk to me. She replied that she would.

I sat on the futon, watching Maggie's every move. She got up from her seated position, and walked in front of the mirror that was nailed to her bedroom door. She tilted her head to the left side of her shoulders and gazed at the right-side of her neck for a few seconds. I asked Maggie if everything was okay. But she opened up the door and sprinted outside. I put on my clothes and since I didn't want to leave the room open, I locked it up to go searching for her. I ran down the stairs to the ground floor; she was nowhere in sight. While I was running up the stairs, I found her on the stairway of the third floor with one of her female friends. I handed her the room keys and departed without any exchange of words."

"How did she get the scratch on her neck?" Ms. Williams asked.

"I don't know. I didn't even know she got scratched. If I scratched her, I had no intentions," I replied. "It might have been my watch. I don't know...she never showed any signs of pain coming from her neck during the incident."

"So did you ever hold her down or place your hands over her mouth?"

"No ma'am...there was no reasons for me to do that," I answered. Ms. Williams started to wrap up our session.

"Is there anything else?" she asked. I was about to say no, but my peripheral vision caught Philip's hand movement of a phone being placed near his ear.

"Oh yeah," I interrupted, retrieving my cell phone. "Ms. Williams, this is the recording of the conversation between Maggie and me. She called me two nights after da incident."

I played the recordings on my speaker phone and placed it in the center of the round table for everyone to hear.

"Hmm," Ms. Williams said. "Okay Mr. Henry, I think we are finished here. I will make my decision within 48 hours and get back to you."

December 21, 2004, the Vermont men's basketball team played the University of North Carolina at Chapel Hill. Prior to game-day, Yogi and Coach K kept on ringing my phone. Their voicemails notified me that they would be attending that game. They were the two main reasons for my American hoop dream success, and I was too ashamed to deliver the disappointing news, especially to Yogi—he would have regretted recommending me to Coach K. I didn't want to be looked at as a failure in their eyes. But they were the least of my problems.

December 23, 2004: I received more pink sheets of paper from the district court. It was a court order filed by Maggie Wilson. It seemed like she appeared in front of a judge for a restraining order against me. The court ordered that I stay 200 feet away from Maggie. It was almost the exact same orders I received the first time, but this time, the orders were enforced for one year. I found it funny when Maggie had already contacted me over the phone. In addition, we'd chatted over the computer several times; and all of the times, she initiated the contact.

When I asked Maggie, "Why you doin' all dat to me?" She said that it was not in her control anymore and her mother also had a major part to play in everything that had happened. I tried my best to stay away from Maggie, but I badly wanted her to write the letter that she promised me—revealing the truth of the incident.

When I finally decided to call my mother, I shamefully lied about everything. "What I hearing about you and some girl?" asked my mother.

"Wha' you talkin' about? Where you hear dat from?" I asked, thinking, *wow, how the hell that news reached all the way to Saint Lucia.* I used everything in my system to fight back the truth—I didn't want to stress her out. My mother was better off thinking that I was continuing chasing success. Her bad leg was enough for her to worry about.

"I don't know. Somebody tell me something about you in problem with some American girl."

"Oh no, doh believe dat. Doh worry about me, Mummy. I'm doing fine."

Chapter 39

The Final Decision

For the first time in my life, I felt like I lived in a home—with a fully-blooded-related, loving, caring, and interracial family (Caucasian and Black). Christmas day felt special. I received a brown beanie as a present, but the best present was that the Cayole family was there for me when I needed them the most. They lifted me up, high enough so that I could still hang on to my dreams. Though lately, my dreams were mainly nightmares about being convicted and then deported to Saint Lucia.

I had written a letter to Coach Brennan and mailed it to his office. In that letter, I apologized for any damages I may have caused towards the program. I hadn't heard back from Coach Brennan or Coach Rush—not once. My teammates hadn't offered their help either.

My New Year opened with the decision made by the university. I received my amended decision letter from Ms. Williams in the mail. My future at the University of Vermont as a student was decided:

"Based on your testimony and the information contained in the incident report, I find you not responsible for violating the following policies: Prohibited Acts i.e. Criminal Conduct/Civil Offenses...

While you were arrested for domestic assault, I do not believe that you assaulted Ms. Wilson. I believe that the two of you argued and that you lost your balance together and fell onto the futon."

I was overwhelmed. Probably one hundred times in a row, I yelled out, "Thank you Jesus...thank you Jesus!"

I wasn't totally let off; in the letter I was notified of my punishment. I was placed on disciplinary probation through fall 2005 and I was required to attend and complete the alternative to violence group through the university's counseling center.

One case down—two more to go.

The following week, I was required to appear in court. As always, Philip stood by my side. I thought I would get the chance for the judge to hear my case—like I did with Ms. Williams—but it was adjourned for one month. The process was wasting my life and time. That day, I informed Erin Smith, my lawyer, of the school's decision to accept my return. She said that the counseling sessions could be used to my advantage if the prosecutor felt the need to pursue my case. I told Keith the news since he was the only counselor I had known. Later on, Keith conducted my weekly counseling sessions—our meetings mostly unveiled the very first chapters of my life. I spoke to Keith about many of the problems in my past, and he advised me on how I should have handled different situations.

Even though I regained my privilege to be a student at the university, it didn't necessarily mean I was back on the basketball team. For that, I needed to end my court case with the State of Vermont. I addressed Mr. Corran about my scholarship for the spring semester. If my scholarship was revoked, it was impossible for me to return to school due to lack of funds. Mr. Corran was kind enough to sustain my scholarship for the remainder of the school year.

January 10, 2005: I showed my support by attending my first basketball game as a spectator—the University of Vermont hosted Dartmouth College. Philip dropped me off at the game. I tried my best to disguise my face from the fans by covering my head with my black-hoodie. Walking through the entrance with my head bowed down, I was hesitant to lift my eyes. I quickly glanced at the team as they warmed-up. I felt envious and sad. In desperate need to hide my emotions, I made an exit back to the lobby and quickly walked to the basement of the gymnasium, to an empty, quiet hallway. I sat on the dusty floor and covered my face between my bent knees. Suicidal thoughts invaded my usually hopeful mind. I felt breathing was useless; my days ahead were pointless. To clear my thoughts, I walked all the way back to the Cayole's home—without returning to the basketball game.

The university reopened for its spring semester on January 17, 2005—by then I had moved back on-campus. If I ever needed a helping hand, the Cayole's were only one phone call away and about a 30 minute walk. I felt like a new person being back in the dorms—but on a team all by myself since all the resources that were available to student-athletes were left back in the fall semester. The only thing that felt the same was Tim still being my roommate; he was the most trustworthy individual I met at school. My social life on-campus was extinct. The false accusation had officially destroyed my image. It seemed like all eyes were on me as though I didn't belong. I assumed people were thinking, *stay away from this tall black guy. He is the guy charged with domestic violence. He beats women.* Even though I was on my best behavior and I flashed fake smiles around campus, deep down inside, the situation was eating me up.

January 20, 2005: I immediately petitioned to modify the restraining order after I noticed Maggie in my Calculus class. That was my first time seeing Maggie since the incident. And when our eyes crossed paths in the classroom, we both quickly rerouted our stares elsewhere. The petition was successful. The only change made was that I could have incidental contact with her at school. The following class period I realized Maggie wasn't in the classroom. Later I learned that she dropped out of the class which made things much easier for me. But my stress still built up. The previous semester I did exceptionally well in the classroom; I was awarded four A's and one B. This semester I found it extremely difficult to concentrate, knowing my future was at risk. I hardly participated and barely paid attention in the classroom. My attitude was lackadaisical with my usual depression phases. And due to many sleepless nights, my professors often woke me up from classroom naps.

During the month of February, the University of Vermont men's basketball team was featured on ESPN2 (The Worldwide Leader in Sports) for a total of three episodes. The popular show was called *The Season*. Every basketball season, ESPN interviewed different college sports teams. During the 2004-2005 season, the University of Vermont men's basketball team was chosen. Watching these episodes was like peeling an onion two inches from my eyes. The ESPN crew captured scenes of the players in their classrooms; at their practices; their social-lives on-campus; and highlighted action from a few basketball games. This would have been a great opportunity for me to call my mother and say, "Hey Mummy, turn the TV to ESPN...you will see me."

One Saturday night, the same night of Hip-Hop rapper Talib Kweli's music concert at the gymnasium, I received a call from a blocked number. "Arnold?" said the recognizable drunken voice.

"Wha' do you want Maggie," I said as I lay in bed, alone in the room.

"I really want to see you...Can you please meet me downstairs?" she asked.

"Why?" I asked. "You know I cah be nex' to you...why you doin' dis to me?"

"Please Arnold, I won't call the cops...I'm tired of all this shit...I really miss you."

Feeling like I needed to maintain a friendly relationship with Maggie (for the sake of her written, truthful letter) I met her outside of Harris-Millis dormitory.

"I miss you so much Arnold," she expressed with a hug.

"Maggie, I really need dat letter from you," I begged, escaping her embrace.

"I know...I screwed up...I just don't want people to think I'm a liar...you know?"

"Yeah, buh it can help me get back on da team."

"I will think about it…but I want you to come over tonight…I want you," she demanded.

I was so naïve, hopeful, and confused that I went with her. But later on, I finally realized that Maggie just wanted to see me for her own conveniences. Every time I went over to her room on Redstone Campus, I broke the laws of the school and the district court.

In the month of March, the University of Vermont men's basketball team ended their season with an overall record of 25 wins and 7 losses. For the third consecutive year, they became the America East Conference Champions; they had also advanced to their third NCAA Division I National Tournament appearance. During spring break, I watched the game alone in my bedroom, as UVM upset Syracuse in the first round of the national tournament—their first ever national tournament victory. It was an epic battle that I wished I could have been part of. UVM's season ended after their loss to Michigan State in the second round of the tournament. That year, North Carolina Tar Heels won their fourth title after being crowned the national champions.

With Coach Brennan finally retired (after 19 seasons), there were speculations that the new head coach was going to be the current assistant coach of the University of Maryland men's basketball team. I was hopeful that I would be able to return to the team. UVM current associate head coach, Jesse Agel, was also fighting for the head coach position. You might think that after 17 seasons under the wings of Coach Brennan, he would easily be hired as the new head coach. Well, he was overlooked and the new head coach of the UVM men's basketball was—as intended—Maryland's Coach Mike Lonergan. Coach Lonergan brought in his own coaching staff. I was pleased with the change; surprisingly, more than half of the players on the team felt the same.

With the conclusion of the season, I tried my best to deal with my court cases by cooperating and being in attendance at my weekly meetings with my counselor, Keith Smith. I was only required to attend seven sessions but at the end of the semester I had accumulated fourteen. From the month of January to April, my court cases were adjourned four times. Four months wasted. I needed to get this dealt with in order for Mr. Corran to make a decision on my future as an athlete.

May 9, 2005: Philip and I went to the District Court of Vermont, expecting something new. Erin, my public defender was finally able to get something out of the prosecutor other than an adjournment. She provided the prosecutor with a letter from Keith Smith outlining my fourteen counseling sessions and somehow provided Maggie's letter. At the end, Erin and the prosecutor signed on a plea agreement. I pled no contest. The charges were reduced to Disorderly Conduct and I was given a five-month deferred sentence. I also paid a $200.00 charitable contribution to the Victims of Crimes Fund. I was told that if I fulfilled the general conditions of my probation, then my sentence would never actually come to pass, and instead, my record would be expunged on October 9, 2005. That same day, I met with my probation officer; I thought he would be strict with me, but it seemed as if he had bigger issues to deal with.

Two cases down—one more to go.

The verdict of my court case had given me more room to breathe. The sun shone a little in my world. The ball was now in Mr. Corran's court, and as the athletic director, his final decision counted the most. I was confident about the restoration of my dreams.

On May 16, 2005, Erin wrote a letter to Mr. Corran on my behalf. In that letter she provided information with my plea agreement. She also wrote, "Arnold has been an extremely conscientious client, and he has taken his duties to address his behavior seriously. In point of fact, he has been much more assiduous than most clients charged with much more serious behavior. He has been forthright with me, respectful and receptive, and I believe he has the character necessary to learn from his mistakes and not repeat them. In my conversation with the alleged victim, I believe she feels similarly. In fact, she indicated to me that the process Arnold has been undergoing has been 'taken too far.'

I believe Arnold to be an individual who has earned a second chance, and I hope he will be given that chance by yourself and those with whom you will meet to discuss his eligibility for re-entry onto the UVM basketball team, and a related scholarship. I would venture to say that Arnold's learning experience, taken seriously, is one by which the whole team can grow stronger."

Every day I patiently waited for the Athletic Director's decision. I had not only waited during the spring semester, I was now waiting during the summer vacation. In the meantime, while everyone returned to their homes, I remained on-campus to work as a painter making $9.00 an hour. As one of the university's workers, I had the privilege to reside in their selected dormitory. After my nine-to-five job, White Mike would picked me up and we would go to hoop at Pomeroy Park (a local outdoor basketball court). Then in the month of June, the pressure was on and I needed answers from Mr. Corran before it was too late.

When I received the decision letter from Mr. Corran, I fell to my knees and knocked my forehead on the floor of my room. One more look at the content of the letter made me feel like inserting a knife through my chest. "Arnold Henry, you will never be allowed to play basketball for the University of Vermont." The letter never broke down or described the nature of my expulsion. It just seemed like Mr. Corran's final decision had already been made back in December, or maybe Coach Brennan had a major role to play. Why did he make me believe that things would be better once my court case was finalized?

I had one final option left. I appealed Mr. Corran's decision to the Appeals Board in the care of the Dean of Students. Seated at a round table with more than ten random affiliates of the university, pleading my case, I realized that the fight for my future as a student-athlete was over. The athletics department did not even offer me any assistance; they just left me to find my own way home. I lost my appeal.

It was already July and I was desperate for help. I needed to find a college that would grant me a full basketball scholarship. I learned that I could not play right away if I was to transfer to another NCAA Division I basketball program; in other words, I would only be able to practice with the team and sit out for the entire 2005-2006 season. If I wanted to play right away then a NCAA Division II program or a junior college program were better options.

I reached out to Coach K for any suggestions—after all, he was the only caring coach I had left in America. During our phone conversation, I broke down and told him what had happened to me over the past few months. I expected Coach K to disown me, but he was reasonable and willing to direct me towards another opportunity. Coach K recommended that I attend a junior college. He gave me two numbers of coaches that might be interested in my position (power-forward). One school was in the state of Arizona and the other one was from the state of Oklahoma. I tried my luck and called the coach from Oklahoma.

"Hello, Men's Basketball, Mike St. John, speaking."

"Hey, Coach, Arnold Henry," I said. "Coach Bruce Kreutzer told me dat you lookin' for a post player?"

"Oh yes. I was expecting your call. So, tell me, you played for the University of Vermont?"

"Yeah Coach buh it did not work out."

"Well we have a place for you here. I understand that you're from Saint Lucia?"

"Yeah Coach."

"We have a six foot ten player on our team from St. Vincent," Coach St. John said.

"Oh really?"

I thought that it would be a great idea to play alongside someone with my Caribbean background, plus my options and time were limited. "His name is Shawn King. Have you heard of him?" I remembered playing against other players from St. Vincent, but Shawn King didn't run through my thoughts.

"No Coach buh I know of St. Vincent," I answered.

"Well, Arnold, I believe Carl Albert State College is the right move for you. You will be able to come in, play right away, and be a starter. The forward position is wide open for you."

Chapter 40

NJCAA Division I
Fall Semester

I was aboard the Greyhound Bus reminiscing about everything I left behind—my dreams, hope, and memories of being a NCAA Division I superstar. Two years in America and I hadn't developed a steady home. I carried four pieces of luggage; everything else I owned was left in the Cayole's storage-room. I had a second chance. My strategy was simple, *one year at this junior college in Oklahoma, and then I'll be right back playing NCAA Division I basketball.*

I glanced into the distance. There weren't many buildings on the outskirts of these States, just farm houses. I sat in the window-seat and wrapped my winter-jacket around my upper-body to keep myself warm from the air-conditioned bus. While my stomach growled most of the time, I used bottles of water to fill up the empty spaces. I couldn't afford meals; I was saving my money for any later expenses because I didn't know what to expect.

From Burlington, Vermont to Fort Smith, Arkansas was over 48 hours on the bus. A one-way plane flight was not affordable; the bus trip saved me over six hundred dollars. My trip consisted of four transfers: Boston, New York City, St. Louis, and Kansas City. I was so tired that I dragged and lagged along whenever I had to transfer my four pieces of luggage from bus to bus. As my new destination became nearer, my hands perspired. I constantly rubbed my hands on my blue jeans.

"Fort Smith, Arkansas," announced the bus-driver. As soon as I stepped off the bus, I stretched my arms to the sky as high as possible, inhaled, and then exhaled to a yawn that lasted longer than usual. My butt was relieved at last. The cool, country air smelt fresh and clean. At first, it looked like I was in the middle of nowhere. But as the bus drove off, I realized civilization was up ahead. I picked up my luggage and went in search of a sign that read my name. Eventually, I met my third American coach. "Arnold, nice to meet you…Coach Mike St. John." At last I could match a face to his country-speaking voice. He was a Caucasian male with a bald head and a black beard that surrounded his mouth and chin.

"Hey Coach, nice to meet you too."

"How was your trip?" he asked, helping me with my bags to his car.

"Long…very long," I complained. He chuckled; his laughed sounded like he was gasping for air.

Poteau, Oklahoma was another thirty minute drive. The ride instantly put me to sleep. The car's hard stop woke me up.

"We're here," said Coach.

I wiped the sleep from my eyes. We were parked in front of a light-pinkish brick building. There were similar buildings surrounding it. It looked like a village with small huts. "You'll be rooming with Shawn and Jay," Coach advised.

I entered through the front door to an already organized room with one unused bed. Shawn King and Jay Elam, who were lying on their beds watching television, introduced themselves. It looked like they were already settled in.

"Tomorrow I'll get you squared away with the school's admission, your class schedule, and your meal plan," Coach mentioned as he placed my last bag on my bed and exited the room.

I remained silent until Shawn asked, "How was your trip?" He had a heavy Caribbean accent and a deep voice—which reminded me of the Vincentian athletes I had met from the Inter-Secondary School Windward Island games.

"Boi, dat was crazy. I fought I was gonna die," I cried out.

"Oh yeah." He got up from his bed to grab a bottle of water from the mini refrigerator. It was then I saw his six-foot-ten, lean frame. I had to look up.

"Boi, you really tall ih." Shawn and Jay joined together in laughter.

"If you think Shawn tall, what you leave for me?" Jay, who was the shortest and looked up to me while standing, asked while trying to sound like he was also from the Caribbean. Jay was Caucasian with ears that poked out. "So why you left Vermont and came here?" he asked.

I slightly paused, and murmured, "Uh, umm…Uh, I jus' eh like it deh no more. It too cold over deh," I said, then changed the subject. "You have anyting to eat?" I asked.

Even though I had two roommates, I was happy with them. They were kind, clean, and respectful. The room was quite spacious; but my bed was not. My six-foot-two, twin-size bed meant, as I slept the night away, five inches of my legs hung off the end.

The next day, I woke up early to plan and catch up with the other students. I had already missed two days of classes. Carl Albert State College opened for the fall semester earlier than the two previous schools I'd attended in America. Before I walked out the door, I needed a tour guide. I approached Shawn. "Yo, where is Coach office and da rest of da school?"

"Every ting pile up over deh," Shawn replied. I laughed really hard.

"Serious ting?"

"Yeah mun, you ting you at Vermont or wha'? A small school dat deh."

"Oh irie." I pointed in the direction of the buildings. "So I just walk over deh?"

"Yeah. You go see everyting over deh."

My walk to Coach's office was brief. There wasn't much to see or hear except trees blowing, birds chirping, and squirrels chattering. The environment was clean and quiet, a perfect, small country-side town. I expected to see cowboys riding around on horses and farms on every street corner.

I learned that Coach St. John was my academic advisor, the athletic director, as well as the head and assistant coach for the men's basketball team. He was like the boss and the manager of his own job—either he didn't like working with others, or he just couldn't afford to hire new employees. I called him a jack of all trades. Whenever I went to his office, he was like an octopus—multi-tasking and moving in a very fast pace. I was lucky to obtain my class agenda during my first visit.

In college terms, I was known as a sophomore—a second year student. I sustained the same Computer Science studies as my major and ensured that I had a sufficient number of classes for the fall semester, since I only had a one-year scholarship. I took eight classes in one semester, an equivalent to twenty-two college hours (12 is the minimum requirement for the number of college hours taken by student-athletes). Academic wise, it was my main concern to graduate on time (May, 2006).

With my class schedule taken care of, I thought of my four priorities: my God always came first, followed by my immediate family, then academics and lastly, basketball. Nothing else intervened; at least not until I added a relationship with a female into the equation.

Throughout my first week on my new campus, I met with all my teammates. Apart from Shawn and me, there were two other international players, one from Jamaica and the other was a seven-footer from the Netherlands. We had a player from Hawaii and three New Yorkers. Most of my teammates were Black—which reminded me of my military basketball team. They were more respectful than my past teammates—likely because of the diversity amongst us.

It was easy to make friends in Poteau, even though I was still in a predominantly white town. Whenever I walked by a stranger on-campus, I always was greeted with big-white-smiles, friendly waves, and hellos. The students, who mostly drove pick-up trucks, always offered me a ride when I roamed the streets. It felt like I was finally welcome in America. And at last, I felt equality.

One month later, I realized a junior college's basketball program was like a downgrade to the successes that I had already accomplished. Coach St. John had no assistance with his coaching. It was my first time being on a team in America with only one coach running the show. Sometimes, I felt like he had a loose screw in his brains. And judging from his operations and team management—he was never concerned with players who were in pain or anyone who complained. "No pain, no gain," he'd say.

As always, basketball season started with conditioning. Guess who was our strength and conditioning coach? Coach St. John. While some of my teammates stayed up late at night, my roommates and I displayed discipline by lying down to sleep by 10:00 in the evening. Weekday mornings we had to be up by 5:30 a.m. to run up Wolf Mountain. It was the steepest hill I'd ever seen in America with an elevation of 1,503 feet above sea level. These dark, early mornings were very chilly. Coach picked us up with the school's minivan; dropped us at the bottom of the hill where he started the race, and then drove up to wait for us at the peak. It was actually scary. High bushes ran alongside the road and there were no buildings in sight. All I heard were crickets creaking and frogs ribbiting. I had a phobia of frogs so I always ran in the middle of the road. Running up Wolf Mountain can either make you or break you. I wanted to be the best, so I ran. At least we weren't running up Cavanal Hill, located in Poteau—the world's tallest hill at 1,999 feet.

The total distance we ran was about three miles—from the bottom of the hill to the top. For the first few, my calf muscles paid for it. During the day, I walked around the campus like I was crippled. However, a limp in my walk was a minor issue. One morning, I felt so sick that I had no idea what was wrong with me. I placed my hands near my neck and it was on fire. I should have stayed in bed to sleep but I couldn't risk my progress. My theory was simple: never show weakness.

"You sure you aight?" Shawn asked after noticing my face. "You know I can tell Coach you eh feeling good."

"Nah dawg, I good, I cah miss nutting," I said, crawling out of bed. I wanted to show-off my toughness.

My stubbornness made me collapse about five minutes after the start of our morning race up the hill, and since my slow start had left me behind the pack, I was alone on the cold, dark road. As I breathed harder and harder, gasping for oxygen, my blurry vision made the stars look distorted. I closed my eyes.

When I opened them, I was gazing at a bright florescent bulb. I found myself lying in a hospital bed with an IV tube stuck in my arm. A white man wearing a white lab-coat was present.

"Wha' happen?" I asked, realizing I was still in my sweat-suit.

"You were rushed into the emergency unit after a driver found you lying in the middle of the road. Give thanks to the driver who didn't run over you." My eyebrows came together, fighting off the sudden headache rush from sitting upright on the bed.

"Wha'?"

"It's nothing to worry about though. You're probably suffering from dehydration. Do you drink sufficient water throughout the day?"

"Not really," I answered.

"Well you might want to make it a habit."

After filling out some paperwork, Coach picked me up and dropped me off at my room. He had excused me from daily practices. I spent the entire day resting and consuming plenty of fluids.

The next day, I was back in action on Wolf Mountain. Coach wanted each of us to clock at least 24 minutes or better for every time we ran up the summit, that way he knew we were progressing. I wasn't even capable of running one mile in eight minutes, far less three, but I tried my very best, unlike my other teammates, especially the freshmen who just walked the entire race. Sometimes Coach just had to pick them up with the minivan on our way down the mountain. Their lack of effort was sickening to me. My times got better through the month and I clocked a best time of 25:12.

Our official practice sessions started much earlier than usual; enough time to develop our team chemistry. The gym was located three-minutes from my room. The size of the gym was probably less than 1,500 seats which was way smaller than UVM's gymnasium. One thing I hated about Coach St. John's intense sessions was that he never gave us water breaks. He considered it to be a waste of his time since we only practiced for two hours. Another thing about Coach was that he showed obvious favoritism towards Shawn; the entire playbook revolved around him. I had to come out of my comfort zone in the low post area to play an unfamiliar position on the wing, to feed the ball to Shawn who posted on the inside—which was the game plan I was used to (the inside game). Though, it was true, Shawn was taller, a tremendous athlete, and hard worker, I felt that he could have been so much better under another coach's supervision. I started questioning Coach St. John's credibility. It felt like I wasn't becoming a better player at all. Coach would have made a great assistant but I didn't believe he had the power to make the right decisions on the court.

We developed our individual skills and strength by ourselves. That was the difference between the junior college I attended and NCAA Division I basketball programs. On my free time, I got stronger in the weight room. I worked on my skills from what I had already learned from my previous coaches. I also watched the NBA superstars on television to learn something new. Whenever I set foot in the gym, I worked my butt off at practice. I was the heaviest and strongest on the team. I was the fourth tallest player. Even though I was six foot seven, weighing 225 pounds, I was also one of the fastest runners. I competed in every drill—pushing myself to the point of nearly puking. I demonstrated tough defense by getting up in my teammate's face. I showed leadership by encouraging everyone. I wanted my team to be winners so I started with myself.

I was no Michael Jordan. I figured replicating Ben Wallace's game was my best bet. Just like Ben, I was dedicated to becoming the best defender and the best go-getter rebounder in the game. Since everyone wanted to be a scorer, I found passion in defending, rebounding, and performing plays that never appeared on the stat sheet, such as taking charges (drawing offensive fouls) or hustling on the court—anything to contribute to victories. I also mirrored Ben's image with my combed-out-afro that boosted my height an inch or two; my pair of UVM's white-long-socks that reached to my knees; a head band around my head and wrist bands around my arms. I tried to get his number 3 jersey number but the number was already taken, so I settled for number 44, one number less than my UVM jersey number.

Chapter 41

Love and No Basketball

It was love at first sight when I laid eyes on Alice Hammond—a beautiful freckle face, Australian—a natural redhead with dyed-blonde hair, who was also a sophomore. Of course, I was attracted by the down-under accent, *"G'day mate,"* but my heart melted when I found out that she played on the women's basketball team. I was being patient, waiting for the right moment to make a connection with her. And I feared my accusations from Vermont would scare her away.

I didn't want to continue living my life fearful of commitments, so one Saturday evening I approached Alice at a house party we both attended. I can't recall the initial words we exchanged, but I found out it was easy to communicate with her and we had an instant connection.

We did everything together—breakfast, lunch, and dinner; studied together; and my favorite moments were our flirtatious, one-on-ones at the gym, improving our strength, endurance, and basketball skills. Both of our families lived overseas so we supported each other, financially, emotionally, and socially. Her sparkling white smile and blue eyes brought joy to my life. I wanted to be the best boyfriend ever, so I sporadically wrote her love poems and notes from my heart. She was so appreciative of my poems that she hung them on her walls next to her bed for all to see. After long periods of classes and basketball practices, we met in her dorm-room. Her roommate was never around so Alice and I had plenty of evenings alone. We became lovers within a month of knowing each other. This was my chance to love again with an open heart and, even though things were moving hasty, it truly felt right. I told her about my incident with my ex-girlfriend. She didn't think any differently of me.

November 1, 2005: I had just finished watching the victory of Alice's first home basketball game for the 2005-2006 season opener. Alice played the same forward position as me and she was a starter. Whenever she contributed towards a great play, the audience chanted, "Aussi, Aussi, Aussi, Oye, Oye, Oye!" But I would chant, "Dats my baby!" Alice's performances hyped me up for my very own home-opener.

Before we charged on the court for warm-ups, we met in the locker-room in preparation for the game and to get Coach's revisions for the match-up. I was all suited up, looking like a miniature version of Ben Wallace. I was so excited that I was shouting, bouncing, and pacing around the locker-room, trying to excite and pump-up my teammates. "Dat is it! You ready?" I yelled at their faces.

Minutes after, my smile turned upside-down as Coach wrote the names of the starting-five on the whiteboard for everyone to see. No Arnold Henry for the starting five line-up. I thought, *unbelievable, after working harder than everyone else.* Before we exited the locker room, everyone huddled in for the Lord's Prayer. Then my teammates chanted, "1, 2, 3, team, 4, 5, 6, family." I felt isolated; I wasn't feeling part of this family. I wanted answers to my starting on the bench. As everyone jetted out on the court for warm-ups, I stayed in. Coach and I were left behind.

"Coach, I didn' com' here to sit on da bench," I protested.

"Me neither Arnold," he responded, making fun of the situation. As I walked out to the court, I accepted his decision and tried my best to focus on the game-plan.

The small community of Poteau showed up in numbers to welcome back their home college team. The walls of the gym were decorated with posters of, "Let's go Vikings," designed by our cheerleaders. And our school mascot, the Viking, entertained our fans.

I waited on the bench for my opportunity to get in the game. Every time Coach walked alongside our bench, I looked him straight in his eyes and kind of shrugged my head so that he could notice me. I even tried invading his walking path by stretching my legs. My selfishness and immaturities neglected the fact that my teammates were playing well.

I understood that scoring points, putting up numbers, and winning games would help me achieve another scholarship from a well-established NCAA Division I program, so I needed to start early to accomplish these goals. I wanted to carry the team on my back by being the leader, since I was the only experienced NCAA Division I player on the team. But Coach was not allowing that to happen.

I looked back at Alice, who sat behind our bench in the bleachers. The frown on her face almost brought tears to my eyes. She felt my pain because she knew how hard I worked for that starting position.

About thirteen minutes passed into the first half when Coach substituted me in, a few minutes later he took me out. In just three minutes, I scored three points and grabbed three rebounds. In the second half, same story—I came off the bench and spent just two minutes on the floor before being taken out, for what I thought was just a simple mistake; I turned-over the possession. Upset, jogging off the court towards the bench, I asked Coach, "Why you take me out?"

He wasn't too pleased that I questioned his authority. He angrily ordered, "Sit the fuck down!" I quickly sat down to save myself from any further embarrassment in front of Alice who witnessed everything. Well, for my actions, I ended up watching the remainder of our blowout victory, 111-65, on the bench. In total, I played only five minutes.

After the game, in the locker room, Coach yelled, "I just hate when players complain for playing time, especially right before a basketball game." Everyone knew Coach was referring to me.

I muttered, "Den why you tell me to com' here?"

"What?" Coach shouted, daring me to repeat my words. I kept my head down.

After receiving sympathy from Alice who always thought I played great, I walked into my room. I dodged everyone else and slammed the doors closed as quickly as I opened them.

"Boi, you aight?" Shawn asked as he entered our bedroom.

"Yeah I safe," I lied.

I remained silent for the rest of the night; resting on my bed, recalling the very first phone conversation I had with Coach, *you will be able to come in, play right away and be a starter...a starter...a starter...*It made me wonder, *hmm, maybe, Coach told all his recruits the same thing.*

The next day though, after a good night's sleep, I figured I better face up to the situation. After I finished my classes for the day, I confronted Coach in his office. Coach was busy as usual with paper work but he took time to allow me to plead my case.

We sat face to face across his desk. After I stuttered a few of my first words, I kept my head down and I said to him, "Coach, it seem like everywhere I go I make da wrong decision—"

Before I could start my next sentence, he interrupted me politely. "Can I have some input as you speak?"

"Um, yeah," I replied, then continued, "...I jus' wanna know why I got treated like dat last night? I mean I work so hard and dis is wha' happen to me."

"Arnold you should have never complained last night about playing time," Coach preached.

"Buh Coach, I really wanna play—"

"I want to play too..." I rolled my eyes. His jokes became annoying. "...You are lucky you even got to get in the game...I

193

usually don't allow guys to play at all after complaining for playing time."

"Coach I understan' buh I jus' wanna help da team win."

"You let me do the coaching, Arnold."

"Buh Coach, I'm like da hardest worker on da team."

"And you just continue doing that."

Coach's last statement kept me speechless. I slowly placed my head on my knees and covered my face, but my sniffing made Coach St. John realized that I was actually crying. Coach remained silent for a minute. He broke the silence. "Before you can practice today, you have to apologize to the team."

I wiped off my tears. I mulled over the discussion on my way to the locker room. As I suited up for practice, I figured Coach had a point—it was a team and I mustn't be selfish. Obeying Coach's wishes, I apologized to the team, telling them that I was sorry for my behavior and promised that it would never happen again. They said, "It's all good...we're family over here." I knew they accepted my apology when I received hugs.

I went on to have another great practice. Before I proceeded outside the gym, I met Coach in the locker-room. I stretched out my hand. "I'm sorry for las' night, Coach." He clasped his hand with mine to terminate the tension we had.

"Just continue working hard, Arnold," he said.

The closer it got to Christmas day, the more homesick I became—a lot of it had to do with Homecoming and Thanksgiving— two of America's annual traditional celebrations. It was a week of enjoyment with various activities to attend. Both celebrations included some kind of family involvement. For Homecoming, most of my schoolmates' families came to visit which made me wish for my mother's presence. I just had to imagine what it would be like if my mother was actually here. *Would she be proud of me? Would she be as happy as the families I glanced at?* I always pretended that she was in the bleachers, watching me play, chanting, "That's my boy!" At least Alice was here. She helped erase flashbacks of my disappointments at the University of Vermont. The loss of my first scholarship was still a burning fire in my heart that somehow made me feel cold on the outside.

One night, lying in bed with Alice, with thoughts of averaging less than five minutes per game, I kept on repeating, "I hate my life...I hate my life!" I broke down in tears, thinking about the betrayal of all the people who I'd trusted with my life and basketball career. Alice was there to dry my eyes, rinse my inner flames, and brighten up my cold, murky days by just holding me tightly throughout my cries and telling me that everything is going to be alright.

I sought happiness amongst my team. If only Coach could have moved on from our differences to give me the opportunity to assist us to victory. He even started a freshman over me; the same guy who I remembered overtaking on our runs up Wolf Mountain during our pre-season workouts. This was unbelievable since everyone knew I was the hardest worker. I had to admit it though—making the right decision was quite difficult for Coach, because all the bench-warmers complained for playing time. Some players truly deserved to be on the court more often, while others' efforts were only hurting our teamwork and chemistry. Seeing that Coach St. John was serious about players' complaining for playing time, I'd found an alternative to show my support from the bench, by chanting for the unit on the court. "Let's go!" or "Defense!"

After every home game, I remained in the gym by myself to either work on my endurance or develop my skills. Alice always joined me as I sprinted back and forth for each shot I missed. I recited, *if I'm not getting enough playing time, then I am still going to work on my skills until I become my Coach's first option on the team.*

November 14, 2005: we played Redlands (ranked 7th in the National Junior College Athletics Association). I played only 3 minutes. We lost. Putting on a fake smile, I remained calm and patient in regards to my playing time. Afterwards, I went back to the gym alone to work on my game.

Next, we played Seminole. I played a few minutes in the first half. We lost in double overtime. Shawn, our center, fouled out, but Coach left me sitting on the bench. We were on a three game losing streak and the season was not looking promising—I blamed it on bad coaching decisions and lack of teamwork. Our overall team record was now four wins and four losses. After the game, Alice joined me to work on strength in the weight-room.

November 18, 2005 was the last day of school before our Thanksgiving break. It was also Alice's birthday. I surprised her by delivering half a dozen red roses during one of her classes. These were actions that I had never done for any of my past relationships. I asked one of my brave male friends to drop off the bouquet while the professor and her classmates were present to make a more romantic scene. Then, I stood outside to watch her reaction through the upper glass door. At first glance, she was thrilled but when she heard, "Aw," from her classmates, she felt slightly embarrassed. But the continuous smile on her face overruled her embarrassment and increased my happiness.

By the end of the day, most of the students had already left home for our one-week break. Again, our basketball games caused us to remain on-campus. The school became emptier, quieter, and boring. I felt we should have gotten the same chance to go home.

I called my mother to decrease my ongoing homesickness. "Mummy, how tings?"

"Not too bad. I still deh struggling with my leg."

"Your leg eh heal yet?"

"No my boy," she cried. "The doctors don't know what's wrong with my leg. Every medicine they gave me, nothing working." I held onto the phone tightly.

"Dats crazy," I said.

Her voice softened and dragged. "My boy, try to hold onto every dollar you can get because I cannot even work. The two-cent Rosalie giving for babysitting Kobie is what me and the children surviving on."

"Ok Mummy, doh worry bout me. I'm okay. Jus' try to focus on getting your leg better," I said, and then changed the topic. "So how's Marvin and Marva?"

"The children okay. They still go to school."

"Dats good—"

"Oh…," my mother interrupted, "…Oh yeah, you haven't heard about Marvin and his basketball?"

"What?"

"The boy tall like a coconut tree. He made his school team. He playing for Bocage Secondary School now." I was proud of Marvin.

While my younger brother participated at the Inter-Secondary School basketball tournament in Saint Lucia, I was going through a couple of early morning practices to prepare for a challenging schedule ahead.

On November 21, 2005, we rode on the bus, 6 hours to Altus, Oklahoma to play against Western. We had defeated Western during Homecoming Week—this time they handed us our fourth straight lost, 72-61. I watched the full 40-minutes of the game on the bench. From my seated position, it was embarrassing to watch some of my teammates play selfishly and sloppy. We went to the locker room to change but I kept my gear on, due to the fact that I didn't even break a sweat. *Coach is still punishing* me, I thought.

I heard one of my teammates ask, "Why didn't Arnold get in the game if nobody wants to rebound?" *At least someone missed me on the court...someone noticed my presence was needed.*

November 22, 2005: we had early morning practice. I could have easily been discouraged (because I truly believe a coach can ruin a player's career), but I pushed myself in practice to prove to Coach that I deserved to get substituted for the three upcoming games at the Road Runner Tournament in Lufkin, Texas.

November 24, 2005: Thanksgiving Day, we played the 25th ranked Lon Morris. Being on a losing streak, we were desperate for a win. But the competition looked challenging. I expected to ride the pine again. But I stayed upbeat, cheered and clapped for my teammates who worked their butts off. And then the unexpected happened: "Arnold—" Coach yelled. That was all I needed to hear. I sprinted immediately before Coach could finish. I knew everyone along my path felt the wind; it took me about one second to remove my warm-up shirt and report to the substitution area.

Upon entering the game, I felt like I had reconnected with life. I was focused. I had to prove myself with consistency.

For the small number of minutes I played, I was all over the stats sheet. I crashed the boards. I scored some points. I stole the ball. I blocked shots. I had a point to prove, and I think I did just that. As I stood at the free throw stripe, a referee smiled at me. "Hey number 44, great hustle." I blushed.

"Arnold, good job. You played well," my teammates said—even Coach St. John commended my performance. But at the end of the game, I felt that my input didn't get it done. I felt like I had gotten in the game too late to save us from losing again. The final score was 92-70.

On the way back to our hotel-rooms, our star player, Shawn, surprised me with some information. "Yo, Arnold, get ready to play tomorrow. Jus' keep your head up. You go start tomorrow. I beg Coach," he said. That set off the waterworks running down my face. I felt like I had won the victory but I believed it should not have gone down like that—Coach should have known from our pre-season that I was a hard working performer.

November 25, 2005: I started in my first game of the season. We played at Angelina College. Everyone in the arena thought that we got cheated by the referees. Their calls favored only Angelina. Despite the referee, I thought that my teammates played great. I had one of my best games: 10 points, 9 rebounds (3 offensive), 2 assists, 1 block shot, and 1 steal. I also had my first dunk of that season. But I still blamed myself because I felt like my lack of input had only contributed to another loss, 75-72.

On November 26, 2005, we played number 14 ranked Kilgore. We defeated them to end our six-game losing streak. The victory finally brought happiness to our team. The highlight of the game for me was when I snatched an offensive rebound in mid-air and slam-dunked it home. My teammates said that I jumped so high my head was above the inner white box of the backboard. Our overall team record was now five wins and six losses.

On December 1, 2005, I wrote in my diary:

Dear Diary,
I am proud of myself for making it this far...

Chapter 42

Commitments

Today's Date: January 8, 2006
Time: 10:06 a.m.

Dear Diary,
I just returned from a three week vacation in Saint Lucia, after being away from home for over eighteen months. I am now back in cold Poteau, reuniting with Alice who is now back too, from Australia. I was missing her so much, but now, I am missing my mother, brother, and sister.
My mother has lost some weight. She and Lucius are now separated. Thank God for that! Her left inner-ankle looked worse; it is now darker than her brown skinned complexion, with pinkish spots and it looks like someone bit a piece of it. The view was hideous.
Marva is more mature and responsible. She helps my mother around the house by washing dishes, sweeping the floors, and washing clothes. And she also knows how to cook. My young sister is not even looking like the teenager she once was. She is chubby, taller, and her chest got bigger.
I was glad to have the opportunity to see Marvin play his last two games of the Inter-Secondary School Basketball Tournament. He was the star player on his team, winning the senior championship. He was awarded the same awards as me when I played back in 2001, most blocked shots and the overall most valuable player trophies.

January 18, 2006: Alice's basketball team was ranked number 16 in the nation, with an overall record of 16 wins and 2 loses. I envied their glories, giving all the credit to Coach Jeff Tadtman. Although he was like Coach St. John, a one-man coaching staff, he was smart enough to utilize his talented players to win games. His team record said it all.

On the other hand, we still struggled to get more than ten wins, with only seven wins so far. We received our tenth loss, 48-44, against Northern-Tonkawa. I scored 10 points—the second highest after Shawn's 15 points.

Two games previous, we slipped by the Rose State Raiders, achieving our eighth win, 84-76. Every game was an improvement with my scoring. This time, I played one of my best games of the season, scoring my season high of 14 points (six of seven shots from the field), with 12 rebounds (six offensive), 2 assists, and 2 steals. And as usual, there were other stats that never show up on the sheet, such as sacrificing my body by diving for loose balls, committing offensive fouls by taking charges, and communicating efficiently on defense.

Next-up was our conference opener for the Bi-State East Conference—these were the wins that counted the most because only the two top teams from each division advanced to the regional tournament—and the winner got an invitation to the National Tournament. Our current team record, 8-13, wasn't posing a threat to our opponents. We all realized that our losing record meant that we weren't mentally prepared as a team. In the locker-room, Coach advised, "We have eight challenging games ahead of us. Let's not worry about our current team record." Coach's words were encouraging. "We still have a chance to clinch a playoff berth for the Region 2 Tournament with these upcoming games," he continued.

On January 30, 2006, we faced our first conference matchup against Northeastern Oklahoma A&M College. I always knew we had a great team; I just never believed in Coach St. John's basketball system. We all knew the consequences of a loss, so for the first time, our team actually united as one; but sometimes players on the court cannot determine the outcome of a game. Unfortunately, we were outcoached as always. We lost our first conference game, 90-78, which set our overall team record as 8-14, and 0-1 in the Bi-State East Conference. Only seven scheduled conference games were left to make-up for our loss.

I was approaching the legal drinking age in America—21. Around that time, I was hoping that the drawers of my dresser would be filled with letters from potential NCAA Division I schools. Instead, I only had offers from Division II schools with coaches who watched my games throughout the season—I didn't want it. Coach's lack of effort to find schools for us was heart-breaking and stressful. If a player doesn't put up numbers like Lebron James, there's a high possibility he'll never get a scholarship offer, especially from a NCAA Division I program. My overall stats weren't that impressive. But my games during the spring-semester showed my improvements—thanks to playing more minutes. However, as I looked into my future, I started to think, *what NCAA Division I coach in their right mind would ever want to recruit at our school with our losing record?*

Two days before my birthday, we were handed our third conference loss, 1- 4. We won our first conference game against

Connors State College but lost the last two, one against University of Arkansas-Fort Smith and the other against Eastern Oklahoma State College. Our chances to qualify for the regional tournament were slowly decreasing. The overall team record was now 9-16. My junior college basketball career was also slowly coming to an end.

I was expecting my 21st birthday to be as boring as any other year; to my surprise, Alice made it special. After I got back from a team dinner, I returned to my room to change before heading to Alice's room. I unlocked and opened my bedroom door to find my bed decorated with balloons and a bag filled with goodies. No one had ever gone so far as this for me. Her birthday card to me read, "Arnold, I know this is not much, but when we go to Australia, I will get you a real birthday present." This was already too much. Her roommate had even gotten me a gift: a comb for my afro and an extra toothbrush to keep in their bedroom for whenever I spent the night.

Since Alice was full of surprises, I had a surprise of my own. With my roommate's assistance, I got Alice the perfect gift for Valentine's Day; though I was a bit skeptical because I didn't know if it was appropriate for our very first time experiencing the day for lovers. On the evening of February 14, after eating some chicken fajitas at a local Mexican Restaurant with some friends, Alice and I had planned to return to our rooms for a good night's sleep. While we all waited for Alice, who was using the washroom, I whispered to her roommate, "Hey Laura, I'm gonna propose to Alice."

"Huh?" she responded as she placed her hands over her open mouth.

I placed my right-index finger over my lips. "Shhh."

"When? Where?" she asked.

"As soon as she comes outside."

"Oh my God. I'm going to get y'all in a picture."

"Okay, cool." I checked my pocket one last time to see if the ring was still in the box. I took it out for easier access. "Shh, dere she is," I whispered.

I held onto Alice's hand as we exited the restaurant and she squeezed mine tightly. She was probably wondering why my hands were trembling, so to prevent the question, I stopped and wrapped my arms around her neck and whispered, "You know I love you, right?"

"Yeah." she held me closely and tightly.

"You know I wanna spen' da rest of my life with you, right?

"Yeah, I know that baby." I slowly placed my hand in my pocket to retrieve the diamond ring.

"I'll always love you. I wanna make you happy." I slowly connected my right knee with the ground while holding on to her soft right hand.

"Oh my…oh my…oh my God," she stuttered. Her eyes and mouth opened widely. She started fanning her face with her right hand as if it was a hot sunny day in Poteau.

"I love you Alice Hammond." I held the ring near her finger-tip, while she used the other hand to wipe away tears. "Will…you…marry…me?" I spoke slowly to ensure that my words were pronounced correctly. I was expecting a very long pause but to my surprise I received an instant answer. "Yes! Yes! Yes!"

There was good news in basketball, too. Coach called me into his office for some unexpected updates. "Hey Arnold, Coach Howard White, assistant coach from the University of North Florida in Jacksonville, Florida, called to speak with you."

"Are dey Division I?" I asked before he passed on any more information.

"Let's find out," he replied, at the same time searching on his computer. "Actually, yes they're NCAA Division I." I looked up, praising God. "Coach White will be calling you on your cell phone sometime soon," Coach St. John added.

Ecstatic, I rushed over to inform Alice. "Oh that's so good," she said with her charming, Australian accent. On the outside, she seemed happy, but I also knew she was worried about our future together. I brushed off the topic by advising her that we shouldn't worry about that right now.

While I waited for Coach White's phone-call, I decided to do some research on the university. With the information I'd gathered, it looked like the University of North Florida men's basketball team was about to finish their first season as a NCAA Division I program. Therefore, their previous year, 2004-2005, was played under a NCAA Division II program. That, combined with their overall team record of winning only 7 out of 29 games, had me reconsidering pursuing their program. But it was my only hope.

Later that evening, Coach White called. "Hey Arnold, I was shopping around for players and I ran across your profile. I noticed that you played for the University of Vermont, correct?"

I thought, *oh boy, here we go again; my past is haunting me.*

"Uh, yeah Coach, I did….It didn' work out."

"I feel ya. We are busy here finishing up our last few games of the season. If you can mail one of your best games down to us…we will evaluate the tape then get back to you as soon as possible."

"Okay, Coach. I'll do it today."

I went back to Coach St. John's office searching for my best game—which was against Rose State College, when I scored 14 points while snatching 12 rebounds. I mailed the videotape to Jacksonville, Florida.

A few days later, I received a follow-up call during my Physics class. This was one call I had to step outside of my classroom for. "Hey Arnold, we really liked what we saw on that tape."

"Oh yeah, thank you Coach."

"I noticed you have an upcoming game, right?"

"Yeah Coach, my las' game of da season."

"I will be doing some recruiting in that area so, on my way there, I will be coming to see you play."

"Oh yeah, dats cool Coach. I'll be ready."

February 27, 2006: Eastern Oklahoma State College hosted my very last junior college basketball game. We had lost to them at home, 16 days ago, with the final score, 103-102. With our Bi-State East Conference record of one win and six loses, there was a zero-percent chance for us making it to the regional tournament.

During my warm-ups, I was greeted by the punctual Coach White, an average height, late-twenties, African-American man with a short, clean haircut. For some reason, I thought Coach White would have been a white man. His attendance allowed me to gain an attitude to a point where it felt like I was fighting for not only a scholarship, but for my life. He exchanged words of motivation. "Yo man, just go out there and do your thing. I'll be watching you. And good luck man."

Coach St. John and all my teammates knew about Coach White's scouting me. It must have been my lucky night because, for the last three games we'd lost, our head Coach started me on the bench. Due to one of our starter's sudden injury, I was selected to be part of the starting-five. Approaching the game's tip-off time, I was supposed to be concentrating on the game; I could not help but keep an eye on Coach White's movements. *Is he watching only me?*

My teammates were very supportive as I played my heart out for a scholarship. Unfortunately, by the end of the game, my commendable performance did not reward us a victory. The final score of 86-79 handed us an overall team record of 9 wins and 20 loses. With the exception of only playing in one official game at Vermont, this was the worst season I had ever encountered whilst playing in Saint Lucia or America.

After the game, I walked to Coach White. He pulled out a white sheet of paper from his pocket and read from it. "You had 18 points (9 of 13 from the field), 13 rebounds, four steals, and two assists."

"Oh wow," I responded as I wiped the sweat off my face. The best game of my sophomore year was put on display at the right moment.

Coach White continued, "I just got off the phone with Head Coach Matt Killcullen. He wants to offer you a full basketball scholarship. I want to take you on an official visit on-campus."

After hearing these words, I truly wanted to run around, somersault and scream, but I kept my cool. "Okay Coach, I tink I wanna do dat. I'm really interested in da program at UNF. I believe I can be a great addition to da team."

"You have any questions for me?" he asked me.

"I jus' have one question for you." I looked him in the eye and asked, "How long you gonna be coaching at UNF?"

"You don't have to worry about that, Arnold. I will be there for a while," Coach White assured me.

My trip to UNF was good. I was only gone for 48 hours and Alice had already missed me. "So you think you going to sign to UNF?" she asked.

"I doh know. What you tink?

"Well, it's up to you babe."

"Yeah, buh can you deal with dat? Wha' if you doh find a school next to me?"

"Babe, it's alright. I'll be fine with whatever decision you make."

"Buh I want you close to me," I said.

"I know, but you don't have many options right now, Arnold," she said. "I'll support you all the way."

Shawn, who always showed concern for my well-being, advised me to sign with them since I didn't have other Division I offers.

I signed the Grant-in-Aid and the National Letter of Intent, in other words, my full basketball scholarship with the University of North Florida. My love for Alice made it very difficult for me to make an easy and quick decision. Since we were about to graduate from junior college, we had planned to attend the same college, or at least be in the same city, or state. I tried contacting the women's coaching-staff at the University of North Florida, but they told me that the head coach was finished with recruitment for the year. With assistance from Alice's head coach, we contacted nearby schools in the Jacksonville area via email, telephone, and mail. Still, the responses were limited.

HANGING ON TO MY DREAMS

On Tuesday, May 2, 2006, while having breakfast in the cafeteria, I finally got a copy of my article from the Poteau Daily Newspaper. The title read, "Vikings' Henry signs with UNF," by Mark Couch. And the following was printed in that newspaper:

"Viking Arnold Henry a 6'7" sophomore from Castries, St. Lucia, signed a letter of intent on April 12, with the University of North Florida.

They are a member of the Atlantic Sun Conference and are coached by Matt Kilcullen.

'The main reason that I came to Carl Albert was to play with Shawn King and we are both from the Caribbean Islands,' said Henry, 'I came to Carl Albert State College to get an opportunity to go play Division-I basketball. The University of North Florida was the first and only school to show interest in me. They came to watch me play and I was able to meet assistant coach Howard White, who told me that I was the missing piece for their team.'

'It is big any time when you have a player sign with a Division-I school,' said St. John, 'It is a two way street for the player, the program, and it is big for recruiting because players want to know where your former players have gone to school.'

'Coach St. John helped me to become a more responsible person and he encouraged me to work harder during games,' said Henry. 'He showed me that I could become a better player, which would allow me to play more minutes. I tried to work at it so that I could make the team more successful.'

'It would have been nice to have Arnold for two years instead of one year,' said St. John, 'I believe Arnold's role at UNF will be the same as it was here at CASC, which was to rebound, take charges, and get on the floor.'

'It was really a hard decision for me to make, because I wanted my fiancé, CASC Lady Viking Alice Hammond, to go to the same school as I did,' said Henry, 'We discussed it and Alice told me that she wanted me to do what was the best for me.'

UNF Assistant Coach Howard White commented the following on Arnold's Henry signing: 'Arnold is a good kid, who came from a good program at CASC. He has a good work ethic and Arnold is the missing piece for us on the low block. Arnold will be one of our leading rebounders, as well as being one of our best post players. I am very excited for Arnold to join the UNF family, as well as continuing his education.'

During the 2005-06 season, Arnold averaged 6.6 points per game, 4 rebounds a game, and he shot 58.5 percent from the field."

On May 5, 2006, Alice and I graduated from Carl Albert State College with academic honors. I graduated with an Associate degree in Computer Science with a grade point average of 3.8—on a 4.0 scale. We decided to skip the graduation ceremony to save money for our summer vacation to Australia. Then it was time to pack up everything and say goodbye to the small town of Poteau. I went back to Vermont for one week before flying to meet Alice Down-Under.

Chapter 43

One More Shot at NCAA Division I

I was now seated on the aircraft on my way to Jacksonville, Florida. It was so hard to say goodbye to Alice. The ring she placed on my wedding finger symbolized our bond. It would be a constant reminder that we were still together even though we were in separate worlds. We proclaimed that we would get married after I graduated from the University of North Florida in two years.

Alice was offered a full basketball scholarship from a four year college in Georgia, but since it was a six hour drive from UNF, she denied the offer. She said that it would be easier if she stayed in Australia with her family and friends.

Australia was the best place I ever visited. I met all of Alice's family and friends. The Hammonds were a really nice family who accepted me. I was so appreciative of being a guest in their home for three months.

I was going to miss everyday basketball practice and morning workouts with the city's NBA team, the Melbourne Tigers; and semi-pro team, the Sabres. The coaches and players assisted me in staying in shape, and I learned some new moves from a different basketball world.

I was surprised to be picked up from the airport by Coach Bowling; I was expecting Coach White. Coach Bowling was the youngest of all the coaches who I had met during my official visit in March. He looked like he was around the same age as me. "So where Coach White?" I asked.

"Oh, he is no longer with us." I remained quiet for the rest of the car ride. I thought, *here we go again...the lying has begun.* After Coach Bowling dropped me off at my apartment, I immediately tried calling Coach White on his cell phone; however, it was no longer in service. I didn't have any other means of getting in touch with him.

My two roommates at our four bedroom apartment were James Grimball—a local six foot eight junior like myself, and six foot six Rashad Williams from Macon, Georgia—the only senior on the team. I remembered them from my spring visit. We all roomed at the Melrose Apartments located about a five minute drive from campus. These apartments were exactly what I needed; and although we shared the same kitchen and living-area, we all had our very own spacious bedroom and bathroom.

"Dawg, wha' happen to Coach White?" I asked James.

"Coach White didn't like how Coach Kilcullen was treating him anymore so he packed up and left," he replied.

James and Rashad became my closest friends. They were quiet, clean, and respectful roommates. Life in Jacksonville, Florida was different from the other cities that I'd lived in. First off, the weather was unpredictable—one day, blazing hot, the day after, freezing cold. I hated its humidity. I could be standing in one spot without making any movements and my body would perspire like I had just run a marathon.

I needed transportation everywhere I went because everything was so isolated. Some parts of the city were only accessible by bridge. Whenever I needed a ride to the school's campus or the stores, my roommates chauffeured me around. I always handed them a small donation for their efforts. The majority of the people I met from Duval County were not as friendly as those in Poteau.

I finally caught up with Coach Kilcullen in his office. He was busy with paperwork. He was all smiles though as I walked in. "Nice to see you back. You enjoyed Australia?"

"Yeah Coach, thanks."

Without me asking him, he commented, "Coach White won't be with us anymore."

"Yeah I hear dat," I replied.

"So let's just prepare for a successful season," Coach Kilcullen said with a smile, but I saw a slight guilt behind his cheeks. I didn't even bother to get into further details of Coach White's disappearance.

I eventually met and greeted everyone affiliated with the basketball program; my teammates, trainers, and Coach White's replacements: Coach Philip and Coach Evans. Coach Evans was the only black coach on the team and he was the easiest to get along with; he acted like he was one of us, a basketball player attending school. Germaine Sparks, Stan Januska, Gallo Charm, and Tom Hammonds were this year's new recruits like me, along with our two walk-ons, Richard Guadagnolo and Herbert Polite. The players on my team were predominantly Black, not especially tall, but we were an athletic, fast paced team. Due to my experiences with previous teams, I realized that we needed plenty of work.

We started pre-season workouts, which lasted for about one month. Every morning at 5:30 sharp, James, Rashad, and I woke up to drive to the gym before 6 o'clock. Our mornings started with exercises conducted by Joe—the strength and conditioning coach. His work ethic reminded me of Chris Poulin at Vermont; he was serious about getting us prepared for the upcoming basketball season. This time, instead of only focusing on my individual development, I was motivated to establish an early leadership role. Whenever we ran drills or lifted weights, I always challenged my teammates to an extra set. For instance, when we finished a morning of workouts, I always suggested to Joe, "Can we do an extra one?" regardless of whether it was one of his running or agility drills. My teammates always whined at me, saying I was only showboating; but I just wanted everyone, including myself, to get better.

Every day, Joe gave us a list of exercises that needed to be completed by the end of our weight-room workouts. I had my first altercation with a teammate during one of those sessions. I was on my own, working on my back, using the lateral pull down machine when I was confronted by Gallo—my six foot six, African teammate. I counted, "1, 2, 3—"

Out of nowhere, Gallo grabbed the handled bar between my reps. "Yo, yo, yo, we ain't done with that machine yet," he shouted. He had this big grin on his face.

Ignoring his rudeness, I continued counting. "4,5,6—" He interrupted me once more. "Hold on boi, Lemme finish dis set," I yelled at him.

"No, you need to get up now," he persisted. I stopped counting to face him. He probably noticed my rage. I felt much disrespected because there were many other students in the gym that morning.

"What you gonna do?" Gallo challenged.

"Who da fuck you take me for!" I shouted and connected the palm of my hand to the left cheek of his face. He held his cheek as if a piece of it had fallen off. I waited for his next move. As he came back to his senses, he tried to attack me but Rashad came between us to terminate any further blows. Coach Kilcullen, who was working out on his own, came to the scene to investigate the situation. He was furious but spoke to me calmly. "Arnold, you cannot be acting like that in public. Everyone is going to think the basketball team can't get along."

"Coach, I'm sorry. But Gallo straight up disrespected me. I deh using da machine and he jus' pull it while I was working out."

"Okay, I know, but if you're having a problem with anyone, you should come see me first."

Coach Kilcullen eventually called out me and Gallo for us to work out our misunderstanding. I didn't want to hold any grudges against my teammate so I apologized with a handshake. He accepted it and returned the sympathy. And just like that, the problem was solved. In order to bring success to a team, we both understood that we needed to establish strong chemistry. If anything, our small altercation brought us closer.

After morning workouts, I spent a lot of time seated in our team's locker-room, appreciating the treatment of NCAA Division I basketball—free education; assistant coaches for individual development; athletic-academic advisors; personal trainers, etc. I had recaptured my dream. The funky smell of my sweaty Nike practice gear made me very proud of my accomplishments. I had to make the best of this situation, so I tried to learn from my past mistakes and concentrate on the present.

Just like my previous American schools, the day official practice began was the same date as the rest of the nation's teams. We would practice during the mornings, before classes, for a maximum of two and a half hours, and be free for study time in the evening. On the very first day that our official practices started being conducted by Coach Kilcullen I saw his inner-mean-monster. Now, don't get me wrong, Coach Kilcullen had his moments for being a happy, benevolent, and quiet man; we saw these when he hosted events such as team dinners, barbeques, or simply whenever we'd drop-by his office. In other words, he was fun to be around—away from the basketball courts. I just wished that Coach White would have at least given me a heads-up about Coach Kilcullen's emotional and verbal abuse towards others. I don't know Bobby Knight, but judging from clips I had seen on ESPN's Sportscenter, Coach Kilcullen wasn't too far off.

After our basketball practice, Coach Kilcullen called an emergency meeting. "I just want y'all to be careful with these social websites," he said.

Initially, I thought Coach was talking gibberish because his indirect message was unclear to me. So, after the meeting I asked James to elaborate. "There's a Facebook group call, Fire Kilcullen, I guess he was just warning us that he sees whoever joins the group," James replied.

When I returned to my apartment, I investigated on my laptop. I placed my hand over my wide-opened mouth, as I read the nasty comments written by UNF basketball supporters. The creator of the group was brave enough to display Coach Kilcullen's image for the profile picture. The first few lines of the group's description read:

"Will the UNF administration grow some balls and fire Matt Kilcullen?? What's it gonna take for them to realize that his players don't like him, he can't recruit, he cuts guys who are good, and he damn sure can't win!"

Visiting this webpage gave me a sickening feeling in my stomach. Once more, I felt betrayed by an American basketball coach. I felt like Coach White escaped without me and set me up for failure. Nevertheless, there was a season ahead.

On November 9, 2006, the UNF basketball team was aboard a flight headed to New York City to participate in the men's college basketball tournament: 2K Sports College Hoops Classic benefiting Coaches versus Cancer. I hadn't been to the liberty state since 2004. Starting my 2006-2007 basketball season in NYC was a pleasure because a few of my friends were finally able to witness, for their first time, a Saint Lucian in action at the highest level of collegiate basketball.

Upon arrival, we were given a brief tour throughout the borough of Manhattan. Some of my teammates who lived in the south all their lives had never been to a busy, energetic city with such an expanse of skyscrapers and bright-lights. For me, it was revisiting my favorite city in America. We spent most of our tour time at Ground Zero; silently, remembering images seen on television, recalling the lives that were lost during the devastating events of 9/11.

November 10, 2006: I played my first game and season-opener as an Osprey against St. John's University Red Storm, which was part of the famous Big East Conference. The game was located at their home court in the borough of Queens, New York. My childhood friends— Olvin, Jermal, and Jovan, who all lived in Brooklyn, attended my game.

I was relieved to be part of the starting five. My hard work over the pre-season paid off. During the game, I played my heart out. I rallied in eight points and eight rebounds. Rashad, our only senior player, led the team in points, racking up 18. In the end, we lost the game, 74-53. We definitely had some room for improvement, especially with the execution of our set plays.

In the locker-room, Coach Kilcullen commented, "I thought you guys did well for your first time playing against a Big East opponent. We will do a lot better and learn from this experience."

I was disappointed in the loss because the winners in our group advanced to the next stage of the tournament which took place at Madison Square Gardens—home basketball court of the city's NBA team the New York Knicks—and these games were televised on ESPN.

After being defeated by Loyola from Maryland in game two the following day, we left New York City and headed back with zero wins and two losses.

On November 14, 2006, UNF basketball was back in Florida, in the city of Gainesville, to compete against the University of Florida Gators. At that time, they were the defending 2005-2006 NCAA Division I National Champions and nationally top-ranked. This was by far the biggest game of my life.

Before the commencement of the game, I tried my best to maintain a high level of focus. While we were doing our regular warm-up routines, it felt like the 12,000 screaming Gator fans that surrounded the center of the court stood inches away from my ears. They called my teammates and I "Gator bait" while they slammed their stretched-out-arms to demonstrate how alligators open and close their mouths. It felt like I was about to be eaten alive.

The Gator's gigantic basketball stadium, The Stephen C. O'Connell Center, was sold-out 20 minutes before the starting of the first half. There were bright lights, cameras, and news broadcasters surrounding the court. On the other half of the court, I spotted the superstars and future NBA prospects that I'd seen play so many times on television: six foot eleven, Joakim Noah; six foot ten, Al Horford; and six foot nine, Corey Brewer. They looked much taller and bigger in person. I wondered how my undersized-team was going to stand a chance.

After we huddled and recited the Lord's Prayer, right before tip-off, Coach Kilcullen cried out, "We are playing the number one team in the nation. I am so proud of you guys. This game will be in your memories forever. Go out and play your hardest." Coach's watery eyes made mine water as well. It was my first time witnessing my coach cry.

Every play we ran, the Gators dominated it with their tenacious defense. It felt like we were playing against NBA superstars. My team and I were just not as powerful as the Gators. I defended Al Horford and he was a brick wall. On the other hand, even though I tried my best to keep Joakim Noah away from the basket, he was so long that it seemed like he never needed to jump to rebound the basketball. We suffered an embarrassing loss to the Gators, 40-86. I'd never in my career endured such a defeat. My stats were awful. I only scored 2 out of 2 free-throws. Rashad did well, scoring 21 points. It was our third lost.

November 25, 2006: there were about 15 seconds left in a showdown against the Northwestern University Wildcats, from the well-known Big Ten Conference. Strategies were discussed over the timeout called by the Wildcats. Victory was near. Then the unthinkable happened: Coach pointed to two of our guards and directed them to be substituted into the game to replace James and me. I wondered, *why is*

Coach putting out two of his tallest players to be replaced by small players?

I had to watch the remainder of the game on the bench. At least we were winning the game by one point, only a few seconds away from pulling the biggest upset in the history of the UNF's NCAA Division I program. I couldn't sit on the bench; I had to tightly grab onto the towel in my hands to stay in my seat.

The Wildcats inbounded the ball and quickly ran their set play. It left a wide open player on the left side of the court's baseline. He was about to shoot a three-pointer even though they just needed a 2-point field goal to win. One of my teammates quickly recovered to prevent a perfect shot. The ball left his hand. We all watched the ball float through the air. The building was quiet. The ball hit the rim. "Yes!" I yelled. But I had spoken too soon. Because, before the time could expire, the Wildcats rebounded their missed shot, and scored an easy bucket. I tilted my head down in disappointment. *We should have our bigger players in the game to rebound the ball,* I thought.

In the locker-room, Coach Kilcullen cried out, "It's my fault. I'll blame that loss on myself." That was the best thing I'd heard him say all season.

Chapter 44

Dismiss

Today's Date: November 15, 2006
Time: Unknown

Dear Diary,
Ever since we lost to the Gators, things went downhill for me. I am no longer a starter on my team. I'm also playing fewer minutes. It seems like Coach don't trust me anymore. I have no problem with starting on the bench; I just hate the fact that I'm playing fewer minutes.
And I am going through a break-up with Alice. I cannot handle the long distance anymore. I broke up with her over the phone. She is trying her best to rekindle our relationship, but I have already moved on. I have a new girlfriend by the name of Allie Parsons, who I met through a mutual friend living in Burlington, Vermont.

My school's winter break was about one month. Since our basketball team had four days off, I flew to Burlington, Vermont to spend Christmas with my new girlfriend, Allie—a tall, pale, gorgeous, young lady with long dark hair. I also reconnected with everyone who had treated me like a friend and family member when I attended the University of Vermont.

Thanks to my former teammate and roommate, Tim McCory, Allie and I received tickets to attend UVM's sold-out basketball game against Quinnipiac. *I should be playing*, my thoughts shrieked. I watched with a watery eye as UVM Catamounts won the game, 101-87.

Being back in Jacksonville for my spring semester, my worries kicked in. Three colleges in three years—four schools in four years—I couldn't get it right.

Before the commencement of our conference games, Coach told us that we were only eligible to participate in the National Invitational Tournament—so that was our goal—to qualify. But in order to succeed as a team, we had to win the most games out of our conference (Atlantic Sun Conference) during the regular season. Since the University of North Florida's basketball team had just converted from NCAA Division II to NCAA Division I in 2005, the program was put under a five year transition period meaning, within these five years, the basketball team wasn't allowed to participate in the Conference Tournament or the National Tournament. Our objective sounded realistic, but summing up our total losses was a dose of reality. In fact, we weren't only losing games, we were also losing players.

Upon entrance to our regular morning practice arena, I noticed that two of our starters, Rashad and Gallo, were seated on the sidelines like spectators. *Are they injured? Are they taking a day off? What happened?*

Coach huddled us and spoke with a shaky voice. "Rashad and Gallo will no longer be playing with us due to academic suspensions."

My heart sunk. We just lost our leading scorer and starting forward who were both above six foot six. How could they be so stupid to fail their classes? Why didn't our coaches follow their academic progress throughout the fall semester? After all, every player on the team was given an academic progress report form to be filled out by our professors so that our coaches or athletic advisors could monitor us all through the semester. If any of my teammates were failing a course, then they would have received immediate assistance such as tutoring. *Someone wasn't doing their job.*

Coach Kilcullen never really went into further details about their academic suspension. But it was obvious Rashad and Gallo's grade point average violated the NCAA academic rules. Rashad saw his last days of collegiate basketball seated from the bleachers. Gallo was still a junior, so he had at least the spring semester to redeem himself before his senior year. I was in no position to judge because my grades weren't as impressive as my previous grades from junior college. For the fall semester, I'd received two C's and three B's which I blamed on playing at least two or three games per week; balancing my school work with practice and scheduled games became too much to handle all at once. My point was proven when a fellow classmate stated, "You Never Finish," in regards to how difficult UNF's courses could be. My grades were mostly affected by the amount of traveling required to play our games. Being a computer science major, as well as an upperclassman, my intense courses needed plenty of attention. However, after an away game or practice session, laziness would pile up on my free time, to be replaced by hours of sleep, instead of catching up on missed assignments or study time.

Eventually I found a strategy to cope. If I noticed my exams were clashing with my basketball schedule, I would try my best to attempt the exam before I left. Otherwise, I would study while away on trips, and then complete the exam upon my return. Luckily, as student-athletes, we weren't penalized for being absent from the classroom thanks to the athletic department's providing letters of excuse.

By February 10, 2007, we lost our twenty-third game in a row against NCAA Division I opponents, after losing at home to East Tennessee State University, 51-56. Allie was seated in the bleachers. It was her first time being able to watch me play collegiate basketball—which reminded me of how Alice used to show her support at my junior college games. Allie had flown in two days prior to that game; an opportunity for us to catch-up on two months of being away from each other and, at the same time, celebrate my 22nd birthday.

After the game, Allie and I decided to go clubbing at a local nightclub. Within an hour of dancing, mingling, and partying, my body temperature suddenly started to rise faster than boiling water in a kettle.

Later, looking in the mirror, I couldn't recognize my own face. I searched between the plaits of my hair. The small bumps were everywhere—all over my body. "What the hell is this?"

"I think you got the chicken pox," Allie said.

On February 15, 2007, I missed my first basketball game against Stetson University—an away game held in DeLand, Florida. I was slowly recovering from my illness.

When I was finally able to return to practice, Coach asked me, "You will be okay for the next game?"

"Yeah Coach," I answered.

"We missed you out there against Stetson. We lost to them by 11 points," he stated as if he was seeking someone to blame for the loss.

By then there were only three more games left in the 2006-2007 season. Against NCAA Division I opponents, we had the worst overall team record in the nation with a total of zero wins and 24 losses—which, when added up from the previous season, summed up to a 22-game conference losing streak, and overall, a 32-game losing streak. I was ashamed to tell people that I played basketball for the University of North Florida. We came so close to winning many of those games. The majority of our games were the same—with five minutes left, it could have gone either way, but we were never able to finish strong. Personally, I blamed bad coaching decisions.

On February 22, 2007, on the day of Saint Lucia's 28th Independence celebration, we faced the Lipscomb University Bisons in our last home game of the season. The first time we played them in Nashville, Tennessee, we lost by 14 points. Win or lose, we had nothing to gain but our pride and dignity. Twenty minutes before the game, in the locker-room, I remembered preaching, "Dawg, it's our las' game. Let just give it our all."

The first half of the game ended with the score, 32-27, in our favor. But that was usually the outcome of our first half. If we only knew how to hang on to the lead, then we would have at least won a game.

With less than five minutes left in the game, shockingly, we were leading 53-51. A few more possessions on both sides with a few attempts at the basket changed the score to 63-56, still in our favor.

I grabbed a rebound after a missed three-pointer by the Bison's shooting guard. They immediately fouled me to stop the clock since we were in the bonus. I hit both free-throws.

Timeouts were called and plays were drawn by both teams. Our small crowd of 697 loyal fans was on their feet eager to finally witness a victory from the UNF men's basketball team. Play by play they screamed with anxiety.

In an attempt to shorten the deficit, the Bisons pushed the ball strongly across their half to quickly put up a three-pointer, but the ball was intercepted by my teammate.

I sprinted ahead of the pack. With only seconds left, I received a pass from my point guard. I took a few dribbles to prevent the defense. I rose up from the floor then slam-dunked the ball with one hand, bringing down the rim as hard as possible to clinch the victory. The energy from the crowd made it seem like the building was sold out. The score was 74-63. As we received a standing ovation from the fans, a few students joined our team in the middle of the court to have a moment of celebration.

It felt like one of those basketball movies when the team facing all odds finally overcomes their struggles at the end. At that very moment, I was finally in high spirits for being part of the university's basketball program. I recorded my first double-double of the season by scoring 11 points and snatching 10 rebounds. In total, I averaged five points and four rebounds per game.

Coach Kilcullen had given us one week to ourselves before we'd resumed post-season practice. I took the opportunity to catch-up on schoolwork that had piled up. I devoted my time and effort to raising my grades. Hopelessness sat upon my desk when I realized that I couldn't handle one of my courses, Data Structures, because I had missed too many lectures. Even if I attempted to study for 24 hours a day; seven days a week; for four weeks straight, I would have never caught up.

Before it was too late, I visited my professor during her office hours for recommendations. "I'm so behind in da class and I doh know wha' to do," I pleaded, hoping she would suggest make-up exams.

"The only thing I can suggest is for you to withdraw from the class. That way you won't hurt your grade point average. And you can retake the course in the fall," she advised.

I went with my professor's proposal and withdrew. That left me with—4 hours subtracted from 13 hours—nine college hours, which made me ineligible for college basketball activities in the upcoming fall semester (sort of what Gallo and Rashad had been through—now I realized how it could happen). NCAA rules require every player to complete a minimum of 24 course hours a year. By the end of the school year, I would calculate 23 hours in total; I only needed one more hour. My plan was to take a 3-hour course over the summer so that I would rack-up 26 course hours for the 2006-2007 school year and regain my eligibility before the fall semester.

Basketball was still playing all across America. Every time I tuned in to watch television, teams were competing in Conference Tournaments, or the National Invitation Tournament (NIT), or preparing for the National Tournament. And at the end of it all, the University of Florida Gators were the repeat national champions. Though our season ended, we started preparing for the next one with post season work-outs.

One week later, I was on my way from class to the gym. As I walked under the bright, sunny, blue skies in Jacksonville, I speed-walked, anxiously ready to capitalize on my years of college experience for my senior year. For the few days I went without bouncing a basketball, I was happy to be back. I arrived in the locker-room and found everyone just as happy as I was.

Somehow, as Coach Kilcullen and his coaching staff joined us in the locker-room, the smiles on everyone's face were wiped-out completely. I remained seated in my corner, quickly tying the strings of my sneakers, before Coach Kilcullen initiated his usual speeches. In the corner of my eyes, I noticed he was staring at my overgrown afro.

"You can't practice like that," Coach Kilcullen said.

"Wha'? Why?" I asked while remembering his idiotic rule: no afros. *If our freshman point-guard had dreadlocks, then what's the big deal with me airing out my hair?* My chicken pox had fully cleared across my body; however, I still had some sores on my scalp that needed to dry out, hence my afro.

"You can't practice with your hair looking like this," he repeated.

I stared him down for a while waiting for his laughter. But his face did not smile. In the back of my mind, I was so frustrated with Coach that I wanted to curse and spit in his face. I thought, *if it is post-season, then why is he taking it so hard on me?* Before I erupted disrespectfully, I changed out of my practice gear into my civilian clothing. But as I walked away, I lost control. "I'm goin' to leave my hair like dis for the rest of my life!" I shouted.

Before I had a chance to exit the locker-room, Coach replied, "No need to come back. You are no longer on this team."

I halted as the locker-room's door shut to my back. *Did I just get dismissed from the team because of my hair?*

I guess that he just wanted to make an example out of me; he wanted the other players to see that he still ran the show. Plus, I sensed my dismissal was coming because I was the only player on the team who'd dare talk back to him.

I took the public bus back to my apartment, thinking about what had just happened. And then two hours later, Coach Evans, the only black assistant coach on the team walked into my apartment, laughing at the situation. "Why did you say that man?" he asked. For me, this was no laughing matter.

"I'm tired of dat man's attitude. He is so annoyin'. I have my hair like dat because of da chicken pox."

"I hear you but you shouldn't have said it in front of the team."

"Coach I know, but we not even playing a game. It's just post-season and he want me to have my hair braided. Dats pure B.S."

Coach Evans placed his hand upon my shoulder. "Well bruda, it seems like you not going to be with us next season. The boss man really wants you gone."

Chapter 45

Now What?

For my brother, Aloysius Marvin Henry, the basketball journey was beginning. As an older brother, I felt it was my duty to find him colleges that would help him succeed as a basketball player and student—great colleges. I saw a brighter future for him than I would ever see for myself. I intended to guide and protect him throughout his progression as if I was his guardian angel. I wanted to relive my American basketball dream vicariously through him.

When I first saw Marvin exiting the gate at the Jacksonville Airport, I remembered my inhalation of American air at the Philadelphia Airport back in 2003. It was now his turn to shine.

"Yo wassup? How was your flight?" I asked Marvin while we exchanged hugs. I couldn't stop smiling for the simple fact that he had grown even taller since our last encounter, now looking like my little big brother. He even had a mustache growing.

"It was aight," he replied. His voice had gotten deeper.

"Boy, you makin' me feel extra short." He laughed. "But I'm happy you are here," I continued. James, who drove me to the airport, was freaking out at my younger brother's height.

When we got back to my apartment, I called our mother to let her know that her second son had made it safely to Florida. The phone call eased her worries. She thought that he wouldn't make it past immigration since he was only "supposedly" coming to visit me and I wasn't a legal resident of the United States. The US Embassy in Bridgetown, Barbados gave Marvin a one year visitor visa; therefore, we had no time to waste.

At the moment, I wasn't concerned about myself. I tried my best to forget the termination of my basketball scholarship. What would Marvin think of me? So, I kept it a secret. I wanted this moment to be all about him. I acted more like a father than a big-brother, one who wanted to provide a better future for my son. I gave him a bed to sleep on, cooked for him, and gave him some of my winter clothes to keep him warm. He never expected that type of treatment coming out of me; Mummy took care of both of us in Saint Lucia.

It was impossible for Marvin to play for any NCAA colleges for the upcoming fall due to the fact that he hadn't written the SAT or ACT exams. It would be too late for him to prepare for these challenging exams. The only other option was to try his luck at a prep school or a junior college. I started in Jacksonville.

The next day, I called Head Coach Stitts from Florida Community College of Jacksonville (FCCJ), to make him aware of my brother's presence in town. "Hey Coach, I'm Arnold Henry from the University of North Florida," I said trying to sound American.

"Hey, what's up?"

"Yeah, I'm calling in regards to my 6'9" brother. He is new in town and I was wondering if you could take a look at him."

"Oh, wow, 6'9?" he replied with a surprised tone.

"Yes Coach."

"Sure, I will take a look at him. We actually have some open try-out runs this week."

After I was done with classes for the day, to prepare Marvin for his tryouts I took him to the UNF arena for a quick shoot-around session. His first step onto a hardwood basketball floor reminded me of my first experienced back at the military school. I could see the glory within him as he dribbled, shot, and dunked the basketball enthusiastically.

I acted like a coach, too. I prepared him briefly. I taught him the essentials for a basketball tryout in America. Our time was limited. During our workouts, I said to Marvin, "Oye, you really need to focus on playin' plenty of defense. Make defense da key as you go out to tryout. You hear me?"

"Yeah," he replied.

"Oye, fa real, dem coaches like to see mun play defense."

"Oh irie."

"And anada ting, try sprintin' back on both offense and defense. Dem coaches like to see an athletic and energetic player."

His game had improved from the last time I watched him play in 2005. For his height, he had terrific ball handles and shot the three exceptionally well; better than most professional big men.

The day of his tryout, I prepared a meal that I believed would give Marvin enough energy. I cooked and fed him a plate of Chicken Alfredo with pasta. His emptied plate put a smile on my face. I wasn't able to show my support during his tryouts because I had classes. Coach Stitts was generous enough to pick him up and drop him back to my apartment.

After two hours of classes, I raced back to my apartment, hoping that Marvin would have some good news for me. He wasn't back as yet, so I waited patiently at the front door.

One hour later, he knocked on the door. I jumped up to open it. Before he planted his foot inside, I asked, "So how was it? How was it? Wha' da Coach say? Wha' he say?" As Marvin spoke, there wasn't any sign of fulfillment.

"It went good. But da Coach tell me to tell you to call him ASAP," Marvin said with a low voice. I dialed Coach Stitts's number before Marvin finished his statement. I put on my American accent once more.

"Hey Coach Stitts. What do you think of Aloysius?" (Just like my mother, I always used our first names for school purposes).

"He is actually a really good player and I would love for him to play for FCCJ," I looked at Marvin and gave him a big smile and a wink. "But—" I rolled my eyes, expecting the worst and thinking, *"but" is never good news.*

"Currently we only have partial scholarships available," Coach Stitts continued.

"Okay coach, I understand," I said.

"Is that something you think he will be interested in?"

"I'm sorry Coach, no. We were hoping for a full scholarship. But thank you for the opportunity."

"No problem."

That was pretty much the end of the conversation and the end of contacting Coach Stitts. I was silent for at least a minute before I broke the *partially* sad news to Marvin.

"Yo, da mun offering a partial scholarship only. We cah take dat cuz school here in America is mad expensive and you already know we cah get any help."

"Oh." His lack of words expressed his disappointment.

"Yo, doh worry. I will check for other schools for you." He nodded, but his reaction implied defeat.

Marvin's time with me was brief and there wasn't much I could have done. He had prior engagements with his Bermudian girlfriend and needed to catch a flight at an airport based in New York City. With monetary assistance from Allie, I purchased a plane ticket for him to fly and stay with his sister until he needed to fly to Bermuda. Before Marvin departed Jacksonville I said to him, "Whatever you do, eh go back to Saint Lucia without a basketball scholarship eh. Have faith, someting go come your way. You were born to play basketball."

My bedroom was once again more spacious with my younger brother hanging on to his own dreams in a different American city. But for me, the big question was, *now what?* I knew it though—it was now time for me to check for myself. Since I only had one year of eligibility remaining, I started wondering what coach in their right mind would offer me a full basketball scholarship? The school year was about to come to an end, so I made phone calls to a few college basketball coaches from all sorts of college leagues—NCAA Division I, II and III; NAIA Division I and II. And as expected, it was nearly impossible to find any programs interested in a player who only had one year to play. The school year ended and I was still saying to myself, *now what?*

Just before I left the university in North Florida, our compliance officer—the man supposedly in charge of ensuring student-athletes are eligible to participate in NCAA activities, called me into his office for an exit interview. Basically, he needed to know about my experience as an athlete. "Arnold, it has been brought to my attention that you will no longer be part of the men's basketball team?" he asked.

"Yeah Sir," I responded, seated at his desk, figuring out that this interview was just a waste of time.

"I will read you some questions and I would like your honest answers." As I answered his questions, the compliance officer jotted them down on a piece of paper.

"How was your overall experience at the University of North Florida?"

"Um, alright."

"Arnold, we are trying to get Kilcullen out of office. If you have any dirt on him, please let me know. Because no one wants him here," he said boldly.

I gazed into space for a moment to reconcile events that took place throughout the season. For the most part, coach Kilcullen was just a bad decision maker for a head coach. I answered all the questions to the best of my knowledge. I could have easily lied to ruin Coach Kilcullen's image as a basketball coach. But I didn't want my conscience slowly haunting me in the future (even though I felt like I would have been doing everyone a huge favor). I left peacefully.

Chapter 46

Still Hanging In There

I returned to Vermont during the summer of 2007. Why did I return to my dead zone? Well, Allie was the number one reason, plus some great friends. Also, I was hoping to be rehired as a painter at the job I worked three years ago. I was assigned to the position, but a week later, after sweating gallons from painting the University of Vermont's residential halls and dormitories, I was let go because of misinformation. Apparently, since I was no longer a student of the University of Vermont, I was ineligible to work on their campus. The recruiting manager was unaware of my status. My continuous employment would have jeopardized the university's credentials with the Internal Revenue Service. I thought that I was able to work at any school in America, as long as it was a job on-campus. Unfortunately, I was only able to work at my current college—which was UNF. Luckily, I was given a check for the week that I'd worked. With no place to live, and no job, I secretly remained at the dorm I was assigned to upon being employed as a painter.

I called the one man who I thought I'd never call for financial assistance. It was pointless calling my mother since she still didn't have a job. I called Tobias. "Hello," I said with a shaky voice.

"Hello, who is this?"

"Dis is Mario," I said to him, gulping down saliva.

"What you doing up there?"

"I need your help please," I begged. "I have no money for food."

"Well I cannot help you."

"Okay thanks," I said before hanging up the phone. *What a waste of an international call,* I thought.

How did I survive that summer without a job? Let's just say, *a friend in need is a friend indeed.* I gained so much respect for that quote. Basically, Vermont was my home away from Saint Lucia. And living there was like living amongst family, regardless of my bad experiences. Whenever I was hungry, I always had a plate of food at someone's home. One meal a day was nearly sufficient for me, but I was losing a lot of weight. I had gone from 245 to 229 pounds. Allie was another big factor in my summer survival. I don't know how I could have survived over three months without her company. Every weekend she washed my clothes, cooked a meal, and shopped for me.

She understood the situation I was going through and stood by my side as a loyal girlfriend.

I made an effort to hang on to my dreams by working out on a daily basis and calling colleges, waiting for an opportunity.

Every day I hopped on the university's shuttle and rode five minutes to the gymnasium to develop my basketball skills. Before I proceeded to the public area within the gym, I made my way through the home basketball court to the weight room. Sometimes, whenever I caught the team practicing on the court, I would watch through a metal gate that separated the public from the players. I saw myself alongside Tim as we practiced for our upcoming senior season. It was very difficult to watch whenever reality disrupted my delusions. It was obvious; *there was no going back in time.*

When I thought all hope was gone, I received a phone call. It was midday. I was lying in bed watching Sportscenter on ESPN. "This is Assistant Coach Eddie Burroughs from Ed-Edward Waters College." I wanted to hang up the phone quickly as he mentioned the name of the school. But I ignored the urge.

"Hey Coach, wassup?" I asked.

"I noticed that you won't be returning to UNF this coming fall?"

In the back of my mind, I thought, *how these coaches always know my business? Who gave them my cell phone number?*

"Oh yeah...yeah, I wanted to leave cause Coach and I wasn't dealing," I answered.

"I hear that...I hear that," Coach Burroughs said, as he softened his tone. "Have you looked at any other schools?"

"Uh, nah. I mean, I lookin' buh nuttin yet."

"Oh yeah!" His toned raised. "Well, we are looking for a post player right now." Coach Burroughs wasted no time in convincing me that Edward Waters College, or EWC, was the right school for me.

"Coach, I only have one year to ball and I'm looking for a full scholarship," I said.

"Oh yeah, for...for sure. We have some scholarships left."

As soon as the call ended, my thoughts shouted, *oh no! Not Edward Waters College!* I couldn't recall the rumors except that I heard it was located in the ghetto of Jacksonville, Florida—a very bad area. And the EWC athletic programs didn't participate in NCAA, they competed in the National Association of Intercollegiate Athletics (NAIA)—a less recognized and less competitive college league. But, EWC was the only hope for my future.

I couldn't make a decision right away. I waited a few more days to see if there were other basketball scholarship opportunities. To clear my head, I took a trip with Allie to New York City for one weekend. It was about a five hour drive. While she took a route to spend time with her friends, I visited Marvin in Poughkeepsie where he now lived with his big sister. My objective of the trip was to find him a full basketball scholarship, but he was doing great on his own. He found a gig with Marist College, a NCAA Division I institute located five minutes from where he rested his head. The basketball coaches were taking great care of him by supplying him with a job and access to the school's gym. I realized that my assistance as big brother was rarely needed. Marvin was in better hands; though my supervision was still present and he was aware that he could have asked me for my opinions on any basketball related topics.

I returned to Vermont as a happy and proud older brother.

A few days later, I had just finished a workout at the UVM's gym when I received a phone call from Edward Waters College's head basketball coach. This time my mind was made up. I took a deep breath. "Coach, I'm ready to sign with EWC," I said.

"Oh yes, I am glad to hear that, Arnold," Coach Mosley said.

"I jus' wanna win a championship; I really wanna win one Coach. It's my las' year and I wanna go out with a bang."

"That's the kind of attitude we are looking for here," he said. "With the addition of you, we believe we have what it takes to win a championship."

I was offered a full basketball scholarship, but I'd immediately run into a problem—I sent in my grades to EWC's compliance officer and I found out that I was academically ineligible to play basketball for the upcoming fall semester. "Oh yeah, of course," I said to myself. I had forgotten I dropped a course at UNF during the spring semester. Coach Mosley was aware of my dilemma. He suggested that I take the CLEP exams—a college level examination program which corresponds to the same credits earned by an institution, but only if the score requirements were met. I wasted no time. Allie was a great support in my preparation; she drove me to Barnes and Nobles and bought me a study guide for the exam. I also researched examples of CLEP exams online to prepare myself. Since I was good at Mathematics, I decided to practice for the College Algebra exams. The information online said that it was 60 multiple-choice questions to be answered in 90 minutes.

I studied for the exams for about three days. After I completed them, I received my results right away. I passed.

Coach Mosley was the first to know my result. He told me that all my documents would be taken care of the moment I arrived in Jacksonville. And just like that, I was back in business.

Chapter 47

The Final College Chapter

Today's Date: August 20, 2007
Time: 1:05p.m.

Dear Diary,
    Edward Waters College, a historically black college (HBC), is now my future. I thank God for allowing me to continue my dream.
    My brother, Marvin, received a full basketball scholarship at a preparatory school in Maine called Maine Central Institute. It is a great way for him to start his basketball journey; the same way I started mine at Massanutten Military Academy, back in 2003. I know his experience will be better than mine. And I am going to make sure. During a phone call, by the sound of my mother's voice, I know she is proud of her sons.

    "You know the school is in the hood, right?" Coach Mosley asked as he swerved to the right to exit interstate 95. "It's not too bad. Just be careful and you'll be alright," he said. I nodded.
    He pulled onto Kings Road. "We're here."
    "Over dere?" I pointed to the buildings on either side of the road.
    "Yeah," answered Coach Mosley (my first Black, American head coach). "That's the dormitories over there. That's the classrooms over there. That's the administrative buildings. You will get used to it." I looked outside the passenger window to my right to hide my disappointment. Coach stopped at the red light. My head went from right to left as a man with ragged clothes crossed, pushing a broken down shopping cart filled with cans and bottles. I thought, *so where is the campus?* I wasn't expecting the school to be right *in* the hood. The campus was in the heart of the community, or should I say, the community was pretty much in the heart of the campus. Either way, for a first-timer, it would have been difficult to differentiate between the students and the residents of the area. It was my first time seeing so many African-Americans in one area, besides New York City. The University of North Florida was only 20 minutes away across the bridge.
    I hesitated to get out of Coach Mosley's vehicle as I noticed the state of the dormitories, which were surrounded by a black metal cage. Coach helped carry my luggage to my room. As I made my first step

through my bedroom door, I instantly backpedaled. I wanted to keep going back to Vermont.

"Coach, I cah live in dere," I cried out. We stood face to face in the lobby.

"You don't like it?" asked Coach Mosley as if he was expecting my reaction.

"Coach, da room wide as my wing span. Dis is too small for me. Plus dey have four beds and one bathroom."

"Um, you know what?"

"No, wha'?"

"Do you have above a 3.0 GPA?" asked Coach, referring to my academic grades.

"Yeah, why?"

"There's the Honors Village. It looks nicer, bigger and you will only get one roommate. It's for students with a 3.0 GPA. I'm sure you can get in there with your grades."

"Please Coach, look into dis for me," I pleaded.

"Okay, I will check it out for you, but for now you will have to sleep in here."

"Okay."

I was not in a sociable mood, so I stayed inside my blistering-hot room as much as possible. The damn air conditioner blew out hot air. Plus, I was afraid that the facility wasn't secure enough. I kept all my belongings locked up in my bags as I awaited Coach's return.

After two nights in the hell hole, I was finally accepted to reside in the Honors Village. My new on-campus residence was more appropriate. When I first walked into my more spacious room, it was sparkling clean. I noticed there were two pieces of furniture. I met my one and only roommate, Travis Morris, a short, African-American young man from Miami, Florida. I was definitely comfortable sharing a bathroom with him after witnessing his clean demeanor. It was easy smiling as I introduced myself. He made me feel welcome as he assisted me with my luggage.

"Wassup?" I asked Travis. Ignoring my question, and picking up my accent, Travis asked, "Are you from Jamaica?" The question was getting old; every time I met someone new, it was the same question.

Travis and I got along great. He introduced me to a job on-campus as a Math tutor. Every week, I worked for 20 hours at eight dollars per hour.

I was now comfortably settled in. All my documents for school were taken care of. I was registered for classes, I obtained my meal plan, and I was issued a student I.D. card. My scholarship took care of all my expenses at the college. The process of getting registered as a student at EWC took longer than at my previous schools. They were lagging in technology; handling all documents with hard copies rather than online application forms. However, I was officially made a student-athlete of Edward Waters College.

I was first introduced to my teammates and the rest of the coaching staff during basketball open-runs at the gym. Comparing myself to my teammates, I measured out to be the tallest, biggest, and only international player on the team. I met with the rest of the coaching staff: Eddie Burroughs, Dannie Pearson, and Shawn Taylor. They were my first all-African-American coaches. Also among us were two associates, Mr. Coleman and Mr. Jenkins, who were somewhat motivational speakers and big supporters of EWC basketball.

For once, I believed and trusted an American coach. Coach Mosley was straightforward and positive about our team's potential to win a championship. And after challenging my teammates during basketball runs, I had no doubts. I recognized most of the faces from when UNF played against them, especially our point guard, Jeffery Winbush, an electrifying jump shooter. He was the most accurate shooter I'd ever played with.

I believed that a pre-season workout and a good solid month of practice would create a power squad among us.

Unlike NCAA athletic programs, the funding for NAIA programs was limited. Well, at least it was for EWC. The outdated weight-room looked very amateur, like a homemade gym; more than half of the machines were broken. Our resources were inadequate but we worked with what was available. Any NCAA Division I basketball player should be appreciative of their position. Being a downgraded college athlete at EWC, I was admiring my former teammates at UNF. Since I was the only experienced NCAA Division I player on the team, I found it necessary to share my knowledge. If they ever complained about Coach Mosley's workouts being too difficult, I said to them, "That's exactly why you not playing NCAA Division I basketball." And if they needed a reason for my statement, I replied, "Because you complain too much."

During pre-season workouts, Coach Mosley always gave us a motivational speech that included our goals for the remainder of the 2007-2008 season. Today, I can still hear him saying, "We need to produce." Coach stated four goals: First, to win 20 or more games; second, to have the most regular season wins against our conference opponents; third, to win the Sun Conference's play-off; and finally, to win the NAIA national championship.

I foresaw the future and our goals were achievable. And for once, it seemed that I was going to be part of something great. Well, until an incident at a local nightclub.

It was after two in the morning when I was awakened by the sound of our residential advisor knocking on my bedroom door. "What's your head coach's cell phone number?" he asked.

"Wha' happen?"

"Something happened at Club Boleros that involved your teammates."

"You have to tell me," I pleaded.

"I really don't know…someone was stabbed."

"What!" I looked straight into his eyes. "Who?"

"Arnold, I don't know, I wasn't there. The school's security needs Coach Mosley's number," he said.

Later that morning, Coach Mosley called my teammates and I in for an emergency meeting. We met in the locker-room at the school's gym. My teammates looked like they had just seen a ghost. It was dead silent, as if we were at a funeral. I noticed two players were missing.

"We all heard about the incident that took place last night at the club," Coach Mosley said. "Josh is on his way back to Jacksonville. He is turning himself in." I noticed the worry on some of my teammates' faces. "A detective will escort everyone who was at the club last night to the police station for questioning," Coach Mosley continued. By then I was thinking, *praise God for the fact I decided to stay in last night.*

After the police investigations, only one of my teammates was charged with murder and aggravated battery. But most of the team suffered consequences in other areas, including emotional depression and life threats from the victims' entourage. Our team was now looked down upon—as if being an all-black team wasn't hard enough in America. In the public eye, we were viewed as thugs. As a basketball team, we had to watch our backs. There were rumors circulating that the victims' family and friends were seeking vengeance on some of my teammates from the club incident. I was out of the loop because I lived at the Honors Village while the rest of my teammates live at Tiger Landing. From that point in time, I only surrounded myself with my team at practice.

After a few days and a team counseling session, the incident eventually faded, and our team regained focus for our upcoming basketball season. We were now down to 11 players. Despite the incident and loss of one of our good guard, I still believed in a prosperous season.

On November 5, 2007, I played my first home game as an EWC Tiger. I was the starting power forward. For my season opener, I scored 14 points, grabbed 11 rebounds, and blocked 2 shots. We lost by 6 points. It was a huge disappointment knowing that we were the better team. We were leading the entire game and the lead was stolen away from us during the final seconds.

November 7, 2007: I sought revenge upon Coach Kilcullen with my newly found basketball team. It was my first encounter with any UNF affiliates since I left back in May. I noticed the surprised faces of UNF's fans, players, and coaching staff when they saw me. I never made any eye contact with Coach Kilcullen.

All my EWC teammates and coaches were aware of my dismissal and desperately wanted to win the game on my behalf. We put up a fight from start to finish and never gave up. But my wishes remained a dream because we lost, 91-82, in double-overtime.

Back in the locker-room, I sat down in the corner with my head on my knees. My teammates placed their hands on my shoulders. "Good job. Sometimes referees determine the outcome of the game, but I thought y'all fought out there tonight," Coach Mosley said. Everyone clapped in support of Coach's comment. "A win would have been great, especially for Arnold," he continued. Even though we lost the match, Coach Mosley thought that we left our blood and sweat on the UNF's home court.

On our way back across the bridge, I received text messages from UNF's students and fans that once rooted for me. They thought that I intentionally left UNF to attend EWC. The messages I read portrayed me as a traitor. I was so crushed by the loss that I just ignored everyone's hurtful comments.

November 29, 2008: 73-81 was the final score of our exhibition game. We lost to NCAA Division I opponent, Bethune-Cookman University from Daytona, Florida. Before the game, my eyes opened widely as I noticed Coach White as one of the Assistant Coaches of their team. *He was only a one hour drive away from Jacksonville and he didn't find it necessary to pay me a visit?* He finally found the courage to speak to me after the game. "Good game, Arnold." My initial thought was to walk away without shaking his hand or engaging in any conversation with him. But I politely shook his hand. "Sorry I didn't get a chance to say goodbye at UNF," Coach White added. I nodded my head slightly and pushed my lips shut so that I could stop myself from giving him a real piece of my mind. As I stared down at him, he continued, "Things didn't go well with me and the old man…sorry about everything. And good luck with the rest of the season."

"Thanks," I responded, and then walked off. I thought, *a simple apology over the phone, one year and a half ago, would have been great…Bastard!*

By January 12, 2008, our overall team record was eight wins and five losses. It was a good start to the season, but I thought that we could have done so much better if we played more as a team. The beginning of the spring semester started rocky. First of all, I lost Allie as a girlfriend. That was the end of our relationship. I'll just leave it as that. Second, one of my teammates quit the team which cut us down to 10 players. Also, our team's manager quit school so he was no longer with us. Last, after the fall semester, we lost Trey Bain—our senior starting shooting guard, for at least three games due to academic suspension. We were now down to nine players, and with his absence, we lost three games in a row. Fortunately, Trey's professor gave him an opportunity to retake the exams that he had failed—he was able to redeem his grades and instantly regained eligibility. We went on winning the next few games.

On January 14, 2008, I missed my first basketball game at EWC. Actually, I was on the bench the whole time—one-hundred-percent healthy and intact. Before tip-off, it was Coach Mosley's decision to count me out of the roster. Once again, my thick afro-hairstyle got me into trouble. It wasn't intentional to disobey Coach Mosley's rules; it just happened that I was unable to find someone to braid my hair before the game. Nonetheless, he ignored my excuse.

Sitting on the bench and watching the entire first half wasn't pleasing. What really bothered me was that Coach Mosley allowed me to play the previous game with my afro. But since this game was less competitive, he sat me down—just to make an example out of me. And he wasn't wrong at all; I just thought that his disciplinary actions should have taken place at the previous game.

I was so pissed-off at the situation, that as soon as I returned to the locker room during halftime I slammed, threw, and broke any object in my way. My teammates watched and dodged shockingly. "I didn' com' here for dat! I jus' wanna win a championship!" I shouted. The racket got Coach Mosley's attention; he had been standing outside the locker-room, deliberating about the first half of the game with the other coaches.

"What's going on in there?" Coach Mosley asked with a furious look on his face.

"Nothing Coach, we were just talking about the game," my teammates replied all together as they hid the damages that I'd caused. But Coach was no fool.

For my actions, I remained on the bench for the second half of the game as well as the following game. And I returned to the starting five only after I proved that I was worthy. I was more disciplined and humble throughout the rest of the season.

February, 9, 2008: two days before my 23rd birthday, I played my last home basketball game as an EWC Tiger. They called it, Senior Night. Including me, we had three seniors on the team. During halftime we were mentioned and honored in front of the students and fans. We were given an appreciation plaque from the college. Upon receiving my award, I held it up high, like I was just handed a championship trophy, and then said to myself, *Yes, five schools in five years, finally I cross the finish line!* But the season was not over; I still sought a championship.

Chapter 48

Ending on a Good Note

February 20, 2008: we lost an away game at Savannah College of Arts and Design (SCAD), 74-81—against a conference team we had defeated by 30 points at home a few weeks earlier. The loss slowed down the momentum that we'd tried to build before the commencement of our conference tournament which was only one week away.

Three days later, we played our last regular season conference game versus the Warner Southern College (WSC) Royals. They handed us our worst defeat of the season, beating us by 34 points. I would say that our selfishness cost us the game—half of the team just wanted to play offense and no defense. We shot 36 percent while the Royals shot 55 percent. Things weren't looking too bright on our side because we were on a two game losing streak heading to the conference tournament. Our overall conference record was six wins and eight losses which ranked our team fifth out of eight places.

After the devastating loss to WSC, we had a quiet five-hour bus ride to our campus. A loss always seemed to make our bus trips longer. Coach Mosley was so mad at our performance that he didn't even speak to us after the game. The only time he spoke was on the bus when he stood up and announced that we had practice at 8 Sunday morning. Then he sat back down. It was my first time witnessing him really mad at us. Coach's announcement of our first Sunday morning practice heated up a controversy amongst my teammates.

Sam Crawford, our back-up point guard spoke out. "Damn that! I ain't coming to no practice on a Sunday." He said it loud enough for everybody on the bus to hear.

Right after, Demetrice Thomas, our starting forward, seconded Sam's remark. "Me neither."

My initial thought was to tell Sam and Demetrice to shut the hell up, but I was so pissed at my own performance that I didn't bother to say a word. I personally thought that it was a great idea for a Sunday morning practice. We were about to face-off against one of the higher ranked conference teams and we needed all the preparation possible.

Sure enough, on Sunday morning, only eight players showed up for practice. Sam and Demetrice were absent without leave. I thought that their actions were selfish. No one knew where they were.

"We just have to work with what we have," said Coach Mosley. I was now more worried than ever. How could we win the conference championship with only eight players? I prayed that night, hoping Sam and Demetrice would show up to practice the following day.

One day before the opening of the conference tournament, Sam and Demetrice showed up for our usual 6:00 p.m. practice. I was pleased to see them. Coach Mosley wasn't. Before we warmed-up, he confronted them. I overheard the conversation. Coach Mosley spoke to Sam and Demetrice individually. "Yesterday we had practice and you chose not to show up; therefore, I'm suspending you for one game." As they shamefully walked off the court, I approached Coach Mosley.

"But Coach we don't have enough players."

"Arnold, we only need five players on the court to play and win the game," he said. I believed him. He had a plan and I saw it in his eyes. I accepted his decision.

Before the tournament commenced, we were given the conference schedule. Our conference consisted of eight teams. Three wins in a row—quarterfinals, semifinals and finals—determined the champions of the conference tournament. The quarterfinal games were played at the home court of the four top-ranked teams; therefore, since we were ranked fifth in the conference, we played the number four ranked team which was SCAD. The semifinals and championship game were hosted by the Northwood University (NU) Seahawks, the number one ranked team in the conference. Besides the Royals, the Seahawks were our toughest opponent; we lost twice to both of them during the regular season.

February 26, 2008: we pulled it off. The final score: 70-75—we displayed great team-work to defeat SCAD on their home court. I thought it was a miracle since we'd lost to them a week ago in the same place. The difference in the game was our shooting percentages and our defensive execution. We shot 42 percent from the field while they shot 32 percent. After the game, I sent a text message to Sam and Demetrice and said to them, "Yo, we won! Get ready for the next game." Their responses were ecstatic.

We had three days to prepare for the semifinals—which meant that we had sufficient time to take care of our academics and two days of practice before we departed for Northwood University located in West Palm Beach, Florida. Sam and Demetrice showed up at practice on time. This time Coach Mosley said to them, "We don't need you." Sam and Demetrice took it lightly; they didn't even flinch. They walked off the court like they were given a paid vacation. I knew if Coach lied to me about an intended one game suspension, I would have gone ballistic when he changed his mind. I thought his last minute decision was outrageous. Was Coach trying to set up us for failure? I thought that we needed all the help we could get, especially when our next opponent was against the towering, nationally ranked, Northwood University Seahawks.

On February 29, 2008, we walked into the building as the underdogs. Win or go home. Well, we weren't ready to go home just yet. We played for the conference championship ring. Our superb defense allowed Northwood University Seahawks to trail throughout the first 20 minutes of action. The first half score was a low 29-22, in our favor.

In our minds, it didn't matter if they had beaten us twice during the regular season, or had seven-foot players, or outnumbered our roster on the bench, or were ranked in the top 25-poll in the nation, or had a more successful basketball program than us. In our hearts, we knew that we were better if we played together as a team. Northwood's big men and star player got into early foul trouble which led to an equal match-up. We out-rebounded the Seahawks, 53-42. They couldn't keep up with our fast paced offense—a perfect strategy for a bigger team—out running them. Three of their players eventually fouled out of the game. We overcame our deepest fear by upsetting the favorable Northwood University, 74-66, at their very own gym, in front of their home crowd. Everyone expected the Seahawks to win the Florida Sun Conference Championship. We proved the critics wrong.

On the other side of the semifinal's matchup, Embry Riddle Aeronautical University (ERAU), also known as the Eagles, had shockingly knocked off the Warner Southern College (WSC) Royals. We were thrilled because we assumed that the Eagles were a better match-up for us—during our regular season games, we were tied for best out of two, splitting the victories.

March 1, 2008: on the day of the Florida Sun Conference championship game the usual gossip streamed through the airways; we had gotten word that no one believed we would win. The filled-up bleachers sat mostly Eagles fans that travelled all the way from Daytona, Florida to support their team. For our support, we only had a few of my teammates' families and friends and our cheerleaders on one end of the court. Even though there were more empty spaces on our bench, we realized that the only support we really needed was each other. We tried to be the loudest in the gym by silencing our opponent's game plan.

The game tipped-off at 7:00 p.m. sharp. The Eagles signed up 12 players and we signed up 8. While the Eagles rotated five players, Coach Mosley only made a rotation of me and VanRossi Holder—our freshman back-up forward from the bench. Therefore, four of my teammates played the entire 40 minutes for the first time during the season. The first 20 minutes ended 39-41 in favor of the Eagles. We were down by two points, but it didn't mean the game was over.

We came out in the second half, firing three-point jump shots by our senior point guard, Jeffery Winbush, who was five-out-of-seven; and our freshman shooting-guard, Johnny Nelson, who was two-out-of-two from the field. But it wasn't easy chopping down the Eagles' wings. They went on a run that caused the game to be tied with less than 10 minutes of action left to play.

The Eagles hit us where it hurt by taking advantage of their bigger size. I sat on the bench due to fatigue. I was dehydrated; I breathed hard. My legs couldn't move. I couldn't raise my hands. VanRossi, who only stood at a height of six foot two, was defending the Eagles' six foot ten center. Coach Mosley inspired me from the bench. He stooped down in front of me, held my head, and said, "Arnold, we need your height, your strength, and we need you to play defense." I'd never seen Coach Mosley display so much passion towards me. I gained strength from his words. I chugged the last amounts of water in my cup and wiped the sweat from my face.

"Coach, I'm ready," I said.

We wanted to re-create the double digit lead we once possessed, so we executed better on offense while dominating on the defensive end. I started our run by scoring three back-to-back shot attempts. We shot an overall of 54 percent from the field, scoring 9-out-of-15 three-point attempts.

With less than five minutes left to play, the Eagles noticed our weak spot and started penetrating our sagging defense. I had no more energy left. I started playing defense with my hands rather than with my feet. I finally fouled out after attempting to commit an offensive charge. I left the game with a double-double, scoring 13 points and snatching 11 rebounds. Upon my exit, I huddled my team. "Yo, doh lose da lead. You can do it," I said. VanRossi replaced me once more. For a freshman, he had a high enough basketball I.Q. to know that we needed him more than ever. I fearfully watched the rest of the game from the bench, biting on the towel, hoping that the time expired before the Eagles caught up.

In the second half of the game, we outscored the Eagles, 46-31. Everyone on our bench was already on their feet celebrating as the time expired. And as the referee blew his final whistle, the score board displayed the final score: EWC-85, ERAU-72.

Our cheerleaders stampeded the court and joined our team while screaming and jumping around like maniacs. Coach Burroughs, Coach Pearson, and I joined in for a big, tight group hug, yelling, "Yes, we did it!" I sprinted to congratulate the rest of my teammates, or should I say, *my family*. When I met up with Coach Mosley, I hugged him tight, clenching my fingers on his back while shouting in his ear, "Thank you Coach...thank you."

The announcer awarded us a plaque with the Florida Sun Conference logo embedded on it that read, "Men's Basketball, 2007-2008 Tournament Champions." Upon receiving it, we raised more hell by chanting and dancing all over the gym. Even Coach Mosley busted out a dance move— which was funny because it was not like him. When it was my turn to hold the plaque, I held on to it tightly like I never wanted to let it go.

We circled around a ladder that led to the basket. We were climbing up the ladder one-by-one to cut the championship net from the rim. Every player and coach had an opportunity to cut off a piece to keep as a souvenir. When it was my turn to cut a piece of the net, for some reason my heart raced faster and faster, even though I took slow and steady steps up the ladder. I watched my every move so that I would not trip, but as soon as I looked up at the rim, I felt overjoyed.

"Arnold! Arnold!" shouted Coach Mosley, snapping me back to reality. "Scissors?"

"Oh right, thanks Coach," I replied then shared a laugh. Coach Mosley handed me the scissors and I continued stepping upwards.

I was hanging on to my dreams...

Cutting the Florida Sun Conference
Championship Net, 2008

Afterword

"I wish you had an extra year to play with us," Coach Mosley told me a week later after a devastating 93-62 loss against number 7 ranked, Eastern Oregon University at the NAIA National Tournament in Point Lookout, Missouri. We stood face to face outside our school's weight room, reminiscing on the 2007-2008 season—my senior year.

"Coach, dat was da best season. I wish I could too."

It was indeed my final year as a college basketball player, and after winning the 2007-2008 Florida Sun Conference title, I was happy it ended at Edward Waters College. But I still had one academic year left to complete my bachelor's degree in Computer Information Systems. That was my goal for the 2008-2009 school year. My younger brother, Aloysius Marvin Henry, had finished his basketball season at Maine Central Institute; after he signed a full basketball scholarship, he was on his way for two seasons (2008-2010) as a freshman and then as a sophomore at Three River Community College in Poplar Bluff, Missouri. Now standing at six foot ten, I believed that he had a great chance to play at the NCAA Division I level in the future.

With Marvin and my achievements, our mother had a lot to be proud of. My graduation was sort of a family reunion in Jacksonville, Florida for my mother, Marvin, and me. Marva wasn't there because I had disowned her, but that's for another story.

That was my mother's first time flying to America. That one week was extra special because I hadn't seen her since 2006. Her leg was doing much better after a successful surgery that allowed doctors to strip a constricted vein. After all her suffering, the problem was a vein causing poor blood circulation. She had lost a fair amount of weight as well to help decrease the pressure of standing on her feet; the affected area was still visible.

I never saw Tobias again but I did find an older sister, Heidi Alleyne of Barbados, after I wrote a song, edited a video, and posted it on youtube.com. It was dedicated to the passing away and the unsuccessful relationship with my biological father, Francis Tobias, who died on May 15, 2010. Heidi was just like me, an outside child. The death of Tobias helped Heidi and I to learn so much more about our father via internet articles and media coverage.

After graduation the plan was to remain in Jacksonville, Florida and live an average American life, perhaps go back to school to attain my master's degree; however, the economy's downfall made finding a job difficult. Unexpectedly, basketball provided an option because the

United States Basketball Association (USBA) announced a franchise for the city of Jacksonville which gave me a reason to hang on to another dream—becoming a professional basketball player. I seized the opportunity and made the roster. As always in my basketball world, another dilemma presented itself. I even tied the knot with a Canadian. But that too, is for another story.

Acknowledgements

I've met many people through my process of self-fulfillment—to a point where there's too many names to be mentioned or remembered. But there are names that can never be forgotten. It seemed as if the following people envisioned my dreams through their own eyes, and they found it necessary to assist me along my journey. They weren't always around to experience my every step; but they always answered my cries whenever I fell down to my knees.

I want to express my deepest gratitude to my Saint Lucian family members; the ones who I still call family today. My mother, Maria Henry; my younger brother, Aloysius Marvin Henry; my wife, Hong Cole; my oldest brother, Kervyn Tobias; my godfather, Peter Flood; my godmother, Susana Thelis; aunty Monica Lucien; and aunty Meuris Weekes. Without y'all I wouldn't be able to breathe.

I truly believe that the people you surround yourself with, are the ones who you'll appreciate forever: Yogi Leo, Jonathan Hall, Terry Finisterre, Dudley Joseph, Sylvia Joseph, Michael 'Midget' Pierre, Ameina Storey, Claudius Francis, Prisca Joseph, Kyshea Thompson, Alice Hammond, Alexandra 'Allie' Parsons, and Barb Howard. At last, you know the important roles you played in my life as a friend or as a motivator.

Family has always been important to me; at times, I wish I had a bigger one. With all my travels around the world, I was adopted into homes which, at some point, I called my second home—depending on my current location. Olivia Cyril (Brooklyn, New York); Philip, Donna, and Michael Cayole (Burlington, Vermont); Felo Kanene Muderhwa (South Burlington, Vermont); Terri and Bill Carroll (Poteau, Oklahoma); The Hammonds (Melbourne, Australia); Deborah Williams and Kimberly Jordan (Jacksonville, Florida).

Although I never pursued Track and Field as a career, there were coaches whom I learned discipline and perseverance from: John Gastor, Gregory Lubin, Mellissa Simon, Archie Gallon, and members of the Saint Lucia Athletics Association.

Anyone can learn the game of basketball on their own, but no one can reach their full potential without the presence and patience of basketball coaches. I've gained so much knowledge from the coaches who taught me the game: Dexter Cumberbatch (Entrepot Secondary School, 1999-2001); Derek Browne (Saint Lucia National Head Coach, 2000-2001); Mathew 'Fudge' Raphael (Sir Arthur Lewis Community College, 2002-2003); Bruce Kreutzer and Brett Phillip (Massanutten

242

Military Academy, 2003-2004); Mike St. John (Carl Albert State College, 2005-2006); Anthony Mosley, Danny Pearson, and Eddie Burroughs (Edward Waters, College, 2007-2008).

To my most valuable teammates who I truly considered to be my brothers from another mother: Ed Desir, Timothy McCrory, Shawn King, James Grimball, Demetrice Thomas, and Sam Crawford. All through my years of playing basketball, I wouldn't have been able to survive emotionally or continue to be inspired without y'all.

And finally, to all my friends, teammates, and teachers throughout season after season: Entrepot Secondary School, 1999-2001; Windward Island Team, 2001-2003; Sir Arthur Lewis Community College, 2002-2003; Massanutten Military Academy, 2003-2004; University of Vermont, 2004-2005; Carl Albert State College, 2005-2006; University of North Florida, 2006-2007; and Edward Waters College, 2007-2008.

I was blessed to have all of you in the first 23 years of my life.

CPSIA information can be obtained at www.ICGtesting.com

232970LV00001B/2/P

9 781602 648128